ASTROLOGY
A COMPATIBILITY GUIDE

NELLIE MCKINLEY

HINKLER
BOOKS

*For my dear friend Kathy, whose support
and inspiration were precious gifts.*

Editor: Carol Campbell
Cover illustration: Courtney Hopkinson
Prepress: Splitting Image
Typesetting: Midland Typesetters
Design and art direction: Katy Wall

Astrology: A Compatibility Guide
First published in 2007 by Hinkler Books Pty Ltd
45–55 Fairchild Street,
Heatherton VIC 3202 Australia
www.hinklerbooks.com

© Hinkler Books Pty Ltd 2007

4 6 8 10 9 7 5 3
08 10 12 11 09

ISBN 978 1 7415 7434 0

Printed and bound in China

CONTENTS

Preface

How many times have you heard people referred to as a 'stubborn Taurean', a 'critical Virgoan', a 'dreamy Piscean', a 'two-faced Gemini', an 'airy-fairy Aquarian' or an 'over-emotional Cancerian'? While these observations are very general, most of us identify with some of the characteristics of our Sun sign. Your Sun sign is determined at the time you are born, when the position of the Sun falls into a sector of the 360-degree zodiac belt, which incorporates all 12 star signs. For example, if your birth date falls on 20 December, you are born under the Sun sign of Sagittarius. The Sun rules outward expression and the way others perceive us. It represents ego, opinion and basic drives; consequently, it reflects the type of partners we attract or are attracted to.

I have always been interested in people and their connections with others, which led me to make a career change some 20 years ago. I left primary school teaching to become an astrologer so I could gain a deeper understanding of the human psyche. I had spent many hours counselling friends about their love relationships and thought it was time to hang up a shingle and professionally help them gain a deeper understanding about themselves and develop some insight into the mysteries of love. I have found astrology to be a wonderful tool that helps people participate more effectively in their relationships. If people can learn to identify their own needs and desires, it follows that they can attract a more compatible partner.

Life with a partner is often a challenge and it usually takes two people to recognise the positive and negative aspects of their partnership. This book – my own interpretations of the individual Sun signs – should be used as a guide to personality traits rather than as a definitive authority. Above all else, we need to love and be loved, which is, sadly, where we tend to complicate our lives. Along life's path, we meet many people who may or may not be our ideal in a long-lasting love relationship. However, for a glimpse of what the future might hold for readers and their loved ones, I have provided a broad analysis of each sign's capacity to give and receive love. Such an analysis I believe is useful to gain some insight into prospective partners and the chances of a long-lasting relationship with them.

Although some signs are more situated because of a compatible combination of astrological influnces, there is no right or wrong pairing. Put simply, incompatible combinations are challenges that can be overcome through an understanding of your astrological make-up. Take, for example, the case of a hard-nosed Capricornian falling for a sensitive, intuitive Piscean. This pairing will have its challenges, but each of these fundamentally different personalities can gain and learn much from each other.

The accuracy of my assessment for each sign and the compatibility of the coupling are, at the very best, a guide. It is impossible to be too prescriptive using just people's Sun signs, given that every individual has a personally defined chart, with many other planetary influences. This book is a snapshot into relationship combinations. It will be a 'try-before-you-buy' handbook for some, while for those already struck by Cupid's arrow, a guide to a better understanding of your mate.

Nellie McKinley

Introduction

What is astrology and how does it shape our lives?

Astrology is a study of the planets and their cycles and how they affect humans and their connection with the universe. The energy of the planets has an influence on an individual's personality and insights. The study of astrology has been evident throughout civilisation and was used in very early times as a guide to the best time to plant and harvest seeds. Now we use it to explore the right moment to germinate our relationships.

Throughout history, educated men such as Pythagoras, Isaac Newton and Danish astronomer Tycho Braher believed in astrology. And today people worldwide are captivated by this ancient science – even the sceptics among us. We read the small print of our horoscopes in our daily newspapers because we all have a fascination with, and desire to know, what the future holds. Astrology opens the door to a new and exciting journey and provides us with a tool to guide our everyday lives.

Once regarded with a degree of scepticism, astrology is now more widely accepted as an aid to self-discovery. In the past, the people who sought astrological consultations wanted a 'quick fix', expecting the answers to come from an outer source rather than relying on their own judgments and actions. However, astrology is now better regarded and seen as an important tool to help people on their journey of self-discovery. It is a fabulous resource that can give us some insight into our drives, our needs, who we are and the people with whom we are most compatible.

We all need a sense of purpose in life: some direction that will make life more fulfilling. This is where astrology enables us to see the path more clearly, helping to cut through the obstacles along the way. It is a defining tool that highlights and stimulates our potentiality. We all need to live with others in a harmonious and enjoyable union. By understanding ourselves better, we can have a more fulfilling relationship.

Horoscopes

A horoscope is an astrological map based on the relative position of planets at the moment in time when and where we are born. The map is a blueprint for each individual, providing vital clues to our personality, energy drives, passion, potential, strengths and weaknesses. It can be compared with a seed that is about to germinate and grow into either a delicate rose, an exotic orchid, an untamed wild flower, an unruly bougainvillea or a strangling vine, each bearing its own unique characteristics yet with a specific connection to the universe.

We are all born with our own set of talents and potentiality. Yet how do we go about managing these individual qualities to develop our true potential? An astrologer can interpret and assess an individual's horoscope to provide a reliable set of sign posts and indicators that can be used for self-improvement and awareness. Through identifying our weaknesses, we can make changes.

Perhaps as a result of certain parental reinforcements, we don't always recognise our talents, so we continue not to believe in ourselves. This behaviour spills into our relationships with others. Astrology can redirect these thoughts and behaviour patterns and help build up our self-esteem to create more healthy and productive relationships.

Astrological charts

An astrologer can prepare a horoscope or 'birth chart' that identifies the positions of the planets in the sky at the moment of our birth. It is a chart unique to each of us because it is created according to the date, time and place where we were born, and is a true reflection of our natural self. Among some of the many things we can learn from our birth chart are the type of partner and relationship that will suit us best and, importantly, the type of person we are.

Comparing two people's birth charts is done by overlaying one chart with the other. The aspects or angles formed between the planets in each chart are then analysed to determine how the energy fields of each person blend and interact. Some couples form more harmonious bonds than others; less compatible bonds offer a greater challenge for peace and happiness in a relationship.

It is through a chart analysis that we can learn to understand ourselves and, if need be, recognise some of our negative behaviour patterns that seem to sabotage our happiness. Each astrological sign has a natural affinity with one or more of the others, so to explore our true relationship potential, we need to study certain aspects of our horoscope.

Astrology is about discovering who we are – the positives as well as the shadowy side of our personality that seems to cause the most trouble in relationships.

Take, for example, the birth chart of Hillary Clinton – US senator and wife of former US president Bill Clinton – which is located on the facing page. Clinton's star sign is Scorpio. By identifying a few key planets in her chart, we can grasp some understanding of her personality traits and how they might affect her relationships.

* *Fire qualities* – show she can be idealistic when it comes to relationships yet she has a hidden vulnerable side.

* *Water elements* – show her to be passionate and sensitive to the feelings of others, although she often hides her feelings to afford her some measure of self-protection.

☽ *Moon in Pisces* – a strong indicator of her emotions and her nurturing requirements. This shows she has a creative, addictive personality and can play the martyr or become a saviour as the occasion arises.

♂ *Mars in Leo* – leads her to crave loyalty. She is attracted to a man who she feels is strong and protective, demonstrative and warm.

☉ *Sun sign* – her Scorpio personality is evident: strong, secretive, controlling, passionate and can face adversity with courage.

♀ *Venus in Scorpio* – Clinton has a certain mystique and sensuality typical of her star sign. In her relationship, she is intense and possessive.

The elements

Each star sign falls under a particular element – earth, fire, water or air – which represents an intrinsic energy quality. Star signs with the same elements usually have the best natural affinity with one another – for example, Aquarius and Gemini have the same energy force and a similar value system. Both being air, they share some mutual affinities.

Fire signs: Aries, Leo, Sagittarius

Feisty and fiery, people under these star signs are destined to lead a life of excitement and adventure. On the downside, their sometimes aggressive and dominating personas can make them appear arrogant and impatient.

Positive traits	Negative traits
Exciting	Aggressive
Optimistic	Bossy
Happy	Impatient
Creative	Tactless
Adventurous	Arrogant
Charismatic	Dominating

Earth signs: Taurus, Virgo, Capricorn

Committed and loyal, the earth signs are 'salt of the earth' characters that make patient and reliable partners. However, they can also be very rigid, stubborn and single-minded, making it easy for them to get stuck in a rut.

Positive traits	Negative traits
Sensual	Mundane
Focused	Rigid
Committed	Materialistic
Patient	Hesitant
Reliable	Conservative
Enduring	Stagnant

Air signs: Gemini, Libra, Aquarius

The air signs are the communicators of the zodiac, always being flexible and open to new ideas with a thirst for knowledge. Partners may find them too detached and scattered in their energies and they can often be accused of being too 'thinking' rather than 'feeling'.

Positive traits	Negative traits
Intellectual	Detached
Flexible	Superficial
Accepting	Opinionated
Creative	Scattered
Communicative	Nervous
Objective	Indecisive

Water signs: Cancer, Scorpio, Pisces

The sensitive, emotional and intuitive water signs are very compassionate and nurturing partners. They are also known to be rather secretive, possessive and intense in their relationships.

Positive traits	Negative traits
Sensual	Moody
Compassionate	Secretive
Nurturing	Possessive
Protective	Needy
Visionary	Passive
Imaginative	Introverted

A ruling planet is a planet of the solar system that, based on certain characteristics, is associated more strongly with a particular sign of the zodiac.

Aries: ruling planet Mars ♂

Aries is ruled by Mars, which represents desires, energy, courage and endurance, all typical traits of an Aries. Astrologically, Mars is a planet of motivation, mobilisation and sexuality – representing items that are urgent and that trigger short-temperedness and arduous pursuit. Those born under this sign usually reflect these traits. In relationships, Aries will never compromise; if action is needed, they will initiate it even if they have to leave the union. Aries will never stay in an unhappy marriage because their single-mindedness will always see them move on to greener pastures. In love, Aries can be hot one minute and, just like the planet Mars, can turn icy the next.

Taurus: ruling planet Venus ♀

Venus is the ruling planet of Taurus and is associated with a strong love of beauty, affection, refinement and sociability. Taurus is very much a sign that represents these desires and Taureans are spurred by the need for material comfort and physical pleasure. Taureans love fine food and wine and, because their emotions run deep, they make very passionate mates. Venus represents harmony and the need for tranquility so Taureans will often stay in relationships long after they have served their purpose. Their need for physical comfort can sometimes override their need for physical intimacy.

Gemini: ruling planet Mercury ☿

In astrology, Mercury represents communication, versatility, alertness and brilliance: all traits that are reflected in Geminis. Mercury has two sides, showing how the planet relates to the two signs it represents – Gemini and Virgo. When Mercury is at its closest point to the Sun, temperatures soar. This correlates with the warmth that radiates from Geminis. This heat is also associated with the spontaneity, enthusiasm and intellect of this sign. In relationships, Geminis will always use their Mercurian energy to communicate logically and let their partners know if they feel they have relationships problems rather than burying their head in the sand as their Taurean cousins do.

Cancer: ruling planet the Moon ☽

Protectiveness, moodiness and kindness are Cancerian traits that typify the Moon's influences on this water sign. The basic personality function of the Moon is to stimulate the responses to our living conditions and relationships. Cancerians reflect the moods of those they are with, just as the Moon reflects whatever it is near. It's also the planet that reflects the mother–child relationship and the influence this has on our lives. In relationships, Cancerians are prone to be moody and the Moon energy tends to bring highs and lows. They are hypersensitive to the slightest hurts and require a partner who understands and is empathetic to these security-conscious crabs.

Leo: ruling planet the Sun ☉

The Sun represents our aspirations and how we direct our energy to achieve and enjoy life. Determination, dignity and vitality are characteristics of both Leo and the Sun. Leos are the creative sparks of the zodiac and they have a natural flair for drama and self-expression. Like the Sun, they shine brightly and like to be considered the centre of the universe. They have a naturally sunny disposition and are very open, proud, generous and colourful. Leos like to shine in relationships – often needing to be in the spotlight – so they should seek a partner who respects and honours them and, in turn, they will do the same.

Virgo: ruling planet Mercury ☿

Since Mercury is a planet of communication, it's no surprise the logical, practical and systematic traits of the Virgo fall under its rule. Virgoans differ from Geminis, who are also ruled by this planet, as they tend to be more analytical and have a more serious disposition. Virgoans also have greater dexterity than Geminis. Mercury, like the Moon, reflects whatever is nearby and therefore Virgos have a tendency to also reflect the moods of people they are with. Virgoans use the Mercurian energy to discriminate, evaluate and process their relationships. They also need a strong element of friendship in their partnerships, which helps them communicate thoughts and concepts more openly.

Libra: ruling planet Venus ♀

Responsiveness and harmony are the two main traits that bind Libra and Taurus to Venus. The two signs differ under this ruling planet insomuch as Libra has an appreciation of visual things, but not always the drive to obtain them, while Taureans enjoy working hard so they can see the fruits of their labours. In the sign of Libra, Venus represents values and what is appreciated in relationships, especially those relating to partnerships. The Venusian influence over Libra creates a desire to be wanted and a need for continuity and solidarity. Venus has the effect of making Librans in love with love itself. They are captivated by beauty and Librans tend to seek out the more superficial qualities in a partner. Librans are romantic by nature and idealistic in love, and will fall in love easily.

Scorpio: ruling planet Pluto ♇

Pluto is the planet of transformation, birth, death, power and sexuality. It rules research, investigation and, like the Scorpio, it focuses on the mysteries of life. Pluto represents invisible energy that encourages Scorpios to unearth what lies deep within their psyche. Many Scorpios go through life-changing events that strengthen their resolve. It is a similar to a process of regeneration – like the phoenix rising from the ashes to be reborn. Pluto evokes intensive emotional responses in Scorpios, who by nature tend to be very untrusting and wary in love. They have a deep emotional reservoir and desire for love, but Pluto's energy can sometimes make them appear over-possessive and jealous. These feelings can stem from childhood experiences where they have lost someone dear to them, which make them look for guarantees in their relationships.

Sagittarius: ruling planet Jupiter ♃

Jupiter is the planet of growth and expansion. It rules higher education, philosophy and travel and these are exactly what the wanderlust archer desires. Sagittarians are drawn to expanding their mind and gaining intellectual wisdom and they enjoy taking things to the max. Jupiter is referred to as the great benefactor and the lucky planet, and that seems to hold true for Sagittarians. Eternal optimists of the zodiac, they appear to have a guardian angel watching over them. Jupiter's influence over this sign encourages freedom and space in relationships. Don't fence the Sagittarian in!

Capricorn: ruling planet Saturn ♄

Referred to as the cosmic cop in astrology, Saturn is the planet of limitations, responsibilities and, at times, frustrations. Saturn makes Capricornians put in the hard yards before they can reap the rewards. Capricornians display this pragmatic approach to life – they're security-conscious and have a tireless drive towards their commitments. Structure and tradition are important elements in the lives of people born under this sign. They are committed in relationships and it is rare that Capricornians leave their spouse or family.

Aquarius: ruling planet Uranus ♅

Uranus is a planet associated with change, freedom, invention and rebelliousness – all of which is attractive to Aquarians, who need mental stimulation, variety, excitement and unpredictability in their relationships. Uranus exemplifies shock, and Aquarians who can't get what they desire from their relationships will often be adventurous enough to move into electrifying territory. Uranus's influence on Aquarians will encourage them to be attracted to the unusual and unconventional. Many Aquarians will have multiple relationships in their lifetimes as they continue to seek further stimulation. Additionally, their ruling planet Uranus will often instigate separations. Uranus is often seen in the chart as a planet of detachment – this extends to the Aquarian approach to relationships because their partners often complain they don't get 100 per cent commitment from their mate.

Pisces: ruling planet Neptune ♆

Neptune is the planet of spirituality and creativity. It is a difficult planet to clearly define because it represents mysterious and evolving spiritual energy. Pisceans often feel confused and sacrifice themselves in their relationships. They are often the martyrs, victims or rescuers. Neptune is also associated with creativity, passion and idealism – all of which Pisceans bring into their relationships. Their compassionate nature can often be their downfall. Sometimes they don't convey what they really mean and see their partners through rose-coloured glasses. They not only seek a physical relationship but also one on a higher spiritual level.

Modes of expression

In astrology each star sign is represented by a mode of expression –
cardinal, fixed and mutable – that represents the energy used by that
sign to accomplish life directions, attain goals and seek out suitable
partnerships.

Cardinal signs

The cardinal signs of the zodiac are Aries, Cancer, Libra and Capricorn.
These people are the initiators of the zodiac, who express their different
energies in accordance with the traits of their specific sign.

Fixed signs

The fixed signs of the zodiac are Taurus, Leo, Scorpio and Aquarius. Fixed
signs are the 'stayers' of the zodiac. These people need to be in a stable
environment and tend to have a rigid outlook on life, rarely compromising
their values.

Mutable signs

Gemini, Virgo, Sagittarius and Pisces are the mutable, or changeable, signs
of the zodiac. These people are the most adaptable of the star signs and
are able to make compromises and move easily from one situation to
another.

Levels of compatibility

We all tumble into relationships throughout our lives – some average,
some good and, luckily, some that are fantastic. But just how suited are you
to your mate? Make a quick check on the grid on the facing page to assess
your chances of a long-term relationship with the current love in your life.

Compatibility overview: which star signs are best suited, according to the zodiac

	Aries ♈	Taurus ♉	Gemini ♊	Cancer ♋	Leo ♌	Virgo ♍	Libra ♎	Scorpio ♏	Sag. ♐	Cap. ♑	Aqua. ♒	Pisces ♓
Aries ♈	A	B	B	C	A	C	D	C	A	C	B	C
Taurus ♉	B	A	B	B	C	B	B	D	C	A	C	B
Gemini ♊	B	B	A	C	B	B	A	C	D	C	A	C
Cancer ♋	C	B	C	A	C	B	C	C	C	B	B	A
Leo ♌	A	C	B	C	A	C	B	C	A	C	B	C
Virgo ♍	C	A	C	C	C	A	C	B	C	A	C	D
Libra ♎	D	B	B	B	B	C	A	C	B	C	A	B
Scorpio ♏	C	D	C	A	C	B	C	A	C	B	C	A
Sag. ♐	A	C	D	C	A	C	B	C	A	C	B	C
Cap. ♑	C	A	C	D	C	A	C	B	C	A	C	B
Aqua. ♒	B	C	B	C	D	C	A	C	B	C	A	B
Pisces ♓	C	B	C	A	C	D	C	A	C	B	B	A

Key to grid

A: Most compatible, but don't take each other too much for granted.

B: Compatible, with some minor concessions from both parties.

C: Challenging, but issues can be resolved with understanding and compromise.

D: Opposed, although can attract and repel equally; however, difficulties might ultimately be too great.

ARIES (21 March–20 April)

♈ Ruled by the planet Mars
Fire sign
Cardinal
Masculine energy

In general ...

Aries is a fire sign and is considered the child of the zodiac because people born under this sign think the universe revolves around them. They are motivated by goals and challenges and tend to pursue their lives in a somewhat selfish manner.

In their childhood Arians strove to please their fathers and often viewed their mothers as the weaker and more suppressed partner in the parental relationship. They tend to see their mothers as women who lacked the strength to change their circumstances and who often stayed in difficult relationships out of fear. This is not what they want in their relationships, so they become very single-minded as a result, which can at times cause problems for them.

Arians are extremely idealistic; many live in a fantasy world. Although easily aroused, they sometimes find the flames of passion can die as quickly as they ignite. They don't realise relationships need to be worked on and that compromises need to be made, with the result that instead of spending time stabilising an existing union they will bow out, usually from boredom. At times they make unrealistic demands on their partner and then feel disappointed when the demands are not met. This idealism needs to be tempered so that their relationships can be brought back down to earth.

Because Arians are so enthusiastic about relationships, they often jump right in with great determination and stamina. Honest to a fault, they want to make a go of this new union, but when it becomes humdrum they can lose interest very quickly and head for hills to search for the excitement of new challenges.

Arians are suited to goal-oriented careers and positions where they can display their strong vitality and physical strength. They need to be the captain of their own ship and lead the way. Being a cardinal sign, they are initiators, especially in relationships, where they like to pursue their potential partners.

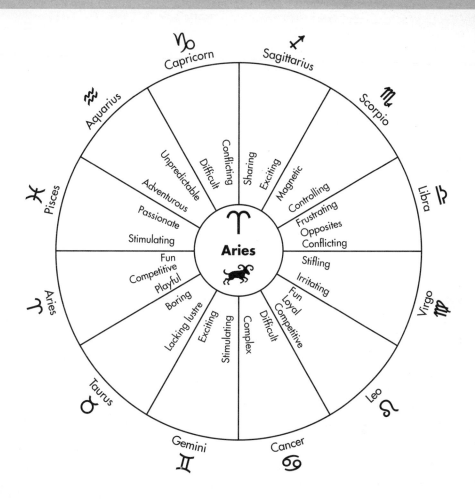

How an Arian personality might match up with other star signs

Ms Aries - an overview

The Arian woman is so passionate in her desire for a relationship that she initiates contact and pursues relentlessly. She will be most enthusiastic in her attempt to orchestrate the entire show from the initial courting to the final stages of walking down the aisle.

Her impulsive nature is often her downfall, as she doesn't allow time to get to know the real essence of her mate. Time and time again, Ms Aries becomes disappointed and disillusioned.

Arian women are passionate, enthusiastic, outgoing, spontaneous and innocent. These essentially child-like qualities are no guide for how to act in a relationship, so Arians can go from one disappointment to another, looking for their knight in shining armour only to become disillusioned because he wasn't what they thought he would be. Not one for letting the grass grow under her feet, Ms Aries is off looking for greener pastures. She seems to be a late bloomer, so perhaps it is best that she has her passionate flings before she makes a lifelong commitment. The experience she gains from this might be what she needs so that she ends up choosing her Mr Right. It is important for Ms Aries to draw from past experiences and reflect on why a relationship might have fallen apart – a hard task when she finds it difficult to admit fault.

Ms Aries' passionate nature can also bring a possessive and jealous quality to her relationships. She will fight for her man if she is under threat, but may find she has overreacted and the threat lay more in her imagination than in reality. However, if the situation calls for it, she will be very ardent in her pursuit, leaving no stone unturned. Arian women are exceedingly loyal in their relationships and this is what they expect in return.

Although Ms Aries will be very enthusiastic about being 'connected', she also has a strong desire to have her independence and freedom. Rarely will she want to be tied by the apron strings so she tends not to be the best homemaker of the zodiac. If you want a tidy house, Ms Aries may not be the woman you are looking for, but if you are after a passionate, honest, loveable and adventurous partner, she can easily fit the bill.

Famous Arian women

* Kate Hudson (actor)
* Elle McPherson
  (supermodel)
* Doris Day (singer)
* Erica Jong (writer)
* Julie Christie (actor)
* Bette Davis (actor)

Combinations

♈ Ms Aries + Mr Aries ♈

Sign	Aries	Aries
Symbol	Ram	Ram
Ruler	Mars	Mars
Type	Cardinal	Cardinal
Element	Fire	Fire

Sparks will certainly fly in this union, but not in the right direction. With both being headstrong and selfish, this pair will be caught in a constant headlock. Aries is all about 'I' not 'we', so when you put two rams together, there's usually only room for one ego.

This combination is a mix of fire and passion. But with both in the relationship usually impulsive and headstrong, there will not be enough give and take to make this a lasting union. Both want to be first to win the race so that rarely will there be a compromise.

It's a catch-22 situation when two rams unite. Both need attention and recognition, so it is hard to give what you're used to only receiving. With all this whirlwind activity and impulsiveness typical of most Aries, there's no one in the relationship to create harmony and balance.

Because Aries is seen as the child of the zodiac, when two Arians meet there's not enough 'adult' wisdom to make a lasting union. But if they can control their impulsiveness and make an effort to be less self-absorbed, they can be happy together, since both are fiercely loyal to their mates. If either of these Aries partners has a nurturing Moon sign they can lend more empathy to the relationship.

In the bedroom: A passionate and electric duo whose chemistry will set the room on fire! Both are good sexual initiators, neither are shy about making the first move and often use the bedroom to make up for their daily head butts.

♈ Ms Aries + Mr Taurus ♉

Sign	Aries	Taurus
Symbol	Ram	Bull
Ruler	Mars	Venus
Type	Cardinal	Fixed
Element	Fire	Earth

Taurus is an earth sign and is far too grounded and stubborn for the quick-footed Arian. Slow and steady usually wins the race, but not when the prize is the impulsive, energetic Arian woman. The steadiness the Taurean can provide is just what Ms Aries needs but sadly this sign is lacking the spontaneity the Martian girl desires. Taurean males are more stay-at-home, play-at-home kind of guys and they need a partner who provides a nice home environment – Ms Aries is many things but domestic goddess is not one of them!

While Taurean men can provide a nurturing and stable environment, this may not be exactly what the Arian girl enjoys. She's driven by unpredictability and excitement so the Taurean man might not present a big enough challenge for her.

Taureans are possessive, obsessive and can become too complacent once entrenched in the relationship. As Ms Aries makes her way around the zodiac, ironically, this is the sort of man she ultimately needs to give her the stability, passion and commitment she is continually looking for.

In the bedroom: Ms Aries may be too selfish and headstrong for the stubborn and inflexible bull. Physically they come from two different spheres – she's into instant gratification for the sake of pleasure itself and while's he's into sex, usually he wants something practical from it – like a family!

♈ Ms Aries + Mr Gemini ♊

Sign	Aries	Gemini
Symbol	Ram	Twins
Ruler	Mars	Mercury
Type	Cardinal	Mutable
Element	Fire	Air

The Gemini man is probably the most suitable air sign for this fiery female. They both love adventure, variety and have an innocent approach to life. Arians thrives on new challenges and experiences, and the mental dexterity Mr Gemini brings to the table can often be an aphrodisiac for Ms Aries.

These signs often start as great pals. Geminis can help Arians expand their mental horizons. They click well because they give one another plenty of space and don't seem to get caught up in the jealousy game. Neither is very domestically oriented, which comes as a relief for the Arian gal, who would rather be out socialising and meeting new people with her Gemini guy than keeping house.

He has a way with words and can provide her with the right amount of flattery to keep her satisfied. He also understands his child-like companion because he, too, is a child of the zodiac. With both on the same wavelength and both liking plenty of freedom in their relationships, this is an ideal combination. Ms Aries and Mr Gemini are not driven by material possessions so they share a friendship that involves mutual ideas and interests. Being a mutable sign, the Gemini is exceedingly adaptable to his whimsical Arian and understands her changeability.

In the bedroom: Sexually these two signs don't always ignite: the Arian is more prone to instant gratification and the Gemini is not noted for his sexual prowess. But if they take the time to fan the flames, they could ignite a fire that is hard to extinguish.

♈ Ms Aries + Mr Cancer ♋

Sign	Aries	Cancer
Symbol	Ram	Crab
Ruler	Mars	Moon
Type	Cardinal	Cardinal
Element	Fire	Water

Think of the two most incompatible energies and you can't go past this union. Mr Cancer's sensitivity, complexity and neediness make him somewhat of a wet blanket for the forthright Ms Aries. His usually strong bond with his mother can be a cause of resentment for his Arian mate, who wants to be number one in his life.

Not particularly adventurous, with home and family life his priorities, this crab will be a bit of a killjoy for someone who craves excitement and fun, like Ms Aries. Cancer's motto is 'I feel' which is in stark contrast to the Arian's 'I am'. She is too unsophisticated for the complex, sensitive crab, who often brings unresolved issues into their relationship. Additionally, she cannot unravel the mysteries of this Cancerian male and quite frankly would rather be spending time with someone more upbeat and dynamic. He, in turn, likes stability and can become somewhat agitated by the flighty nature of the freedom-loving Arian woman.

Initially, Ms Aries will be drawn to Mr Crab's gentle nature but as time moves on she will become frustrated and bored with him. Unless he meets Ms Aries at the end of her journey through the zodiac, he will find her ultimate rejection heartbreaking.

In the bedroom: It's likely that the watery crab will extinguish the fiery and passionate flames of Ms Aries because his heavy-going energy will be a turn-off for the playful ram, who likes to jump up and down and get excited in the sack.

♈ Ms Aries + Mr Leo ♌

Sign	Aries	Leo
Symbol	Ram	Lion
Ruler	Mars	Sun
Type	Cardinal	Fixed
Element	Fire	Fire

Charming, charismatic and sociable, Mr Leo will sweep Ms Aries off her feet. Finally she's met her knight in shining armour, who has all the right moves and even more of the right lines for this needy, idealistic ram. At last – someone she can have some fun with!

Leos enjoy socialising and are drawn to creative pursuits. While most lions enjoy being the centre of attention, they are happy to share the spotlight with their attention-seeking ram partner. This is a happy union where both partners respect and enjoy each other's qualities.

The father figure played an important role in the early lives of both Leos and Arians. Accordingly, both need a certain degree of strength from and solidarity with their partners. Even though Ms Aries is more emotionally idealistic than her intellectual Leo, they both carry a strong sense of loyalty and commitment to each other.

Because both are constantly seeking approval, it makes them understand and recognise this need in others. Providing they don't try to overshadow each other and keep their idealistic natures in balance with the practical side of life, these two signs will continue on a journey of passion throughout their relationship.

In the bedroom: When fire meets fire, the flames of love will spark a competitive love match in the bedroom. Ms Aries and Mr Leo are highly sexually charged and both will last the distance.

♈ Ms Aries + Mr Virgo ♍

Sign	Aries	Virgo
Symbol	Ram	Virgin
Ruler	Mars	Mercury
Type	Cardinal	Mutable
Element	Fire	Earth

The personal habits and instinctive emotional responses that define these two signs make their union fraught with ups and downs. The sensitive, nervous nature of the Virgo male will often be tried and tested by the blunt and brash Arian female.

Although both Ms Aries and Mr Virgo strive for the unadulterated truth in all situations, there are some basic differences in their makeup that can make them uncomfortable with each other. Ms Aries tends to act on a whim, which can rattle poor Mr Virgo, who likes to weigh up the pros and cons of a situation rather than diving straight in. He will find that he plays servant to the demanding and headstrong Ms Aries, who can find the perfectionism and over-critical nature of her mate hard to take. Both of these signs will need to make plenty of adjustments to make their relationship work.

On the other hand, because both Ms Aries and Mr Virgo have a predisposition to physical activities – the Virgo more in his dietary needs and the Arian in her sporting prowess – they can find common ground to express their interests in outdoor pursuits and health.

In the bedroom: The self-controlled nature of Mr Virgo will initially attract Ms Aries, but again this earth sign will be too grounded and practical to hold a long-term sexual attraction for the fiery, quick-fix Arian woman.

♈ Ms Aries + Mr Libra ♎

Sign	Aries	Libra
Symbol	Ram	Scales
Ruler	Mars	Venus
Type	Cardinal	Cardinal
Element	Fire	Air

Sparks will fly at the initial meeting between Ms Aries and Mr Libra. Although opposites attract, the differences will prove too great in a long-term relationship. Mr Libra will crave the closeness an intimate relationship provides. He will be concerned with society's expectations and will always want to be seen to follow traditional standards. Mr Libra will put Ms Aries on a pedestal but ultimately she won't fit the mould of the perfect, doting wife.

Idealistic and always looking at the world through rose-coloured glasses, Mr Libra will become frustrated with messy Ms Aries, who'd rather be outdoors climbing mountains than sitting at home playing house. She, in turn, will become irritated with her Libran guy. His indecisiveness and inability to make quick decisions will drive her crazy, along with his laziness. While his airs and graces will seem quite charming to Ms Aries, once he's won her heart he will have a hard time keeping it.

Libra is the sign of balance and harmony and he will always want to please his mate. But on this occasion the scales will rarely tip in his favour. Once again, Ms Aries, as in many of her other unions, will be in the driver's seat of the relationship and will soon tire of the fence-sitting Mr Libra.

In the bedroom: Air will fuel the flames of passion bursting in Ms Aries. These two will have a good sexual union as he can sweet talk the ram into bed and knows exactly how to please her.

♈ Ms Aries + Mr Scorpio ♏

Sign	Aries	Scorpio
Symbol	Ram	Scorpion
Ruler	Mars	Pluto
Type	Cardinal	Fixed
Element	Fire	Water

Ms Aries will be attracted to the deep, sensual nature of Mr Scorpio, making this union overflow with all the trimmings of a passionate love affair. But the security-craving Scorpio may become too intense for the easy-going Arian woman, who will find herself drowning in a sea of emotions – his, that is!

Mr Scorpio is secretive and non-trusting by nature, which is the opposite of the trusting, direct and open Arian woman. She will have no qualms about telling him what she thinks but will find it frustrating that he doesn't share the same frankness with her. He will have a lot of time for her spunk and her get-up-and-go attitude but his need for emotional closeness will make her jumpy.

Ms Aries is fairly down-to-earth, simple and spontaneous, while her Scorpio lover is a far more complex character. His brooding, jealous and controlling nature will suffocate Ms Aries, who doesn't have the energy or inclination to fight a losing battle. She is an impulsive and independent woman, while he's much more secretive and anti-social.

In the bedroom: Slowly the sparks will fly, but no longer in the bedroom. Ms Aries will pack her bags and head to greener pastures where she will feel free from the ever-present constraints of the sexually charged Mr Scorpio.

♈ Ms Aries + Mr Sagittarius ♐

Sign	Aries	Sagittarius
Symbol	Ram	Archer
Ruler	Mars	Jupiter
Type	Cardinal	Mutable
Element	Fire	Fire

This couple's love of sport and the great outdoors makes for a compatible union. They both embrace life with equal enthusiasm and will derive pleasure from experiences they can share together. Mr Sagittarius will be a breath of fresh air for Ms Aries, who will flourish in a relationship free from the controlling and manipulative clutches of some of the other signs of the zodiac.

Both fire signs, these two are open and honest with each other – what you see is often what you get. Although Mr Sagittarius is known for his 'foot-in-mouth disease', he is more charming and refined than Ms Aries, a trait she finds appealing. The archer's thirst for knowledge and his need to try new experiences is what keeps Ms Aries on her toes. She loves adventure, so these two would have a great time globetrotting.

Mutual understanding between these signs is strong; neither likes boundaries in their relationships. Since both have a tendency to rush headlong into any situation, there is little room for peace and quiet in this union. Ms Aries and Mr Sagittarius live in the moment, sometimes with little regard for tomorrow. But as fire signs, both love the idea of being in love and might quite easily end up walking down the aisle together.

In the bedroom: Both the ram and the archer are extremely passionate lovers who will make responsive and affectionate bedfellows. Ms Aries may become jealous or miffed when he breaks his promises, but the sensual and energetic archer will make up for that in more ways than one!

♈ Ms Aries + Mr Capricorn ♑

Sign	Aries	Capricorn
Symbol	Ram	Goat
Ruler	Mars	Saturn
Type	Cardinal	Cardinal
Element	Fire	Earth

Mr Capricorn is interested in guarantees and long-term security, which Ms Aries will struggle to provide. Astrologically, these two signs square each other, which suggests that there will be difficulties in finding a happy medium.

Mr Capricorn is ambitious, pragmatic, conservative and single-minded, and ruled by the planet Saturn, which represents hard work, tenacity and direction. He will make an excellent provider for Ms Aries, who may admire his success and the trappings of wealth. Ms Aries will be initially attracted to the strength and commitment Mr Capricorn gives her and he'll equally enjoy her free-spirited approach to life and her bubbly personality.

The fiery warmth of the Arian persona will melt the cold heart of the Capricornian. But since the goat can sometimes keep his true feelings under wraps, he may end up losing the woman he loves because he simply can't tell her how he really feels – unlike Ms Aries who calls a spade a spade and has no problem doing so. But ultimately his seriousness and lack of frivolity will not be enough to keep the home fires burning. Ms Aries will crave a more carefree union and will break free from this structured and rigid relationship that may stifle her creativity.

In the bedroom: Mr Capricorn is self-disciplined and cautious, even in the bedroom, which can be extremely frustrating for a voracious woman like Ms Aries, who jumps headlong into most situations.

♈ Ms Aries + Mr Aquarius ♒

Sign	Aries	Aquarius
Symbol	Ram	Water bearer
Ruler	Mars	Uranus
Type	Cardinal	Fixed
Element	Fire	Air

This dynamic duo will find much common ground in a relationship. Both idealistic and adventure loving, Ms Aries and Mr Aquarius will entertain and amuse each other to no end. Mr Aquarius will find her child-like qualities endearing and, for her, his quirky sense of humour and *joie de vivre* will be a breath of fresh air.

There's no stopping this pair, who'll share an insatiable thirst for new adventures. They embrace life with open arms and are interested, particularly Mr Aquarius, in the greater good of mankind. Mr Aquarius will teach Ms Aries to broaden her outlook and perspective on life, which will lead to her embarking on her own journey of self-discovery. Ms Aries will admire and respect the intellect of the water bearer and will learn a great deal from him. But she may find his detached, aloof nature a little confusing because she can't really tell what he feels. The Aquarian guy might hide a sea of emotions under his cool exterior for fear of revealing a vulnerability that may not be fully understood by the Arian woman.

Despite their obvious compatibility, Aquarius is a fixed sign, making this guy stubborn and rigid in his outlook on life. This can be frustrating for Ms Aries, who may find him a bit too opinionated and set in his ways.

In the bedroom: She likes to lead but, being a fixed sign, he doesn't like to follow. However, her frankness – especially about what she needs physically – will appeal to her Aquarian lover, who can be as adventurous in bed as she can be hungry for sexual gratification.

♈ Ms Aries + Mr Pisces ♓

Sign	Aries	Pisces
Symbol	Ram	Fish
Ruler	Mars	Neptune
Type	Cardinal	Mutable
Element	Fire	Water

The longevity of this relationship will depend on how patient Ms Aries is getting to know this sensitive, romantic, idealistic man. The ram, known for her impulsive and headstrong persona, will appeal to Mr Pisces. He will be attracted to her direct and confident approach, but can he use his sixth sense quickly enough to tune in to what this woman wants, and not let her get away? Mr Pisces needs to act quickly and show her his mystical and creative qualities, and then he may start a fire in her heart.

Both Ms Aries and Mr Pisces can bring some wonderful delights into their union, as they share a love of adventure and excitement. This duo need to live their lives in creative and spirited ways, exploring all the possibilities that lie before them, instead of being bogged down by the mundane aspects of life.

Fire and water are often at odds with one another and, true to form, this Arian girl may be rather blunt and insensitive to the more passive and gentle Mr Pisces. If he can keep his over-sensitive nature under wraps and recognise that her outbursts are over in a flash, this duo could have a lot of fun. Mr Pisces should be aware that his brooding and, at times, detached and private temperament can dampen the spirits of this bubbly girl.

Ms Aries will be the stronger and more controlling of the two, as Mr Pisces will always make the sacrifices in the relationship. However, that is just what this girl desires and needs. As long as Mr Pisces is living the higher side of his persona and not falling prey to the addictive, destructive side, this relationship will teach the Arian girl and her Piscean man a thing or two about love.

In the bedroom: Both want a sexual experience that offers great intensity and passion, and these two will take every chance to fulfil their fantasies behind closed doors. They are both extremely creative when it comes to sex, which can lead to endless possibilities!

Celebrity Ms Aries: Bette Davis

Actor, born 5 April 1908 in Lowell, Massachusetts, USA

```
Personal planets: Sun in Aries
                  Moon in Gemini
                  Mercury in Gemini
                  Venus in Gemini
                  Mars in Taurus
```

The act of sex, gratifying as it may be is it may be, is God's joke on humanity. It is man's last desperate stand at superintendency.

– Bette Davis

Bette Davis was a strong, fiery Arian who, as a self-motivated and outspoken actor in her time, played a variety of complex roles in her long career and carved her name in the film industry as a tenacious and driven woman. Davis was married four times, her relationships suffering as her career expanded. By her own admission, her acting took precedence over her intimate life, which is a general assessment of an Arian woman, who drives her life hard and will never compromise her goals for a relationship. Davis's marriages lasted from three years to 10; if it didn't work, she didn't hang around. As an Arian, she needed to be free of any constraints so she could tap into her creative potential; her relationships appear to have been an encumbrance to her goals.

Davis referred to actor Gary Merrell, who fell in love with her on the set of *All About Eve*, as her 'favourite husband', which is understandable because he was a Leo. These two had the same fiery energy that would draw them together instantly. However, that same quality led to a turbulent relationship and they fought frequently during their 10-year marriage. Because both were fire signs, these two were high-spirited, competitive and self-centred. Merrell's chart, however, also contains the sensitive and nurturing qualities of Cancer, meaning that he was the more domestic and nurturing of the two. His abundance of water elements made him super-sensitive. He would rather hide behind the protective wall of his Leo persona rather than show his emotions. His need for financial and emotional security may have seen him stick with the marriage longer than he might have otherwise.

Davis's chart consists of fire, earth and air, showing she had her feet on the ground, and held a burning desire to grow intellectually and learn as much as she could. She needed a mate who was interested in communication and diversity and believed her life to be a kaleidoscope of vast potential. She had a strong focus on achieving professionally, so she didn't let the grass grow under her feet in more ways than one. Mars in the sensual sign of Taurus would have made her loyal in her relationships with a healthy appetite for the finer things in life.

The man Davis was reputed to have 'loved the most' was film director William Wyler but the pair never married. She was attracted to him because of his ability to communicate and because he, like her, was open to all of life's possibilities.

Mr Aries — an overview

Arian males are born leaders and are attracted to anything that is risky — they are the risqué type of men. Mr Aries is as assertive as his female counterpart and finds the challenge of the pursuit exciting and even exhilarating. The Arian man needs a woman who can share his passion for adventure, be it in the bedroom or on the sporting field.

The male Arian has a strong physical stamina so he rarely runs out of steam. Being a fire sign, his passion ignites very quickly but, unless he feels cherished and adored, he may lose his desire very quickly and the flame may die. Although he portrays an air of confidence, a feeling of insecurity lies beneath that shining armour. This macho disposition is only bravado to compensate for feelings of inadequacy.

Arian men fire on all cylinders when the relationship is new and invigorating but have a tendency to become easily bored, hence they need a woman who will keep them on their toes. The Arian male is very impulsive and when he sets his sights on someone, he has to have them. Single-minded in their approach, the Arians want it all their own way. They need a relationship where they have plenty of room to move and, although they can be very possessive, they become frustrated if their partners are demanding. They need a mate who is understanding, yet also adventurous.

Mr Aries is bossy and not always able to make compromises and tolerate his partner's opinions. Arians are seen to be selfish in relationships, thinking of their own pleasure first. They see their partners not as individuals but as an extension of themselves. Because their desires are plentiful, they often think one relationship is not enough. So for women who require great intimacy and attention, such as the more sensitive and emotional water signs, Mr Aries will prove fickle. Emotionally, they don't understand what women want because they are too preoccupied with their own needs.

Lovemaking is high on the Arian male's agenda – they have a reputation as the Casanovas of the zodiac – and at times have difficulty discerning the difference between lust and love. He is idealistic in love and expects his partner to be 'the one'. However, he is very honest in his approach and love's desires, so what you see is what you get. If you have your sights set on a relationship with an Arian man, it is important to remember these guys enjoy the thrill of the chase and love a challenge, so never make the first move. Tease him a little and let him come to you.

Famous Arian men

* Vincent Van Gough (artist)
* David Letterman (talk show host)
* Leonardo da Vinci (artist)
* Russell Crowe (actor)
* Quentin Tarantino (film director)
* Hans Christian Anderson (writer)

Combinations

♈ Mr Aries + Ms Aries ♈

Sign	Aries	Aries
Symbol	Ram	Ram
Ruler	Mars	Mars
Type	Cardinal	Cardinal
Element	Fire	Fire

This combination is a fiery mix because both these fire signs display virtually the same drives and temperament. The Arian male is just as headstrong as his female counterpart so there are no winners or losers in this match. Mr Aries will be attracted to the quick step and versatility of this female but not by her at-times overbearing personality. This match is great for pursuing adventure and fun-loving activities but, because the Arian man seems to be initially attracted to the silent and mysterious type of woman, this union may never get off the ground.

Both need some direction with their long-term goals and dreams in this union but their wilful temperament doesn't allow them to take guidance easily. They want instant gratification and may not have the staying power to make this union last. Initially passionate and excited by one another, as the relationship progresses, unrealistic expectations of one another will start to emerge. With neither wanting to take a backseat, they will never be willing to compromise for the benefit of their partner. They will tend to accuse each other of being too single-minded and selfish.

The need for excitement will draw these two signs together; both have a strong sense of adventure and will always try anything new. This union will be a success if either can show willingness to compromise – and it is more likely be on the part of Ms Aries. However, if she is willing to compromise, things might just work out for the good.

In the bedroom: This passionate and electric duo's chemistry will set the room on fire! Both are good sexual initiators, neither are shy about making the first move and often use the bedroom to make up for their daily head butts.

♈ Mr Aries + Ms Taurus ♉

Sign	Aries	Taurus
Symbol	Ram	Bull
Ruler	Mars	Venus
Type	Cardinal	Fixed
Element	Fire	Earth

Mr Aries will be attracted to the strength and comfort of this steadfast earth sign. Ms Taurus can give him much of the sensual pleasures he desires and he will relish her nurturing and stable qualities. Initially, he finds this endearing and, in turn, she finds him a breath of fresh air in her somewhat grounded life. The problem these two may face can be found in the Taurean woman's need for reliability, commitment and security – qualities she can readily provide but that he has great difficulty in reciprocating because it is not in his makeup.

Both these signs are persistent in their pursuit of goals and can therefore encourage one another. The fiery temperament of the Arian man needs at times to be grounded and earthed, and this is what his Taurean mate can achieve. He is appreciative of her Mother Earth nature and loves the security and comfort she provides. He also finds the strength she displays particularly attractive. On the downside, however, she is not as energetic and active as him and her lack of spontaneity can at times frustrate the hot-blooded Arian male.

Taurean females are more stay-at-home, play-at-home types of gals and need a partner who provides a nice home environment, something that Mr Aries is quite capable of supplying. This pair can have a good relationship if they learn to appreciate one another's qualities. Mr Aries needs encouragement with and reinforcement about love and his Taurean mate will be only too eager to please. This union can have some wonderful success because Ms Taurus will constantly enjoy her boyish, impish knight in shining armour, but only if he keeps his Casanova ways in check.

In the bedroom: Here these two can have considerable fun. Both Arians and Taureans have a strong desire for sex although each has a different approach. Arians are quick and spontaneous and don't need much foreplay, whereas the Taurus gal needs to be wooed before the game starts. If Mr Aries is willing to linger a little longer, sparks will fly in this combination.

♈ Mr Aries + Ms Gemini ♊

Sign	Aries	Gemini
Symbol	Ram	Twins
Ruler	Mars	Mercury
Type	Cardinal	Mutable
Element	Fire	Air

These signs often become friends before a romance starts. Geminis can teach the Arian a lot about communication skills. The Gemini woman excites the Arian guy because she will always be naturally curious and interested to learn what makes him tick. This pair can have a lively and entertaining relationship because they both share the same enthusiasm and zest for life.

Ms Gemini will always flatter and tell Mr Aries what he wants to hear, and as long as he has the ability to mentally stimulate her, she will enjoy their times together. This couple are more interested in having fun – whether it's Ms Gemini surrounded by her books or Mr Aries off mountain climbing – rather than being bound by domestic duties. They give one another plenty of space to pursue their own hobbies and interests.

Ms Gemini and Mr Aries are not possessive or clingy types and both crave excitement, change and adventure. Because neither is materialistic, their relationship will be based more on experiencing life through travels and hobbies rather than building a traditional domestic existence. Being a mutable sign, the Gemini is very adaptable to the whimsical Arian, who understands her changeability. The natural curiosity this couple shares will allow them to be open to new experiences and challenges. Both have a natural curiosity and need mental stimulation so they will be able to communicate well with each other. Aries being a fire sign can, however, turn up the heat and warm the cockles of this woman's heart. The combination of fire and air is a positive flow of energy; fire needs oxygen to keep the Arian invigorated, and Ms Gemini had plenty of air to give

In the bedroom: Sexually, however, the Gemini and her Arian mate don't always combine well – Geminis are interested in the stimulation of the mind whereas the passionate Arian male is more interested in the stimulation of the body. Although the Arian male is more sexually driven than Ms Gemini, with the right attention they can grow together and appreciate each other's needs and desires.

♈ Mr Aries + Ms Cancer ♋

Sign	Aries	Cancer
Symbol	Ram	Crab
Ruler	Mars	Moon
Type	Cardinal	Cardinal
Element	Fire	Water

Mr Aries and Ms Cancer don't have much in common. Her sensitivity, complexity and neediness make her very different from the forthright, insensitive and selfish Arian. Although often initially attracted to Ms Cancer's sensitive and silent energy, the independent Mr Aries finds her neediness becoming too overbearing.

Arians find it difficult to commit to one person, let alone to the institution of marriage, whereas the Cancerian woman craves security and commitment. She can at times display her moody tendencies, which will only aggravate the Arian guy. He has neither the insight nor the patience to deal with her changeable emotions. And although Mr Aries' sense of fun and adventure appeals to Ms Cancer, she will find his childlike ways infuriating, which will frustrate her complex and emotional nature.

Cancer's motto is 'I feel' which is in stark contrast to the Aries' 'I am'. The Arian man is too unsophisticated for the complex, sensitive crab and her tendencies to bring unresolved issues into the relationship. He can neither fathom nor appreciate the complexities of Ms Cancer, and quite frankly would rather be spending time with someone more outgoing. In turn, she likes stability and gets somewhat agitated by the flighty nature of the freedom-loving Arian. Ms Cancer's over-protectiveness and clingy nature will turn the crab into a crab apple as far as Mr Aries is concerned.

In the bedroom: It's likely Ms Cancer will extinguish the fiery and passionate flames of Mr Aries, because the watery crab's heavy-going energy will be a turn-off for the playful ram, who likes to jump up and down and get excited in the sack.

♈ Mr Aries + Ms Leo ♌

Sign	Aries	Leo
Symbol	Ram	Lion
Ruler	Mars	Sun
Type	Cardinal	Fixed
Element	Fire	Fire

This combination is a particularly compatible one and these signs can bring some wonderful energy to the table. The charismatic and sociable Ms Leo will sweep Mr Aries off his feet. Finally he has met the charming and expressive self-confident woman who can share in his enthusiasm for life. Both fire signs, their need for approval is very strong, so each will encourage the other all the way. This highly idealistic combination shares similar interests and hobbies and will be out to have fun. The lioness seems to be more mature than her Arian guy, and understands the importance of compromise and tolerance in a relationship. She is loyal and committed and will give Mr Aries the acknowledgment and support he is after.

Both enjoy socialising and are drawn to creative pursuits. While most lions enjoy being the centre of attention, they are happy to share the spotlight with their attention-seeking ram partners. This is a happy union where partners respect and enjoy each other's qualities. The father figure played an important role in the early lives of both these signs, with the result that their standards, ethics, morals and codes of behaviour are very similar. Respect features strongly in this union, which seems to be the basis of a strong and committed relationship.

Both Arians and Leos require a certain degree of strength and solidarity from their partners. Even though Mr Aries is more emotionally idealistic than his intellectual Leo, they both carry a strong sense of loyalty and commitment to each other. Providing they don't overshadow each other and keep their egos in check, this will be a lasting and exciting relationship.

In the bedroom: Not only will these two light one another's fires but an added insatiable thirst for sexual gratification mixed with a strong need for tenderness will make this a lasting and satisfying union for them both.

♈ Mr Aries + Ms Virgo ♍

Sign	Aries	Virgo
Symbol	Ram	Virgin
Ruler	Mars	Mercury
Type	Cardinal	Mutable
Element	Fire	Earth

The personalities of these two don't mix well, making a love relationship more of a battlefield than a loving union. The sensitive, nervous and critical nature of the Ms Virgo will often be tried and tested by the blunt and brash Mr Aries.

Both Arians and Virgos are honest in their feelings, which sometimes can be the basis for long-term disharmony. Ms Virgo's critical nature can wear down Mr Aries, who needs constant adulation, support and encouragement. Instead of interpreting her analytical comments as the constructive criticisms she intended, he will view them as personal attacks he can live without. Since both signs seem to have an underlying lack of self-confidence, their differing natures don't give them the ability to make the other feel their worth. This can lead to feelings of rejection and insecurity on both sides.

Mr Aries is too impulsive for Ms Virgo, who likes to weigh up the pros and cons of a situation rather than diving straight in. She will find she plays servant to the demanding and headstrong Mr Aries. On the other hand, as both have a predisposition to physical activities – the Virgo more in her dietary needs and the Aries in his sporting prowess – they can find some common ground to express their interests in outdoor pursuits and health.

In the long term, however, although the self-controlled and self-contained nature of Ms Virgo will be initially attractive, this earth sign will be too grounded and practical to hold a long-term attraction for the fiery, quick-fix and non-committed Arian man.

In the bedroom: If Mr Aries can be patient with Ms Virgo, who may not share the same sexual stamina as him, then he will be rewarded with a caring and loving partner. She will also need to take care and not criticise his techniques in the bedroom!

♈ Mr Aries + Ms Libra ♎

Sign	Aries	Libra
Symbol	Ram	Scales
Ruler	Mars	Venus
Type	Cardinal	Cardinal
Element	Fire	Air

Opposites attract but, by the same token, the differences might become too great in a long-term relationship between these two. Ms Libra needs to have a relationship and will go to great lengths to have a union. Initially she will be attracted to the impulsive, innocent and charming Mr Aries but his overbearing nature and bossiness will eventually become a turn-off. She will put him up on a pedestal but will learn as time goes on that he won't fit the mould of the perfect, doting husband. His hot-tempered Arian nature will be too much for the Libran lass, who craves peace and harmony in her love relationships.

Idealistic and always looking at the world through rose-coloured glasses, Ms Libra will become frustrated with the somewhat unromantic Mr Aries, who'd rather be climbing mountains than sitting at a fine restaurant. He, in turn, will become irritated with Ms Libra's indecision and superficiality. While Ms Libra's natural good looks and refinement will charm him, his bossiness and demands will make her very unhappy because she needs peace and balance in her life – not an altogether ideal recipe for a perfect union.

And although Ms Libra might exemplify the perfect woman in charm and looks, underlying her perfect exterior is a very strong and demanding personality. When tested, she can become highly volatile, which is likely to prompt Mr Aries to end the relationship.

In the bedroom: Ms Libra should let her ram take the lead in the bedroom. He is headstrong and likes to lead the way. But being a woman of great charm and diplomacy, she will let her man take charge and sit back and enjoy herself.

♈ Mr Aries + Ms Scorpio ♏

Sign	Aries	Scorpio
Symbol	Ram	Scorpion
Ruler	Mars	Pluto
Type	Cardinal	Fixed
Element	Fire	Water

Mr Aries will be attracted to the deep, sensual nature of Ms Scorpio, making this union overflow with all the trimmings of a passionate love affair, but the security-craving scorpion might become too intense for the easy-going ram, who might find himself drowning in a sea of emotions.

Ms Scorpio is secretive and non-trusting by nature – the opposite of the trusting and open Arian man. The nature of this water-sign girl is needy, controlling and possessive, traits that will eventually drive her Arian mate away. She will show the ram a strong sense of loyalty and commitment but the intensity will overwhelm him. His forthrightness and openness will be refreshing for the Scorpio woman, however, her secretive nature will make him feel insecure. Ms Scorpio is passionate about anything she undertakes and requires considerable depth to her relationships, whereas Mr Aries is fairly simple, and sees the world on a more superficial level.

Communication between these two will not flow: Ms Scorpio has a tendency to not share her feelings and consequently Mr Aries will be left in the dark. Eventually this tension will erupt, causing anger and frustration on both sides.

Ms Scorpio's brooding, jealous and controlling nature will suffocate Mr Aries. Scorpios have a tendency to control their relationship through sex, which does initially attract him; however, it is commitment and emotional consistency she seeks. Unfortunately, Mr Aries is not that intense and needy. Because Scorpio is a fixed sign, change doesn't come easily, whereas Mr Aries is constantly attracted to change. What started out as a promising relationship has nowhere to go. Slowly the flames will die and Mr Aries will pack his bags in search of a far less complex and needy relationship.

In the bedroom: These two sexually charged signs will share plenty of erotic pleasures. Ms Scorpio will let her man take the lead but by no means will she be a passive lover.

♈ Mr Aries + Ms Sagittarius ♐

Sign	Aries	Sagittarius
Symbol	Ram	Archer
Ruler	Mars	Jupiter
Type	Cardinal	Mutable
Element	Fire	Fire

Both these signs enjoy freedom, independence and sporting pursuits. Because the ram and the archer are enthusiastic about life's pleasures, they will relish a relationship that gives them the freedom and space they need. These fire signs are open and honest with each other – what you see is often what you get, which can be a carefree combination of frivolity, playfulness and spontaneity. Both are very open-minded and will be honest about what they need from a relationship.

The archer's thirst for knowledge and her itchy feet for greener pastures keep her Arian lover on his toes. She loves adventure and will never let the grass grow under her feet, a vitality particularly attractive to Mr Aries. He enjoys that his partner has an open-mind and a non-judgmental view of the world, which he can share.

Mutual understanding between these signs is strong; they don't like boundaries in their relationships. Mr Aries and Ms Sagittarius live in the moment, sometimes with little regard for tomorrow. Both have a tendency to rush headlong into any situation, so there is little room for peace and quiet in this union. But, as fire signs, they love the idea of being in love and might quite easily end up walking down the aisle.

In the bedroom: As lovers, the sparks can fly because the archer and ram are both are highly sexed and adventurous in the bedroom. There will be no stopping the bedroom antics of these two fire signs!

♈ Mr Aries + Ms Capricorn ♑

Sign	Aries	Capricorn
Symbol	Ram	Goat
Ruler	Mars	Saturn
Type	Cardinal	Cardinal
Element	Fire	Earth

Astrologically these two signs are in a difficult aspect, which indicates that there will be differences in their natures. Ms Capricorn is ambitious, pragmatic and practical, and her ruling planet Saturn requires her to work hard at her relationships – and that's what she expects from her mate. Although she can teach her Arian lover about the practicalities of life, she is too conservative and serious for this Casanova. Her lack of spontaneity and her serious disposition do not fit well with the playful frivolity of the Arian male.

Ms Capricorn is very serious about her relationships and not as spontaneous as Mr Aries. Before she allows herself to become too passionate, she needs some form of commitment. If he persists in his efforts to crack through her tough exterior, he will find a committed and successful woman, but rarely does he have the patience or tenacity to persist with such a seemingly arduous task.

The fiery warmth of the Aries persona will melt the cold heart of Ms Capricorn, but ultimately her seriousness, lack of frivolity and managerial qualities will be too heavy going for adventurous Mr Aries. He will crave a more carefree union and eventually break free from this structured and rigid relationship which stifles his creativity.

In the bedroom: These two rarely make it to the bedroom because Mr Aries finds Ms Capricorn too straight-laced and conservative to make an exciting lover. She'll lack spontaneity, preferring sex in the bedroom, while the impulsive and excitable ram can hardly make it beyond the backseat of the car!

♈ Mr Aries + Ms Aquarius ♒

Sign	Aries	Aquarius
Symbol	Ram	Water bearer
Ruler	Mars	Uranus
Type	Cardinal	Fixed
Element	Fire	Air

This dynamic duo will find much common ground in a relationship. Both idealistic and adventure loving, Mr Aries and Ms Aquarius will entertain and amuse each other to no end. She will find his child-like qualities endearing and, for him, her quirky sense of humour and *joie de vivre* will be a breath of fresh air.

This Aquarian girl will teach her Arian mate to broaden his outlook and perspective on life, which will lead to a journey of self-discovery. He will admire and respect the intellect of the water bearer and will learn a great deal from her. On the downside, however, he might find her detached, aloof nature a little confusing because he can't really work out what she feels; she has a tendency to hide her emotions under a cool exterior for fear of revealing a vulnerability that her mate might not fully understand.

Despite the obvious compatibility between this pair, Aquarius is a fixed sign, making this woman stubborn and rigid in her outlook on life. This can be frustrating for her Arian partner, who might find her a bit too opinionated and set in her ways. While he enjoys freedom and space in his relationships, it's usually on his terms and he might find his Aquarian mate's equal need for solitude a bit unsettling.

However, Aquarians are altruistic people and if Mr Aries can share his partner's interest in humanitarian causes and intellectual exchange, this could end up a decidedly rewarding union.

In the bedroom: The Aquarian woman is not as sexually needy as her Arian mate and can sometimes be a bit detached when it comes to their lovemaking. She'll need to summon up some enthusiasm and be interested in his sexual advances, otherwise this air girl might find she has extinguished his fire.

♈ Mr Aries + Ms Pisces ♓

Sign	Aries	Pisces
Symbol	Ram	Fish
Ruler	Mars	Neptune
Type	Cardinal	Mutable
Element	Fire	Water

Mr Aries will be drawn to the sensitive, intuitive, gentle Piscean woman. Pisceans yearn for an ideal love and are romantic by nature, so these two signs will be able to give each other the passion they need. A Piscean woman tends to give her all in a relationship and will make her mate her number one priority, which her Arian mate will find very appealing. He will be attracted to the Piscean's sense of adventure, and loves the fantasy world she lives in and her desire to nurture his every need.

The Arian's ability to be open, honest and direct in the relationship will comfort Ms Pisces because she is often unsure of her direction in life and likes her mate to take control. She has a vivid imagination and is highly creative, both qualities that can stimulate the ram in and out of the bedroom. Her sixth sense will be tuned into just the right frequency to know what her Arian mate wants.

Ms Pisces will have a tendency to tire easily from the mundane rituals of life, providing Mr Aries with a legitimate reason not to let moss grow under his feet. However, as long as Ms Pisces sticks to the higher road of her persona and does not fall prey to her addictive, destructive side, then this union will have no boundaries. Mr Aries will never allow himself to become the rescuer or the martyr in this relationship.

In the bedroom: Think Romeo and Juliet or Adam and Eve, and you've got a sexual union like no other. The sensitive and intuitive Piscean will know exactly how to satisfy and fulfil her ram lover's every desire.

Celebrity Mr Aries: Warren Beatty

Actor, born 5.03 pm 30 March 1937 in Richmond, Virginia, USA

Personal planets: Sun in Aries
Moon in Scorpio
Mercury in Aries
Venus in Taurus
Mars in Sagittarius

Marriage requires a special talent, like acting. Monogamy requires genius.

– Warren Beatty

When songstress Carly Simon coined the words 'you're so vain, you probably think this song is about you, don't you', she was painting a fairly accurate insight into the typical self-centred and restless soul of Arian Warren Beatty.

Beatty is notorious for his relationships with a multitude of women over the years, which include high-profile conquests such as Madonna, Joan Collins, Liv Ullman and Carly Simon.

Although he has an impersonal tone to the way he relates, his Venus in the sign of Taurus makes him loyal, physical and highly sensual. He needs comfort, beauty and a Mother Earth type to turn him on, and had a tendency in his younger years to fall in love quickly and frequently, often leaving a trail of heartbroken women in his wake. With a Scorpio moon, Beatty is secretive and mistrusting; however, he also enjoys the emotional intensity of what a relationship can offer and has a strong preoccupation with sex. The need to be closely connected with a partner, yet at the same time wanting his freedom and space, is a source of internal conflict for this man. Women find it hard to understand and interpret him because of this and fear rejection.

From Beatty's chart we can see he is lacking air, which makes him curious about many things. He is always open to learning something new, which extends into his love relationships. He will seek out women who have a strong intellect that can help stimulate his inquiring mind and quench his thirst for mental stimulation.

Beatty has four earth planets, which make him desirous of material comforts. And although he is keen to be in a relationship, he will never compromise himself if it is not working. By the same token, he is direct in his needs and rarely takes no for an answer. His Aries Sun makes him enthusiastic, eager and idealistic in his relationships and a man who can be critical and discriminating. This is perhaps why he has found it difficult in his younger days to find his perfect woman.

Challenge is important to him; this is what makes him maintain interest in a relationship. Because he is easily bored, he has a strong desire for new and exciting adventures. However, a Gemini woman, actor Annette Bening, has captivated this Don Juan and seemingly transformed him into a loving husband and father over the past decade. Beatty and Bening have a magnetic attraction for one another based on her Venus in Aries and his Aries Sun, and they share the same interests and cultural pursuits. They also have a strong physical attraction, each having a heart-thumping impact on the other. As time goes by, their relationship will only become deeper and more transformative. It seems that the Casanova years of Warren Beatty are now well behind him.

TAURUS (21 April–21 May)

☊ Ruled by the planet Venus
Earth sign
Fixed
Feminine energy

In general ...

Taurus is a fixed earth sign, which makes people born under this star sign grounded, practical and fixed in their opinions. They are considered to be the 'nurturers' of the zodiac because they have an innate desire to create stable and comfortable environments for their partners. All the earth signs, which include Taurus, Capricorn and Virgo, contribute significantly in this capacity; however, the Taureans have a stronger desire for material comforts and security and can anticipate their partner's desires. Taureans are also regarded as the 'builders' of the zodiac because their desire for material possessions is high on their list of priorities. Taurean folk will work hard to accomplish their goals.

Venus – the planet of love – rules Taurus, so bulls need to be in a satisfying and stable union. They display certain cautiousness in their relationships until they are satisfied that their partner is on the same wavelength. Taureans are known for their slow and steady pace, which applies to their relationships as well. Although passionate beings, their passion is slow to surface because they need to feel a certain mutual response and desire from their mate. Taureans are emotionally insecure and, despite their air of confidence and security, they need to feel wanted and tend towards possessiveness in relationships.

Like their Libran brothers and sisters, who are also ruled by the planet Venus, they need to be in a relationship to make them feel complete. Difficulties arise in relationships with Taureans because of their tendency to dominate and take charge. Taureans feel they know what their partner needs and, as a result, can be resentful if they feel that their advice is not needed. Because they come from such a genuine space and are extraordinarily helpful, it is disappointing to the Taurean when people do not always respond in the way they expect. A possible limitation for Taureans is that they stay in relationships long after they should have moved on. Emotional and physical security is such a driving force that too much of their life is lived for others; they need to learn to address their own needs in their relationships.

In summary, Taureans are sensual, nurturing and generous individuals and make wonderful partners. If you want a stable, practical and grounded individual in your life, then the bull fits the bill.

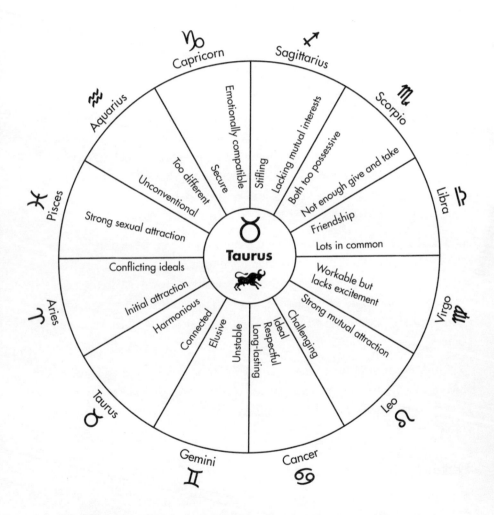

How an Taurean personality might match up with other star signs

Ms Taurus – an overview

The Taurean female exemplifies the saying 'the way to a man's heart is through his stomach'. So if you want a woman whose homemaking skills are near to perfection, this is the girl for you! She is often referred to as the Mother Earth type, because she has a natural and distinctive knowingness, which makes her male partner feel nurtured, comforted and protected. As well as her expert homemaking skills, she is a very loyal and faithful partner and has a high moral code, and so she expects loyalty and faithfulness in her relationships.

Ms Taurus is a true romantic – passionate and sensual around the man she loves. Although often attracted to the creative, fiery and fun-loving members of the zodiac, she adjusts more readily to a partner that can, in the long run, offer her a stable, practical and comfortable environment. Taurean women have strong leadership qualities and, as such, are often the initiator in relationships. Within their psyche, they have a natural flair for accessing their partner's needs and desires. Because of their practical application they often get what they want from their mate.

The Taurean woman can be single-minded and stubborn in her outlook and at times will railroad her mate into doing things the way she wants without considering any other perspective. However, her great capacity to appreciate and enjoy the finer things in life will be an attractive quality for any individual who shares and engages in life with this sensual person.

Once committed in a relationship, Ms Taurus will want to leave it this way. If you are prepared to accept the qualities of the Taurean female, and not try to change her at all, she can make for a committed, enduring and stable partner.

Famous Taurean women

* Shirley Temple (actor)
* Florence Nightingale (nurse)
* Katherine Hepburn (actor)
* Cher (singer)
* Barbra Streisand (singer)
* Donatella Versace (fashion designer)

Combinations

☿ Ms Taurus + Mr Aries ♈

Sign	Taurus	Aries
Symbol	Bull	Ram
Ruler	Venus	Mars
Type	Fixed	Cardinal
Element	Earth	Fire

Mr Aries will be attracted to the strength and comfort of this steadfast earth sign. Ms Taurus can give him much of the sensual pleasures he desires and he will relish her nurturing and stable qualities. Initially, he finds this endearing and, in turn, she finds him a breath of fresh air in her somewhat grounded life. The problem these two may face can be found in the Taurean woman's need for reliability, commitment and security – qualities she can readily provide but that he has great difficulty in reciprocating because it is not in his makeup.

Both these signs are persistent in their pursuit of goals and can therefore encourage one another. The fiery temperament of the Arian man needs at times to be grounded and earthed; this is what his Taurean mate can help him to achieve. He is appreciative of her Mother Earth nature and loves the security and comfort she provides. He also finds the strength she displays particularly attractive. On the downside, however, she is not as energetic and active as him. Her lack of spontaneity can at times frustrate the hot-blooded Arian male.

Taurean females are more stay-at-home, play-at-home types of gals and need a partner who provides a nice home environment, something that Mr Aries is quite capable of supplying. This pair can have a good relationship if they learn to appreciate one another's qualities. Mr Aries needs encouragement with and reinforcement about love and his Taurean mate will be only too eager to please. This union can have some wonderful success because Ms Taurus will constantly enjoy her boyish, impish knight in shining armour, but only if he keeps his Casanova ways in check.

In the bedroom: Here these two can have considerable fun. Both Arians and Taureans have a strong desire for sex, although each has a different approach. Arians are quick and spontaneous and don't need much foreplay, whereas the Taurean gal needs to be wooed before the game starts. If Mr Aries is willing to linger a little longer, sparks will fly in this combination.

♉ Ms Taurus + Mr Taurus ♉

Sign	Taurus	Taurus
Symbol	Bull	Bull
Ruler	Venus	Venus
Type	Fixed	Fixed
Element	Earth	Earth

This combination can be a blissful union or one fraught with disaster. Both Mr and Ms Taurus are fixed signs so the conflict could arise from their uncompromising nature or their unwillingness to be flexible. On the other hand, two bulls can really connect through their similarities: a desire for comfort, material and physical security; appreciation of the finer things in life; and a nurturing nature.

These two could not be happier than sharing the intimacy of a candle-lit dinner and a good bottle of vino; however, their stubborn, obstinate personalities will see them often at loggerheads because this Taurean duo have wicked tempers when pushed to the limit.

On the plus side, she really appreciates her partner's ability to participate in the domestic side of the relationship. And because sensuality is strong on both sides, their intimacy is focused on what they can do to please the other. Both are able to draw material wealth into their lives, as they create a certain structure in their working environment. She is very committed to giving her Taurean mate the emotional and physical support he needs and he responds equally.

Although Ms Taurus will often be stimulated by flighty, fiery types, her desire to stay in her comfort zone with all the material trappings tends to make her realise that Mr Taurus is the one for her. If they can both overcome the hurdle of being so similar, this pair can lead a tranquil existence, indulging in their passion for gardening and homemaking, and anything that falls into their much-loved routines.

In the bedroom: Both male and female bulls have a tendency to over-indulge and sex will be no exception. When these two lock horns, it will be a sexual union where they can most definitely satisfy their physical desires.

♉ Ms Taurus + Mr Gemini ♊

Sign	Taurus	Gemini
Symbol	Bull	Twins
Ruler	Venus	Mercury
Type	Fixed	Mutable
Element	Earth	Air

Fixed with mutable is not a good astrological mix. Ms Taurus is grounded, earthed, practical and sensible, which in the eyes of Mr Gemini is staid and boring. These two signs share no common ground. Ms Taurus has a serious disposition, and her love for order and practical application differs from Mr Gemini, who loves constantly dynamic conditions. She will see him as too fickle and inconsistent, flitting from place to place and with too superficial a view of the world. He needs to move into new situations on a regular basis and constantly seeks out new stimuli, whereas she needs someone with his feet planted firmly on the ground.

At times the bull may even attempt to be more flexible and will feel angry that she can't get out of the mud quickly enough to respond to the ambidextrous Mr Gemini, who will be far too quick-footed and elusive for her. This Taurean woman will drive her Gemini mate to distraction with her responsible and dutiful approach to life. Being an air sign, he is tuned in to his Mercurial mind, which is all about reason and logic and communication; Ms Taurus, however, is the silent type and delivers her passion through actions and deeds. She is particularly consistent in her behaviour within her relationships, unlike the fickle Mr Gemini.

In the bedroom: Ms Taurus is an all-or-nothing kind of women and expects the same from her lover. She'll expect and demand not only sexual fulfilment, but emotional stability from her Gemini mate. She is likely to become resentful if she thinks he's only physically there, which is probably the case since this air man often has his mind further afield.

♉ Ms Taurus + Mr Cancer ♋

Sign	Taurus	Cancer
Symbol	Bull	Crab
Ruler	Venus	Moon
Type	Fixed	Cardinal
Element	Earth	Water

This connection is a match made in heaven because these signs are particularly compatible, sharing similar goals and visions. Ms Taurus is an earth sign and her loyalty and practical approach to life will be greatly appreciated by her Cancerian mate, who needs shelter, nurturing, stability and, above all else, security – which she can supply in abundance. Mr Cancer can, in turn, give Ms Taurus the respect and appreciation she desires.

Because he is prone to emotional highs and lows, she will always be a positive support and has an innate understanding of what her crab needs. When he feels like retreating from the outside world, he can come home where the fires always burn brightly and the warm chicken soup for the soul is in good supply. This relationship has all the ingredients of a loving and lasting combination. With both sharing the traits of sympathy and protectiveness, they know how to ensure their mate feels 100 per cent secure. Domestic bliss is assured because both crave a happy and loving home environment for their families.

In the bedroom: Sexually . . . wow! The Taurus–Cancer pairing is a powerful union because their lovemaking is an extension of the friendship they have cemented. Their relationship carries a lot of depth and is not based on any of the superficial trappings of lust, greed and ego.

☉ Ms Taurus + Mr Leo ♌

Sign	Taurus	Leo
Symbol	Bull	Lion
Ruler	Venus	Sun
Type	Fixed	Fixed
Element	Earth	Fire

These two signs form a difficult astrological aspect, which equates to challenges and competitiveness. The conflict between this pairing is that both are fixed modes of expression, which makes them stubborn and uncompromising. However, if Ms Taurus and Mr Leo are willing to put aside their egos, they can both share some common goals.

They have similar interests, share the same values system and have high moral standards. Their sense of fairness, justice and loyalty is also on the same footing, but their intrinsic personalities are too polarised. The obstinate bull will never bow to the bold, proud lion, who will always need to be in the limelight of the relationship. If Ms Taurus can find a pussy cat among the pride, she might be happy with this more docile, domesticated pet.

Being an earth sign, the Taurean female will always be attracted to the colourful, flamboyant fire sign personalities because they can lift her out of life's predictability. But the speed at which Mr Leo moves, and the adulation Ms Taurus requires from other admirers, tends to bring her insecurities to the surface.

Who's the boss? This can be tricky since both Ms Taurus and Mr Leo will continually fight it out to be on top in their relationship. Since both find it difficult to compromise and can be somewhat obstinate, it is likely they will reach an impasse and be unable to move forward from that point on.

In the bedroom: The makeup sex between Ms Taurus and Mr Leo will be right up there with the best she's ever had! Actions speak louder than words as far as the Taurean woman is concerned so she'll lap up the lion's sincere and passionate lovemaking and in turn make him feel like king of the world!

♉ Ms Taurus + Mr Virgo ♍

Sign	Taurus	Virgo
Symbol	Bull	Virgin
Ruler	Venus	Mercury
Type	Fixed	Mutable
Element	Earth	Earth

Ms Taurus and Mr Virgo can support one another on many levels. The Virgoan shares similar interests and hobbies with her Taurean mate – both earth signs like practical pursuits. Ms Taurus will appreciate Mr Virgo's attention to detail and the extra effort and energy he puts into the relationship. He is skilled at catering to her every whim and, in turn, will value the loyalty and security his Taurean mate provides.

These two are both particularly faithful when it comes to love, and it will take a long time for them to give up on each other. However, their strong desire to please people does not always lead to an equally strong understanding of what each other needs on an emotional front.

Ms Taurus will provide an excellent home environment for her mate; she'll cook the gourmet meal while he'll do the washing up. Although this pair will do well in most aspects of their lives together, their main challenge will be communicating, because people born under these signs tend to lose themselves in their own world by focusing on the practicalities of life.

Since both Taurus and Virgo are earth signs, they can be practical and self-sufficient. Neither will need to exploit the other's generosity and good nature. On the downside, Virgoans can be quite critical, and their constant nagging might frustrate Taureans, who will soon tire of the analysis of their actions. Likewise, the methodical and somewhat slow energy of Ms Taurus will aggravate the energetic and alert Mr Virgo. Ultimately, these two can have a lasting union if they don't get too bogged down in the functionality of life.

In the bedroom: Silent sex is probably the best way to describe these two in bed. Taureans prefer to get down to the business of making love rather than talking about it and Mr Virgo is simply not a man who's into talking dirty. Mr Virgo will be most concerned about pleasing his lover and Ms Taurus will be the eager recipient of such TLC!

♉ Ms Taurus + Mr Libra ♎

Sign	Taurus	Libra
Symbol	Bull	Scales
Ruler	Venus	Venus
Type	Fixed	Cardinal
Element	Earth	Air

Venus, the planet of love, rules both these signs so you might think this is a match made in heaven. The Taurus–Libra couple have a lot in common: an appreciation of the arts, beauty, comfort and material delights. However, Taurus is a more practical and grounded sign, preoccupied with wealth acquisition, while Librans are more interested in accumulating people rather than objects in their life's journey. Additionally, Ms Taurus doesn't possess the same gracious, light energy of the charming Mr Libra.

This relationship is more workable as a friendship rather than a loving union. They can learn much from each other: Ms Taurus can learn to loosen up and sharpen her communication skills, and Mr Libra can become more decisive and practical.

The Libran male is more open to social interaction and a willingness to please and often won't express his needs in the relationship, whereas his Taurean mate will call a spade a spade and not waste precious time weighing up the pros and cons.

In the bedroom: These two signs are both ruled by Venus so their union has the potential to be hot and heavy. She desires a strong physical bond and he'll want a creative kitten in the sack, so if they meet somewhere in the middle then there'll be no turning back!

♉ Ms Taurus + Mr Scorpio ♏

Sign	Taurus	Scorpio
Symbol	Bull	Scorpion
Ruler	Venus	Pluto
Type	Fixed	Fixed
Element	Earth	Water

Passion will ignite this pair because they both share a deep level of commitment, loyalty and security, and are also extremely possessive. Fundamentally they are compatible; however, Ms Taurus is less complicated than, and not as intense as, Mr Scorpio, who will at times try to manipulate her good nature. The scorpion is too demanding and has a tendency to play power games in his relationships, whereas the single-minded bull, who is fiercely loyal, has a less-controlling nature.

Although both will show a strong sense of commitment in the relationship, Ms Taurus will at times become overwhelmed by Mr Scorpio's nasty sting and power games. Sexually they can complement each other as they are both strong, sensual beings.

The Taurean woman will have no qualms about standing up for herself, which is where the union may fall apart because Scorpio's temperament is also unrelenting – rarely will one make the first move and back down. But, if they can temper their combative streaks and enjoy the sensuality the relationship has to offer, the compatible bull and the scorpion can be very happy together. Both have a faithful nature and, when committed, will be intensely loyal to each other. Ms Taurus will make her mate feel secure and nurtured, which is comforting to the secretive and suspicious Scorpio, who might have suffered rejection in his childhood and is looking for guarantees in life. This is something his Taurean mate can provide.

In the bedroom: There'll be a strong physical chemistry between Ms Taurus and Mr Scorpio. He will enjoy his woman's possessive nature and she'll understand the deep-seated passion that burns within him!

☿ Ms Taurus + Mr Sagittarius ♐

Sign	Taurus	Sagittarius
Symbol	Bull	Archer
Ruler	Venus	Jupiter
Type	Fixed	Mutable
Element	Earth	Fire

Ms Taurus and Mr Sagittarius don't seem to have much in common. Her practical no-nonsense attitude to life is in complete contrast to the adventuresome, freedom-loving archer. Ms Taurus will find her Sagittarian man attractive and, in some respects, be in a bit in awe of his ability to move so freely through life with such an optimistic and philosophical outlook. She is more materialistic and comfort-oriented and gets too bogged down with the nitty-gritty of daily life. The archer appreciates some of the grounding qualities that his lady bull provides, but her complacency and smothering tends to stifle his outward expression.

Ms Taurus is ruled by Venus, making her needy with a partner and wanting the comforts and security of life, whereas Mr Sagittarius prefers a less-structured and more dynamic lifestyle where he can come and go as he pleases and satisfy his lustful nature. Ms Taurus will seem like a mother-like figure to the impish archer. He likes to fire his arrow in many directions and finds her too stifling as a love interest. She in turn will find the archer too fickle and will not share his passion for energetic, daredevil pursuits, instead preferring a mate who will be happier to work alongside her pulling out weeds in the garden.

The bull is a domesticated creature and her archer companion will not provide her with the luxuries and comforts she desires. She would much prefer a weekend in a five-star resort than a tent in the Himalayas.

In the bedroom: A Taurean woman shows her love best through touch and a Sagittarian man needs to express himself both physically and verbally. They will have different sexual needs, but a little give and take will go a long way in helping these two reach nirvana in the bedroom!

♉ Ms Taurus + Mr Capricorn ♑

Sign	Taurus	Capricorn
Symbol	Bull	Goat
Ruler	Venus	Saturn
Type	Fixed	Cardinal
Element	Earth	Earth

These two earth sign possess a favourable combination of similar qualities. They share the same ideals and values and are both driven to accumulate resources to help them lead a comfortable and secure lifestyle. Taureans will provide the perfect home setting for the Capricornian man who will appreciate his partner's ability to be the perfect wife, hostess and homemaker.

Ms Taurus and Mr Capricorn will stay committed to one another and see divorce as a last resort. Both have supportive natures and a mutual understanding of the practicalities of life and it is the interest of materialistic security that helps keep this pair together. Mr Capricorn is interested in social status and respect, so Ms Taurus is the ideal partner to help him in his rise to fame and fortune. Loyalty, integrity and commitment feature very strongly in this match. They will provide each other with tenderness and love in and out of the bedroom, and be appreciative of the other's enduring love and devotion.

Money is important to both the Taurean and Capricornian, but only as a means to provide comfort and security to the former, and power and prestige to the latter. Behind every great man there's an equally strong, determined woman and Ms Taurus is no exception. She and her earth sign mate will make a formidable couple – he as a great leader and she alongside him as his loyal supporter.

In the bedroom: The goat never finds it easy to express his desires but, with the right encouragement, Ms Taurus and her man will be swinging from the chandeliers in no time!

♉ Ms Taurus + Mr Aquarius ♒

Sign	Taurus	Aquarius
Symbol	Bull	Water bearer
Ruler	Venus	Uranus
Type	Fixed	Fixed
Element	Earth	Air

Too many fundamental differences exist between the straight and inflexible Taurean and the rebellious and independent water bearer. Ms Taurus is attracted to predictability and safety and will not dip her toe into unchartered waters, while Mr Aquarius loves nothing better than adventure, excitement and surprises. Both are fixed signs and as such are inflexible in their ability to compromise – neither will be pushed into doing anything they don't want to, making it difficult for them to find common ground.

Ms Taurus will find Mr Aquarius not reassuring enough because he will always display an impersonal and aloof detachment that will frustrate the security-conscious bull. He seeks adventure, attracting him to the unconventional – he would prefer to live in a commune where he can spread love everywhere, unlike the domestic goddess Ms Taurus, who could think of nothing worse than not having a cosy, comfortable home.

One of the fundamental differences in this love relationship is that Aquarians are attracted to people from all walks of life, and friendship is sometimes more important than love and intimacy. This can be frustrating for the single-minded, loyal Taurean woman who might not know where she stands in the relationship. Such uncertainty can lead to feelings of insecurity in Ms Taurus, who likes to know the status quo.

Such differences can be insurmountable, with one's requirements in love rarely being met by the other. The sooner they recognise the incompatibilities, the easier it will be to move on and find a more suitable partner.

In the bedroom: The element of surprise will feature strongly in the bedroom of Ms Taurus and her Aquarian lover. He will shock her with his wacky and outlandish sexual antics; she should try to lighten up and enjoy the ride!

♉ Ms Taurus + Mr Pisces ♓

Sign	Taurus	Pisces
Symbol	Bull	Fish
Ruler	Venus	Neptune
Type	Fixed	Mutable
Element	Earth	Water

Both Ms Taurus and Mr Pisces seem to have a mutual respect for each other and their qualities. The fish may be seen at times to be swimming in a sea of his own emotions, but his lady bull's sensitivity, understanding and patience will nurture and support his fragile and introspective soul.

He will be drawn to the practical, earthed and stable influence of Ms Taurus, who will not pander to the escapist tendencies he displays at times. She will never take advantage of her vulnerable mate, instead instilling in him a sense of confidence and self-worth because she appreciates and admires his creative flare, kindness and compassion. The bull will ensure her fish swims upstream instead of going in different directions and will not tolerate any wayward behaviour.

Ms Taurus is more pragmatic, predictable and self-assured than her Piscean mate, making her able to keep him on the straight and narrow and steer him away from his negative addictions. In turn, he will thrive and enjoy the supportive and nurturing home environment the bull creates. Both share a passion for music and the arts, creating a strong bond between them. Ms Taurus loves to be wooed and pursued and is a true romantic at heart, like her equally sensual Piscean man. Ms Taurus and Mr Pisces will find solace and comfort in a happy and harmonious love relationship.

In the bedroom: He'll be a sensuous and romantic bedmate for the equally loving and caring bull. Her feminine energy will be hugely appealing to her ethereal and intuitive Piscean lover and these two will unleash pleasures from out of this world!

Celebrity Ms Taurus: Cher

Actor/singer, born 7.25 am 20 May 1946 in El Centro, California, USA

```
Personal planets: Sun in Taurus
                  Moon in Capricorn
                  Mercury in Taurus
                  Venus in Gemini
                  Mars in Leo
```

I don't need a man, but I'm happier with one – I like to have someone I can touch and squeeze and kiss. But I don't fold up and die if I don't have a man around.

– Cher

Cher is a Taurean and has both her luminaries – the Sun and Moon – in earth signs. This gives her a craving for security and an ambitious desire to succeed in life. In addition, her Moon in Capricorn gives her a predisposition to become younger as she gets older and to enjoy her later years; like a good wine, she gets better with age. However, she has an intense fear of being rejected, so she doesn't always communicate her needs.

This Moon sign is a good placement for professional success, yet it isn't sympathetic to creating intimacy. Cher also has a bundle of signs in Gemini which adds to her youthful image. Her one water element makes her need to experience intensity in her relationships; she can be dependent on a relationship which provides her with nurturing and support. Conversely, Cher is also a woman who is inclined to fall impetuously in and out of love in the same way, leaving a trail of confused men in her wake. She is not naturally self-assured and has had issues about her self-image for many years.

Her chart reflects a need for respect and approval from her relationships, and she commands commitment and loyalty from the individuals with whom she aligns herself. However, she also has a strong urge to control her relationships and can be a very demanding mate. Communication is high on her agenda and she needs a partner who is mentally challenging and can keep her on her toes. Her Mars in Leo gives her a sense of the dramatic and she will always be attracted to a man she can be proud of and respect. Her need to share her thoughts and ideas and just 'hang out' with her mate is very important.

Cher has had two significant relationships. The first of these was with singer Sonny Bono, who was an Aquarian and complemented her Venus in Gemini, so there was an attraction of the minds. The second was with singer Gene Simmons, who is a Virgo, and again the strong Mercurian quality that they shared in their mental exchanges is what kept this relationship alive. Gene's Sun sign in Virgo complimented her Sun sign in Taurus, which brought stability into their fiery union.

A great mate for this woman would be someone who can genuinely instil a sense of confidence in her. He would have to be a strong and reliable person, and someone who would allow himself to be manipulated.

Mr Taurus – an overview

The Taurean male exudes a practical, stable and reliable force. This man requires his life to be complete in all aspects, from his working life to his personal, intimate relationships. Mr Taurus is insatiable in his desires, and his sensuality and passion is directed towards the best things in life. The Taurean man is single-minded in his desire for a stable and grounded mate and, like his female counterpart, will be initially cautious when first establishing a relationship. He needs to feel secure in his relationship before he can commit. However once shot with Cupid's bow, Taureans plummet hook, line and sinker into the throes of passion.

They are committed, loyal and generous in their relationships and willing to share their hard-earned rewards with their partner. Taureans make ideal companions on the domestic front because they are happy to play their part on a practical level – from running the house and cooking a meal to doing the gardening. He does not expect his partner to be the sole nurturer in the relationship because he too has wonderful instinctive qualities, knows what his mate needs and is always keen to provide her with the best he can offer.

The Taurean male has, however, a fixed mode of expression and, although stable by nature, carries a degree of rigidity and stubbornness. As a result, he has certain opinions and beliefs that are difficult to change. Because of his rigidity, it is difficult for him to adapt to his partner's requirements. This inability to change and be flexible can make Taureans become too complacent in relationships, which can result in partners feeling that their lives with them are a little like being stuck on a never-changing treadmill.

Famous Taurean men

* Andre Agassi
  (tennis player)
* Sigmund Freud
  (psychologist)
* George Clooney (actor)

* Adolf Hitler (dictator)
* David Beckham
  (soccer player)
* William Shakespeare
  (playwright)

Combinations

♉ Mr Taurus + Ms Aries ♈

Sign	Taurus	Aries
Symbol	Bull	Ram
Ruler	Venus	Mars
Type	Fixed	Cardinal
Element	Earth	Fire

Taurus is an earth sign and far too grounded and stubborn for the quick-footed Arian. Slow and steady usually wins the race but not when the prize is the impulsive, energetic Ms Aries. The steadiness the Taurean can provide is just what Ms Aries needs but sadly this sign is lacking the spontaneity the Martian girl desires. Taurean males are more stay-at-home, play-at-home kind of guys and they need a partner who provides a nice home environment – Ms Aries is many things but domestic goddess is not one of them!

While Taurean men can provide a nurturing and stable environment, this may not be exactly what the Arian girl enjoys. She's driven by unpredictability and excitement, so the Taurean man might not present a big enough challenge for her.

Taureans are possessive, obsessive and can become too complacent once entrenched in the relationship. As Ms Aries makes her way around the zodiac, ironically, this is the sort of man she ultimately needs to give her the stability, passion and commitment she is continually looking for.

In the bedroom: Ms Aries may be too selfish and headstrong for the stubborn and inflexible bull. Physically they come from two different spheres – she's into instant gratification for the sake of pleasure itself and while's he's into sex, usually he wants something practical from it – like a family!

♉ Mr Taurus + Ms Taurus ♉

Sign	Taurus	Taurus
Symbol	Bull	Bull
Ruler	Venus	Venus
Type	Fixed	Fixed
Element	Earth	Earth

The Taurean man exemplifies everything a woman requires from her mate. He is exceedingly generous, even when he is down to his last penny, and will wine and dine her and be a faithful and loyal companion – an ideal mate for most.

However, the combination of Mr Taurus and Ms Taurus is a particularly compatible one. These two earth signs like the same things and identify one another's needs very well. They both are into comfort, security, pleasure and stability and will both work hard to achieve this in their union. With both being committed individuals, issues of trust, loyalty and honour are high on the list of virtues they seek from one another. Ms Taurus will give her Taurean man all the nurturing and home comforts he desires and, in turn, he will supply her with the financial and physical comforts she so enjoys.

The only difficulty is that both being fixed earth signs, they have a streak of stubbornness that can creep into their union. These two bulls butt heads and do not let up. Together, these Taureans are single-minded individuals and will rarely give in unless one or the other has a more compromising streak in their nature – usually the Mother Earth Ms Taurus who wants to keep the family unit together.

This match is highly passionate; they are both lusty individuals who have a healthy appetite for life's pleasures. It is this quality that will always be a driving force in this union.

In the bedroom: Both male and female bulls have a tendency to over-indulge and sex will be no exception. When these two lock horns, it will be a sexual union where they can most definitely satisfy their physical desires.

♉ Mr Taurus + Ms Gemini ♓

Sign	Taurus	Gemini
Symbol	Bull	Twins
Ruler	Venus	Mercury
Type	Fixed	Mutable
Element	Earth	Air

The Taurean male and Gemini female personalities are totally out of sync because they have vastly different perspectives on life. The security-conscious bull is fixed in his opinions and has firm ideas and, although generous to a fault, is possessive and single-minded. This is in stark contrast to Ms Gemini, who is fickle in her emotions and changeable in nature, and who needs to be in a dynamic atmosphere where she can buzz around and gather people and information along the way. Hers is an air sign, which is all about communication, so she lives very much in her headspace compared with the grounded, slower earth character of Mr Taurus.

These two will never be able to live in a harmonious union because the Taurean man has a strong nesting instinct and hankers for the predictable. He needs a domesticated partner who can provide him with his comforts and earthly pleasures, and someone with Ms Gemini's vacillating nature will drive him to distraction. More of a one-to-one man, Mr Taurus will find the elusive Gemini too hard to pin down and tame. Ms Gemini, on the other hand, has a tendency to intellectualise her feelings and needs a mate she can communicate with and with whom she can share her love of variety and texture.

Ms Gemini is a mutable sign so she can readily adjust to new situations and circumstances and will be more adaptable than her Taurean mate. Ask Ms Gemini how she feels and her answer will be 'I think', and there lies the difference between these two signs. Ultimately, Ms Gemini is too changeable for the slow and steady bull, who likes to know exactly where he is heading.

In the bedroom: Gemini women are extremely changeable and flighty and enjoy flirting, unlike the loyal Taurean who is more of a one-woman man who likes to fast-track it to the bedroom rather than talking about sex. However, it's rare the day when these two will even make it to the bedroom.

♉ Mr Taurus + Ms Cancer ♋

Sign	Taurus	Cancer
Symbol	Bull	Crab
Ruler	Venus	Moon
Type	Fixed	Cardinal
Element	Earth	Water

This is a great match because people born under these signs have a mutual rapport – earth and water are a good mix. Mr Taurus is a loving sort of guy who really appreciates a sensitive woman, and Ms Cancer is a nurturer and a giver. With both having a great capacity to nourish and support their partners, they will bring out the best qualities in one another.

The crab is ruled by the Moon, which can make her more prone to mood swings and depression. Mr Taurus will provide the understanding and steadfastness to assist her when she needs that extra loving care and support. In turn, she will provide him with the traditional family values and instinctive loving qualities for which Mr Taurus yearns.

The crab is a feeling individual who understands her Taurean mate's outbursts of jealousy and possessiveness as she too shares these qualities, so both have a mutual rapport on an intimate level.

These two like predicability and don't like to venture to greener pastures once they have found their little plot to set up a safe and secure home. Both have strong family ideals and values, which is an important ingredient for this match.

Both Taureans and Cancerians have a record of longevity and commitment, and rarely will they abandon their union until they have exhausted all possibilities. Theirs is a staying power with a sense of endurance. Home life is an important feature of this union and Mr Taurus will value his Cancerian mate's input in creating a comfortable environment for him. Both have their own individual style and artistic streak, which will be reinforced in this union.

In the bedroom: Neither Mr Taurus nor Ms Cancer gives themselves completely unless they're truly, madly and deeply in love. This will be a physically loving union as both are able to nurture and support their lover.

♉ Mr Taurus + Ms Leo ♌

Sign	Taurus	Leo
Symbol	Bull	Lion
Ruler	Venus	Sun
Type	Fixed	Fixed
Element	Earth	Fire

The glamorous and generous-spirited Ms Leo will be a natural drawcard for the Taurean male. Her appealing looks and vivaciousness will charm this man off his feet. However, she is not one to commit as easily as he would like, so this match will take some time to get off the ground. If the relationship is taken to a new level, these two will need to keep their controlling natures in check because both are fixed signs and share the same stubborn streak.

The flamboyant Ms Leo will be expressive in her needs and desires, all of which Mr Taurus can readily provide. However, owned by the world, she is too elusive and the Taurean's possessiveness will really need to be tempered if he wants to keep his girl. Mr Taurus is looking for constancy and requires a mate to keep the home fires burning but, alas, Ms Leo wants to be on stage, her name flashing in neon lights.

The Taurean male is possessive and inclined to see his lioness as a possession to be proud of. And, although she will appreciate his overwhelming generosity and loyalty, she has the same values – she needs a partner who shares the same outgoing broad-mindedness.

Although Ms Leo has a strong ego she does respond to her mate in a very loving and committed way and that can be a great contribution to this match. Sadly, however, Mr Taurus will be too needy because his sense of security is based on ownership. This is not what the lioness is about. She is too regal and too 'out there' for the more home-loving bull.

In the bedroom: Mr Taurus is a man who enjoys the sensual pleasures of life. His lioness lover will turn him on with her passion and beauty, and these two will share a fulfilling sexual union. But Ms Leo must temper her ego if she wants to stay in the loving embrace of her earthly man forever.

☿ Mr Taurus + Ms Virgo ♍

Sign	Taurus	Virgo
Symbol	Bull	Virgin
Ruler	Venus	Mercury
Type	Fixed	Mutable
Element	Earth	Earth

These two earth signs are very comfortable with each other. They share a strong need for the physical and both are very ready to please their partner. She is a perfectionist and will always want to be seen in her best light. The virgin has a tendency to give it her best shot and her Taurean companion will be very appreciative. As long as Ms Virgo can keep her critical nature under control, this pair will have a mutual respect and an underlying empathy for one another.

The Taurean male's requirements are very simple – honesty, loyalty, integrity and commitment, and these are the same for his Virgo lover, making this a union of many common interests.

Both Mr Taurus and Ms Virgo have personal issues with security that can affect their relationships. She is too critical of herself and he sometimes tries too hard to accumulate money and possessions. Because she is a mutable sign, Ms Virgo is the one who will always be accommodating in the relationship and will bend to allow her fixed bull to think he is in control. But little does he know that beneath this seemingly passive-natured girl lies a tower of strength. The ice maiden doesn't get her nickname for nothing.

In the bedroom: Sexually, both are sensual beings and will revel in their compatibility in the bedroom. Ms Virgo is loyal, supportive and practical and will be easily seduced by the generosity of her Taurean man.

♉ Mr Taurus + Ms Libra ♎

Sign	Taurus	Libra
Symbol	Bull	Scales
Ruler	Venus	Venus
Type	Fixed	Cardinal
Element	Earth	Air

This is a good match and can be a very workable arrangement because both are ruled by the planet Venus and share an appreciation of the finer things in life. Ms Libra represents the goddess of love, and her beauty, style and charm captivate all the signs, especially the Taurean male who has an eye for beautiful objects.

Although they are both ruled by Venus, each has an individual approach to what they need in their relationships. The Taurean relates more to what makes him feel comfortable and secure in terms of physical belongings, while the Libran is more into finding comfort from her relationship rather than possessions. This can transcend their union as Mr Taurus shows his love by providing the physical pleasures his Libra mate desires and she in turn supplies him with love and desire expressed through words and actions.

They each need a partner who can share their lives and be ready to please the other and give of themselves. The Taurean man will adore his Libran woman and will be impressed by her grace and tact; in turn, his strong and supportive energy will be a turn-on for her.

In the bedroom: Both Ms Libra and Mr Taurus are hopeless romantics who together can make mind-blowing love. Both are very physical and will be able to fulfil each other's wildest fantasies.

♉ Mr Taurus + Ms Scorpio ♏

Sign	Taurus	Scorpio
Symbol	Bull	Scorpion
Ruler	Venus	Pluto
Type	Fixed	Fixed
Element	Earth	Water

Sex will be the driving force in this union as lust and more lust is primarily what these two signs have in common. Both Scorpios and Taureans desire a close, possessive relationship where they feel they are number one. Because people born under these two signs are in a fixed mode of expression, they are not adaptable to change and so can become totally committed once they feel they have trust in their relationships.

Ms Scorpio is often afraid of rejection and will engage in certain controlling behaviour patterns to feel in charge of the relationship and her Taurean mate will lap up the attention. These signs share a similar intensity in their relationship: both are very devoted and will become extremely protective of their loved one. Pity help anyone that does an injustice to their lover, because they will rise to the occasion and become very angry. Loyalty is what seems to keep these two on an even keel; it is the common thread that binds this couple. Mr Taurus will find Ms Scorpio vulnerable and will always ensure that she is in a safe haven. In turn, she will use her mysterious charm to woo her man.

Taureans and Librans do not communicate their emotions easily. Ms Scorpio is secretive and distrusting and Mr Taurus has a tendency to bury his head in the sand. Hence it is important for these two to recognise that this trait might cause some difficulties. All in all, however, this is a good and powerful combination because the watery Scorpio will always shower her bull with much love and affection.

In the bedroom: Erotic and devouring best describe the love-making between Mr Taurus and his Scorpio lover. They both expect to be loved completely and not simply because they're great in the sack!

♉ Mr Taurus + Ms Sagittarius ♐

Sign	Taurus	Sagittarius
Symbol	Bull	Archer
Ruler	Venus	Jupiter
Type	Fixed	Mutable
Element	Earth	Fire

The key words for Ms Sagittarius are growth and idealism. She is the optimist of the zodiac and the adventurer who craves knowledge – always looking to spread her wings and travel to greener pastures. Mr Taurus will not find this conducive to the type of relationship he desires, which is steadfast, predictable and conservative. The Sagittarian woman will find him too limiting and boring and, although she will be appreciative of his grounding influence on occasions, in the long run she will see it as a form of control and restriction. Because she values her freedom above all else, she will feel like a caged bird while her Taurean mate, resentful of her ability to soar, will try to clip her wings.

This is not a good mix as the fiery Sagittarian does not want to be grounded; she needs excitement and is not interested in the same material trappings as the Taurean man, who loves security and comfort.

Ultimately these two are likely to head in different directions but if Mr Taurus is willing to give Ms Sagittarius some space, she will come home from her adventures to recuperate and enjoy the burning home fires and cosy environment he has created. If things don't fall into place for the security-loving Mr Taurus, he will eventually stamp his hoof and demand an end to this lopsided union.

In the bedroom: The initial sexual chemistry will be strong between the earth man and fire woman. He'll love her raw sex appeal and animal instinct; in turn, he'll make her feel complete.

♉ Mr Taurus + Ms Capricorn ♑

Sign	Taurus	Capricorn
Symbol	Bull	Goat
Ruler	Venus	Saturn
Type	Fixed	Cardinal
Element	Earth	Earth

This combination has a strong connection and seems to get on well, with both thriving on building a structured lifestyle with all the trappings of wealth. These two will work hard to achieve this and will support and appreciate one another's desire for material accumulation.

Ms Capricorn can appear a little detached and aloof – in fact, rather cold and pragmatic; however, she is also very defensive of her mate and will protect him with all her might. In turn, Mr Taurus will thrive on Ms Capricorn's practical application to life and will value her support to attain success.

Earth signs need to learn how to express these needs verbally so that partners can gain an insight into each other's frustrations and, if these two can break down the communication barriers, they will build a close-knit and secure future together and enjoy the fruits of their labours.

Because this pair shares a conservative attitude towards life, they will proceed with caution until they feel a genuine trust. Then things will start to speed up. Both are also interested in long-term commitments and will always prefer marriage to merely living together. Mr Taurus will be attracted to the ambitious quality Ms Capricorn displays and she, in turn, will support and encourage her man at every turn.

Mr Taurus desires a partner who will give him the security he craves and who is genuine in her affection. These earth signs have a mutual affinity and are often considered to be the builders of the zodiac – the ones who create a comfortable and secure lifestyle for themselves.

In the bedroom: Although suited on many levels, physical passion is unlikely to be the driving force behind this union. But that's not to say they won't find a comfortable physical relationship together. Romance and long-lasting sexual compatibility is on the cards for these two earth stars.

♉ Mr Taurus + Ms Aquarius ♒

Sign	Taurus	Aquarius
Symbol	Bull	Water bearer
Ruler	Venus	Uranus
Type	Fixed	Fixed
Element	Earth	Air

The Taurean man will find Ms Aquarius too independent, wilful and flamboyant for his more conservative and structured personality. She values her freedom above all else and so Mr Taurus will always be trying to tame his free-spirited mate. Unfortunately, because Ms Aquarius has the same fixed mode of expression as him, she will be unwilling to temper her desire for universal love.

At times the Aquarian might show a conservative streak because she is, on the one-hand, traditionally oriented yet, on the other, attracted to a bohemian lifestyle. This can confuse Mr Taurus who thinks he has her figured out until she is off saving the world on one of her humanitarian pursuits, leaving him out in the cold. When she returns, hoping to pick up where they left off, she'll be most surprised to find that he has finally lost patience, which usually takes some time for the loyal and patient bull, and is fussing over the next woman in his life.

Both these signs are generous spirits and are always willing to lend a helping hand but while Ms Aquarius expects nothing in return, Mr Taurus is more calculating in his approach. He will find the water bearer too cold and detached for his sensual nature and will feel his efforts to ensure she feels secure and comfortable are not always appreciated.

One of the fundamental differences in this love relationship is that Aquarians are attracted to people from all walks of life, and friendship is sometimes more important than love and intimacy. This can frustrate the single-minded, loyal Taurean, who likes to know the status quo, and lead to feelings of insecurity. This couple's requirements in love will rarely be met by each other, and the sooner each recognises these incompatibilities, the better for all.

In the bedroom: The detached air woman will be a little confusing to read for the down-to-earth Taurean. She's more into a meeting of the minds than a melding of the bodies.

♉ Mr Taurus + Ms Pisces ♊

Sign	Taurus	Pisces
Symbol	Bull	Fish
Ruler	Venus	Neptune
Type	Fixed	Mutable
Element	Earth	Water

These two romantics of the zodiac will find a loving partner in each other. The attraction between them lies in Mr Taurus's ability to ground the dreamy Piscean and create stability and structure in her life. Ms Pisces, in turn, will introduce her mate to a more spiritual and creative way of life.

Pisceans are particularly intuitive and have an innate knowledge of what their partner needs, and Taureans love the closeness and intimacy that their Pisces mate injects into the partnership. The Taurean man loves to be wanted and needed, and will value his partner if he feels appreciated, while Ms Pisces will always feel grateful for the loving and stable environment her mate can provide. His pragmatic and practical approach to life enables the bull to keep his dreamy, and sometimes wayward, escapist Ms Pisces on the straight and narrow. If she receives the right encouragement and nurturing, Mr Taurus will be privy to a Pandora's box of amazing spiritual, artistic and aesthetic delights.

Although the Taurean man is not always seen as the most exciting partner of the zodiac, his Piscean companion has the ability to transform his earthly approach to life and create a more ethereal and spiritual affair. This really is a wonderful union with both having the ability to nurture and encourage each other's more positive aspects.

In the bedroom: It might not be the thunderbolt sex experienced by some other combinations but there'll be a fair share of tenderness and affection between Mr Taurus and his gentle Piscean lover. They are both extremely sensual; he's into romance and she's into fantasy, which creates a utopian union.

Celebrity Mr Taurus: Jack Nicholson

Actor, born 11 am 22 April 1937 in Neptune City, New Jersey, USA

Personal planets: Sun in Taurus
Moon in Virgo
Mercury in Taurus
Venus in Aries
Mars in Sagittarius

I only take Viagra when I'm with more than one woman.

– Jack Nicholson

Jack Nicholson is a man who likes to call the shots in his relationships. He has six earth elements in his chart making him rigid, stubborn and exceedingly single-minded. Furthermore, he is also tuned into the material comforts of life, which give him a sense of emotional and physical security. He feels emotionally isolated and his bravado often conceals an inner sensitivity, and so he requires a mate who can encourage him to develop a greater sense of self-worth.

As an earth sign he is very sensual and requires a responsive partner who can appreciate the skilful art of his love-making, which can incorporate much fun and playfulness. Nicholson is frank about his sexual desires, and is spontaneous yet also has a high standard of morality.

His relationship difficulties occur as a result of his Venus in Aries which can make him particularly selfish and impersonal. His chart is coloured by the unpredictable planet Uranus, which gives him an excitable and unpredictable quality in his interactions. Nicholson is turned on by constant, new stimulation and the conquering of new frontiers. In his relationships he has an independent and impersonal streak and because he is egocentric he can be insensitive to the feelings of others. His Mars is in the sign of Sagittarius, so the motto 'don't fence me in' is synonymous with Nicholson's desire to have a mate who allows him to have space and freedom.

He enjoys the thrill of the chase more than the conquest and the journey is more exciting than the actual arrival. Nicholson desires his partners to blend into what he wants and cannot empathise with what their own needs are. He has a strong and protective quality and, although committed in his undertakings, he can become obsessional when it comes to his relationships.

His early long-term partnership with Angelica Houston, who is a Cancerian, would have complemented his Taurean energy because earth and water are always a good combination and her fluidity would have encouraged his growth and development. In addition, his next relationship with Rebecca Broussard, a Capricornian, links with his Taurean sun; both are earth signs and have a mutual affinity.

Nicholson's priorities in a relationship are honesty, respect and approval and he will always be motivated by a partnership that will bring about a transformational quality to his life.

GEMINI (22 May–22 June)

Ruled by the planet Mercury
Air sign
Mutable
Masculine energy

In general ...

Geminis are the butterflies of the zodiac. They need constant stimuli and ever-changing conditions. As they become dissatisfied with one phase of an experience they will move on to new pastures where they believe the grass is greener. However, it is usually not that long before they are on the move again.

To understand these creatures, you need only to look at their ruling planet Mercury, which is the planet of communication. Mercury is the messenger of the gods and likes to be constantly imparting and receiving knowledge. Hence, Geminis like to keep active as they move about their environment, flitting from place to place and collecting bits and pieces of information along the way.

Gemini is an air sign and people born under this star sign love to be involved in new experiences, conquering new frontiers and expressing themselves in a warm and lively manner. Often referred to as the sign of the split personality, Geminis can be passionate about a particular belief system yet will change dramatically when the occasion suits. This makes it very hard for their partners to accept and understand them.

Both the Gemini man and his female counterpart find emotional intimacy stifling. They would love to be in a committed relationship as long at it does not restrict their freedom and their independence. They love to be in love, but without the commitments that successful relationships usually demand. Needy and claustrophobic involvements will stifle them, causing them to flee and leave a bewildered partner behind. In the first blush of romance, their Gemini mate seemed so eager to please.

If you want stability and reliability, steer clear of Geminis because they don't have a long concentration span and will move from one idea or thought in an instant, leaving some confusion in their wake. Emotionally immature, but without malice, Geminis are like small children in a candy shop: they like to try before they buy and make their way through the selection. But just when they think they've found the sweetest on offer, something else turns up to tempt them.

Geminis tend to be on the unstable side and it will take a particularly easygoing personality to join in the quickstep of the excitable and dynamic twin.

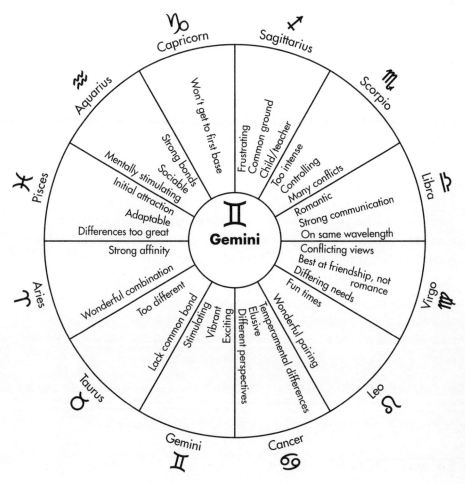

How a Gemini personality might match up with other star signs

Ms Gemini - an overview

Ms Gemini is outgoing and gregarious and in a relationship will always assume the role of what her partner wants her to be, which often is not how she really feels. She can create much confusion within her relationships because although she knows her own mind well, she doesn't always say it as it really is, so her unsuspecting partner has little warning that things are not travelling smoothly.

Geminis are the mutable air sign, flowing from place to place and person to person, constantly stimulated by new, more interesting and diverse companions. Ms Gemini needs a partner who is lively, fun-loving and as zany as herself. Don't wait around too long for this lady, guys, because she is likely to be off in search of someone more interesting, leaving you wondering where it all went wrong. Geminis are the chameleons of the zodiac, fitting in to whatever mood and situation takes their fancy.

These flirtatious souls can be inconsistent when it comes to feelings, wanting something one minute and then vacillating to something else the next, and often driving their partners crazy with their duplicity. Geminis seem to have multiple relationships in their lives; they marry more than once and always seem to end up with the same problem – an inability to keep their feet firmly on the ground and settle down.

The Gemini woman has a tendency to be attracted to partners with a high intellect. Since her planetary ruler is Mercury – the ruler of communication – she will demand that her partner has a good mind and can challenge her. She enjoys being the eternal student and is always gathering snippets of information from every experience.

Gemini women fall in love frequently but if a relationship comes with strings attached and the union is too restrictive, she will be off like the wind, in search of freedom and another wild ride on the train of love.

Famous Gemini women

* Marilyn Monroe (actor)
* Gladys Knight (singer)
* Steffi Graff (tennis player)
* Nicole Kidman (actor)
* Joan Rivers (comedian)
* Judy Garland (singer/actor)

Combinations

♊ Ms Gemini + Mr Aries ♈

Sign	Gemini	Aries
Symbol	Twins	Ram
Ruler	Mercury	Mars
Type	Mutable	Cardinal
Element	Air	Fire

These signs often become friends before a romance starts. Geminis can teach the Arian a lot about communication skills. The Gemini woman excites the Arian guy because she will always be naturally curious and interested to learn what makes him tick. This pair can have a lively and entertaining relationship because they both share the same enthusiasm and zest for life.

Ms Gemini will always flatter and tell Mr Aries what he wants to hear, and as long as he has the ability to mentally stimulate her, she will enjoy their times together. This couple are more interested in having fun – whether it's Ms Gemini surrounded by her books or Mr Aries off mountain climbing – rather than being bound by domestic duties. They give one another plenty of space to pursue their own hobbies and interests.

Ms Gemini and Mr Aries are not possessive or clingy types and both crave excitement, change and adventure. Because neither is materialistic, their relationship will be based more on experiencing life through travel and hobbies rather than building a traditional domestic existence. Being a mutable sign, the Gemini is very adaptable to the whimsical Arian, who understands her changeability. The natural curiosity this couple shares will allow them to be open to new experiences and challenges. Both have a natural curiosity and need mental stimulation so they will be able to communicate well with each other. Aries being a fire sign can, however, turn up the heat and he can warm the cockles of this woman's heart. The combination of fire and air is a positive flow of energy; fire needs oxygen to keep the Arian invigorated.

In the bedroom: Sexually, however, the Gemini and her Arian mate don't always combine well – Geminis are interested in the stimulation of the mind whereas the passionate Arian male is more interested in the stimulation of the body. Although the Arian male is more sexually driven than Ms Gemini, with the right attention they can grow together and appreciate each other's needs and desires.

♊ Ms Gemini + Mr Taurus ♉

Sign	Gemini	Taurus
Symbol	Twins	Bull
Ruler	Mercury	Venus
Type	Mutable	Fixed
Element	Air	Earth

The personalities of the Gemini woman and the Taurean man are totally out of sync because they have vastly different perspectives on life. The stable Mr Taurus is security conscious and fixed in his opinions and ideas. Although generous to a fault, he is possessive and single-minded compared with Ms Gemini, who is emotionally fickle and needs to be in a dynamic atmosphere, where she can buzz around and gather people and information along the way. Gemini is an air sign, making this lady all about communication. She lives very much in her headspace compared with the more grounded, earthy Mr Taurus.

These two will never be able to live in harmonious union because Mr Taurus has a strong nesting instinct and needs a domesticated partner who can cater to his comforts and earthly pleasures, particularly his need for the predictable. Ms Gemini, on the other hand, has a vacillating nature that will drive her Taurean mate to distraction. She needs someone she can communicate with and with whom she can share her love of variety and texture, but he is more of a one-to-one man and will find the elusive Gemini too hard to pin down and tame.

Born under mutable and air signs, Ms Gemini can readily adjust to new situations and circumstances and will be more adaptable than Mr Taurus. She also has a tendency to intellectualise her feelings. Ask Ms Gemini how she feels and her answer will be 'I think', and there lies the difference between these two signs. Ultimately, Ms Gemini is too changeable for the slow and steady bull who likes to know exactly where he is heading.

In the bedroom: Gemini women are extremely changeable and flighty and enjoy flirting, unlike the loyal Taurean who is more of a one-woman man who likes to fast-track it to the bedroom rather than talking about sex. But given their differences, it's pretty unlikely that these two will ever make it this far.

♊ Ms Gemini + Mr Gemini ♊

Sign	Gemini	Gemini
Symbol	Twins	Twins
Ruler	Mercury	Mercury
Type	Mutable	Mutable
Element	Air	Air

These twins have a great deal in common and seek the same things from each other. They have a notorious flirtatious streak so that neither can claim they are making the other jealous. Both are daring, expressive individuals who seek to throw themselves into life with enthusiasm. They are independently minded and will value their freedom and shun any form of restriction. They will not try to control each other but will always encourage and support the other's interests. On most occasions they will share a passion for the same activities and pursuits.

Because Gemini is a mutable sign, this man and woman have adaptable natures and are more understanding of each other's need for freedom and flexibility. They verbally communicate how they feel, which is important in any relationship, and enjoy fun and frivolity together.

However, this banter doesn't always lead to a solid union. Ms and Mr Gemini may not have the power to hang in because both relate more on a superficial level. When the going gets tough, these two agile creatures will not want to work through the difficult times; they want fun, not hard work and a commitment to maintaining a sustainable relationship.

Sexually these two will ignite one another as they are drawn to the charm and elusive quality that each displays. Air signs exude a detached persona, which can often incite emotional insecurity in the earth and water signs; however, it is a quality that really turns on Ms and Mr Gemini, and makes for a more unpredictable quality that keeps the relationship alive and challenging. The twins become bored if things are too predictable. They need emotional freedom and tend to become panicky if they feel too trapped and stifled.

In the bedroom: The sexual escapades of two Gemini lovers have no limits. Since the changeability they each feel is reflected in the other, they will be able to satisfy each other's whims and double the magic of the occasion.

♊ Ms Gemini + Mr Cancer ♋

Sign	Gemini	Cancer
Symbol	Twins	Crab
Ruler	Mercury	Moon
Type	Mutable	Cardinal
Element	Air	Water

Ms Gemini tends to fall in love with men who are mentally agile and can stimulate her mind. She is a great conversationalist and will always be attracted to a man who has a lot to say. Alas, Mr Cancer is too introverted, serious and sensitive for the restless Ms Gemini. She doesn't have the understanding of the intuitive and emotionally sensitive crab, who is far more of a feeling type than her.

Geminis and Cancerians come from different perspectives. He will start to communicate his feelings only when he feels sure of the relationship. Security is an important ingredient for this guy. On the other hand, his Gemini interest will profess love in an instant only to change her mind the next day, leaving the confused crab feeling even more insecure.

These two signs have a different approach to relationships. Ms Gemini will verbalise what she feels putting Mr Cancer at a disadvantage. He doesn't have the same dexterity with words. Instead he will show how he feels with great sensitivity and depth, ways not so easily understood by his Gemini lover.

At first the silent crab will mystify Ms Gemini because she will see this brooding quality as a sign of significant sensuality; however, the fickleness Ms Gemini so often displays will create much tension between this pair. His strong need for security will drive a wedge between them and Ms Gemini will feel too trapped and stifled by what she interprets as clingy and somewhat controlling behaviour.

In the bedroom: The sex life of Ms Gemini and Mr Cancer will be surprisingly good – he's perceptive enough to go with the flow when she changes her mind about what turns her on. She'll appreciate his warm and caring approach to sex and feel very safe from the world in his arms.

♊ Ms Gemini + Mr Leo ♌

Sign	Gemini	Leo
Symbol	Twins	Lion
Ruler	Mercury	Sun
Type	Mutable	Fixed
Element	Air	Fire

The mental agility and desire to have fun and constant stimulation will herald a partnership that is a success – both in and out of the bedroom. Mr Leo leans more to the side of commitment and will want to have Ms Gemini by his side to show her off. And as long as he loosens the reins on occasions and gives her enough freedom to be herself, this relationship has the makings of a wonderful pairing.

She will be attracted to the lion's sense of adventure and has the power to control his arrogance and temper his desire to be in the spotlight. She has a way of cutting Mr Leo down to size. He seems to be able to take instructions rather readily from Ms Gemini, who will always critique his actions with typical Gemini explanations.

They both love to be involved in myriad activities so the constant variety will appeal to Ms Gemini. It is all about being able to provide enough stimulation for this flighty female and Mr Leo has a way of clipping Ms Gemini's wings without her knowing it. The sun-ruled Leo has great aspirations and the Gemini will use her air qualities to inspire her man to bigger and better things. This couple will walk side by side in their external search for stimulation, variety and excitement, all of which they can equally provide.

In the bedroom: The twin might put out the fires of passion burning deep within her Leo with her cool and detached approach to sex. The proud lion likes to be king – even in the bedroom – and might become insecure if he thinks he's not satisfying his changeable Gemini lover. She'll need to be more in 'bed' than in her 'head' if she wants a compatible sexual union.

♊ Ms Gemini + Mr Virgo ♍

Sign	Gemini	Virgo
Symbol	Twins	Virgin
Ruler	Mercury	Mercury
Type	Mutable	Mutable
Element	Air	Earth

Gemini and Virgo are ruled by the planet Mercury; hence they both feel the need to communicate despite coming from different angles. Although they need to feel mentally stimulated, Mr Virgo is more practical and down to earth than Ms Gemini, who tends to talk fast and doesn't really think before she opens her mouth.

She is too impractical and messy for the discriminating and analysing Virgo, who likes routine and order. He is a germ freak and, with her being no domestic goddess, there won't be time for the dust settle on this relationship. Domestically they are poles apart and, in the long run, will start to irritate one another.

Any initial attraction will not be long lasting because these two have very different needs in a relationship. Ms Gemini is a restless individual, full of enthusiasm and who likes to roam freely, which annoys the serious, heavy-going Mr Virgo. His constant disapproval and criticism leaves Ms Gemini feeling unhappy, meaning she won't stick around for long.

Earth and air don't seem to mix well. Mr Virgo likes to spend his time plodding away at various projects until they're completed systematically, while Ms Gemini finds it hard to concentrate on one thing for any sustained period of time with the result that boredom usually prompts her on to move on to the next pursuit.

In the bedroom: Sexually speaking, Mr Virgo is unlikely to set the bed of Ms Gemini on fire. He is not prone to sexual abandonment but, given that Ms Gemini is light and airy in her approach to sex, it might just work.

♊ Ms Gemini + Mr Libra ♎

Sign	Gemini	Libra
Symbol	Twins	Scales
Ruler	Mercury	Venus
Type	Mutable	Cardinal
Element	Air	Air

Astrologically, the combination of Ms Gemini and Mr Libra is what is referred to as a trine aspect, which means the flow of energy between these two signs is one of harmony and unity. They are both fairly impulsive in love, more so Ms Gemini, and both being air signs means they have a natural affinity. Ms Gemini is attracted to the charming, dedicated, romantic Mr Libra, who is equally charmed by her ability to keep him on his toes.

Air signs seem to lack the depth and intensity of the water and earth signs, meaning their relationships work on a more superficial level. Ms Gemini may at times become impatient with Mr Libra's indecisiveness because she is very quick to make up her mind, but his Venusian charm will always manage to win her over.

Both these signs are characterised by a narcissistic streak, resulting in the Gemini and Libran being preoccupied with themselves and often clouding their ability to truly understand what they need from the relationship. Mr Libra will be far needier in a relationship than Ms Gemini, who is more inconsistent about what she wants and doesn't always convey her true feelings or desires to a partner. Instead, she will often tell him what she thinks he wants to hear rather than being truthful and straightforward.

Mr Libra is idealistic in love, putting his beloved on a pedestal and seeing her as something more than mortal. He needs to be more realistic in his relationships and Ms Gemini needs to be less fickle and more honest in what she wants if this is to be a lasting union.

In the bedroom: Although these two air signs will become one in bed, it is unlikely they will experience the same wild abandonment and consuming passion of two earth or fire combinations. But sex between Ms Gemini and Mr Libra will be changeable and delightful.

♊ Ms Gemini + Mr Scorpio ♏

Sign	Gemini	Scorpio
Symbol	Twins	Scorpion
Ruler	Mercury	Pluto
Type	Mutable	Fixed
Element	Air	Water

Mr Scorpio is too deep and intense for the light-hearted Ms Gemini, who loves to spread her wings and fly, not like a soaring eagle high into the sky, but rather like a butterfly, flitting from one flower to another, spreading her light and captivating audiences along the way.

Mr Scorpio will start to brood and become insanely jealous because he doesn't understand the flighty ways of the ever-changing Gemini lass. He needs her in his corner, under his thumb, where he can control her movements and keep a watchful eye over his possession. But Ms Gemini will never allow any man to control her impulsive ways; she can't be tamed and the more her Scorpio mate tries to hold on to her, the more elusive she will become until she has vanished from sight.

Mr Scorpio is a fixed water sign, so his inflexible attitude will create tension in this union. He will find that Ms Gemini is too interested in her own world and will not give him the attention he so desperately craves to feel wanted and desired. This man is a passionate being and needs depth and intensity in all his undertakings, especially in his relationships. He is guided by a keen sense of intuition and will be put off by Ms Gemini's flirtatious yet harmless ways. Because Mr Scorpio is so untrusting he will never really believe the many truths and non-truths she tells him.

Mr Scorpio needs a lady that he can smother with love but Ms Gemini will find this claustrophobic and uncomfortable – this girl needs loads of space.

In the bedroom: Sex to a Scorpio is the meaning of life itself, but to a Gemini woman it's simply one of life's little pleasures. Ms Gemini is likely to find her Scorpio lover far too serious about sex and her mind may wander off into the ether during their lovemaking.

♊ Ms Gemini + Mr Sagittarius ♐

Sign	Gemini	Sagittarius
Symbol	Twins	Archer
Ruler	Mercury	Jupiter
Type	Mutable	Mutable
Element	Air	Fire

These two have some common traits and understand each other on some levels but Ms Gemini is a communicator in a superficial sense, whereas Mr Sagittarius is the eternal student, the philosopher and the adventurer and cannot be bogged down by the inconsequential issues of life.

Ms Gemini has a lot to learn from her archer who is constantly aiming his arrow higher at the horizon and, if she is patient enough to listen to his wisdom, this could be an exciting partnership. Both have a strong sense of adventure and love to horse around, although she lives more in her head and is not as physically active. And with neither of them being domesticated, they are happiest following their passions rather than playing house.

If Ms Gemini is willing to let her archer guide her through the journey of life, this bond could last an eternity; however, the ever-changing faces of the twin will, at times, frustrate the deeper, more philosophical Sagittarian guy. On the bright side, both Geminis and Sagittarians look for greener pastures and are motivated by new frontiers, so life together will never be dull. The combination of air and fire signs means they will have a certain idealism in their relationship, despite a tendency towards a wandering eye. This, however, gives them common ground for greater understanding of each other.

The qualities that define this relationship are freedom and independence, which are extremely important to both parties. Mr Sagittarius has an ability to relate well to people and will understand his Gemini mate's need to socialise, which he will not interpret as flirtatious but rather as an expression of her personality.

In the bedroom: He might be more physical than he is mental, but that doesn't mean the twin and archer won't blend in bed to become one. The archer will definitely be the more demonstrative and fiery mate in this sexual pairing.

♊ Ms Gemini + Mr Capricorn ♑

Sign	Gemini	Capricorn
Symbol	Twins	Goat
Ruler	Mercury	Saturn
Type	Mutable	Cardinal
Element	Air	Earth

The energy is so different between these two that rarely would they attract each other as a prospective partner. Ms Gemini values her freedom and will find the goat too conservative and boring to keep her interested. He is a pragmatic and steady creature who values integrity, loyalty and commitment from his mate – traits that Ms Gemini definitely lacks. She is not the sort of woman who can help this ambitious goat further his status in life. He needs someone who will walk methodically and slowly beside him, sharing in his quest to achieve fortune and success.

Ms Gemini doesn't share Mr Capricorn's persistence and interest in commitment and success and his desire for social status and security. His ambitious streak is fuelled by his ruling planet Saturn, often referred to as the 'cosmic cop'. He values tenacity and hard work and is far too disciplined in his approach to life for Ms Gemini. He will judge harshly her sense of frivolity and fun and lack of commitment. She will be too much of a featherweight to compete in his corner of the ring.

The Capricornian guy requires solidity and dependability from his partner and, although they both seek independence, he still will want to be the boss in this match. In turn, Ms Gemini will not give up her independence for the promise of security and financial gains.

In the bedroom: Both the Gemini and Capricorn approach sex from the same perspective. Neither is necessarily after a mind-altering experience but rather a comfortable and pleasurable one. He'll skip with joy if his Gemini lover is receptive to his playful, physical advances; in turn, she'll appreciate words to arouse her desires.

♊ Ms Gemini + Mr Aquarius ♒

Sign	Gemini	Aquarius
Symbol	Twins	Water bearer
Ruler	Mercury	Uranus
Type	Mutable	Fixed
Element	Air	Air

Ms Gemini and Mr Aquarius will have a great time together because both are communicative and love to be surrounded by people. They share a passion for the unpredictable, especially the Aquarian, so these two will have no trouble striking up a friendship.

Since neither likes to be fenced in, they will respond well to the other's need for independence. Both are a little zany and have a sense of adventure and will be willing to try something new at the drop of a hat. Ms Gemini is more adaptable than her fixed-sign Aquarian mate and is likely to be more flexible in the relationship. Although he has an appetite for the new and exciting, he can be strong-willed when he wants his own way – a stubborn streak that might frustrate his Gemini mate. Both seem to have an erratic disposition but, as long as they can temper this side of their personalities, they will have a great meeting of the minds.

Both air signs, this pair can be a little cool in their expression of affection and might be accused of not knowing how to give themselves properly in love. However, since they share this trait, they seem to understand each other very well. Neither is romantic by nature and both like to experiment in love, often leaving them open to being labelled promiscuous. It is not that they are fuelled by sexual desire; instead they love people from all walks of life and are naturally drawn to different experiences and situations.

In the bedroom: 'It will happen but it won't happen overnight' is the best way to sum up the consummation of the relationship between these two air signs. Sex is not a priority for either and they might end up spending more time on mental stimulation than the physical. But when they eventually remember that lovers actually do have sex, it is sure to be uncomplicated and exciting.

♊ Ms Gemini + Mr Pisces ♓

Sign	Gemini	Pisces
Symbol	Twins	Fish
Ruler	Mercury	Neptune
Type	Mutable	Mutable
Element	Air	Water

Although these two signs are challenging astrologically, they are often drawn to one another. Ms Gemini is attracted to the Piscean's complex, sensitive nature and is fascinated by what lurks in the depth of his mind. He is intrigued by the verbal agility she displays. Both have very different personalities but share an inability to commit, giving them both their own time and space.

The main challenge in this Gemini–Piscean relationship is that they are both elusive and fail to adequately express their needs, which can result in difficulties when it comes to cementing their union. Ms Gemini will try to accommodate her partner's needs, only to become resentful down the track when she finds out that her needy-in-love Piscean relies on her strength to give him the self-esteem that he needs to keep him on the straight and narrow. Ms Gemini, however, is unlikely to have the commitment and endurance to support the needy Mr Pisces; often he will be the one having to prop up his unpredictable and highly strung Gemini mate.

Geminis and Pisceans carry too much baggage and, in a relationship, will allow each other to indulge in their addictive tendencies. Although Ms Gemini values her freedom, she also needs a strong arm to lean on at times and can take advantage of her compassionate and devoted Piscean, who may be too weak to stand up to his demanding mate. Ms Gemini, despite her reliance on him, will see his martyr-like qualities as a sign of weakness and will walk all over him on her way to the next challenge.

In the bedroom: With both approaching sex from a different perspective, Ms Gemini is likely to be too selfish and immature for the sensitive and ethereal Piscean. The fish may also become insecure and jealous of her sometimes casual attitude to lovemaking.

Celebrity Ms Gemini: Marilyn Monroe

Actor, born 9.30 am 1 June 1926 in Los Angeles, California, USA

```
Personal planets: Sun in Gemini
                  Moon in Aquarius
                  Mercury in Gemini
                  Venus in Aries
                  Mars in Pisces
```

Before marriage, a girl has to make love to her man to hold him; after marriage, she has to hold him to make love to him.

– Marilyn Monroe

Marilyn Monroe was a Gemini who had an abundance of planets in water and air but lacked a healthy dose of earth and fire elements. This resulted in an exaggerated need for love and attention. She was fundamentally insecure and always sought to find herself through others. Being a Gemini, her life was about interactions with people, and communication was a strong feature in all her relationships. She had a strong desire for emotional and physical security but hid her insecurities to avoid exposing her inner self. This protective wall she built around herself made it difficult to know the true Monroe. She lacked self-confidence, which was manifested in her tendency to grab on to love in personal relationships, even if it proved dissatisfying and unproductive.

Monroe's Moon was in the detached sign of Aquarius so, as needy as she was, she also had to have some space and independence within her relationships. She was attracted to unconventional liaisons but was at times delusional and had no clear perspective on who her partner really was. Because she lived in a fantasy world, she could be deceived by others. Her strong escapist tendencies, upon which her relationships were founded, were the result of her Mars in the sensitive sign of Pisces, making her desire the secretive and clandestine. Her attraction to men was based on her idealistic perception and involved a great deal of romanticism and fantasy.

Monroe had an insatiable desire to explore her sexuality. From this perspective she could be rather impulsive and would jump into entanglements impetuously without assessing the consequences. However, she had a strong sense of loyalty and commitment to her partners. And although her willingness to merge with her partner's persona and become what he desired might have given her a lot of pleasure, it was also her downfall.

Her first marriage was to professional baseball player Joe DiMaggio, a Sagittarian, and although the union was short lived, he remained a strong influence throughout her life. He and Monroe would have had an immediate attraction because his Sun sign, Sagittarius, was in opposition to her Sun in Gemini, and opposites attract. He encouraged her and gave her the self-confidence she lacked. Another lover former, US president John F. Kennedy, was a natural drawcard for Monroe. He was a fellow Gemini and their Suns were linked by three degrees of separation, so they certainly had a significant effect on each other.

Mr Gemini - an overview

He is a man on the move, a talker. You can pick the charming Gemini lad in a crowded room as he will be the one with an array of females around him hanging off his every word. But be warned, girls: this man is hard to tame. He adores women but is slow to commit because he doesn't want to forsake any potential opportunities that might be just around the corner.

The Gemini man has a great intellect and is also versatile and knowledgeable. He needs a partner with whom he can share his ideas and concepts because he is not known so much for his sexual prowess as for his mental agility. Because his is a mutable sign, he can adjust to his partner's demands to some degree; however, he will stay strong in his convictions to do the things he feels are important to him. He is flirtatious and seems to win his way to a woman's heart through his flattering words, which at times might be insincere.

Characterised by a split personality, Mr Gemini can be changeable in his desires and needs. This duality leads to great highs and lows, so he needs a girl who can adapt to this often radical swing of moods. At times he can be rather detached emotionally because all air signs have a cool disposition and partners often feel left out in the cold.

Gemini males love the challenge of the chase so allow him the space to make his own moves. He makes a formidable partner once he commits but he needs to be kept stimulated and challenged, otherwise he is sure to wander.

Famous Gemini men

* Johnny Depp (actor)
* Paul McCartney (singer/songwriter)
* Paul Gauguin (artist)

* Bob Hope (comedian)
* John F. Kennedy (US president)
* Bob Dylan (singer)

Combinations

♊ Mr Gemini + Ms Aries ♈

Sign	Gemini	Aries
Symbol	Twins	Ram
Ruler	Mercury	Mars
Type	Mutable	Cardinal
Element	Air	Fire

The Gemini man is probably the most suitable air sign for this fiery female. They both love adventure, variety and have an innocent approach to life. Arians thrives on new challenges and experiences, and the mental dexterity Mr Gemini brings to the table can often be an aphrodisiac for Ms Aries.

These signs often start as great pals. Geminis can help Aries expand their mental horizons. They click well because they give one another plenty of space and don't seem to get caught up in the jealousy game. Neither is very domestically oriented, which comes as a relief for the Arian gal, who would rather be out socialising and meeting new people with her Gemini guy than keeping house.

He has a way with words and can provide her with the right amount of flattery to keep her satisfied. He also understands his child-like companion because he, too, is a child of the zodiac. With both on the same wavelength and both liking plenty of freedom in their relationships, this is an ideal combination. Ms Aries and Mr Gemini are not driven by material possession so they share a friendship that involves mutual ideas and interests. Being a mutable sign, the Gemini is exceedingly adaptable to his whimsical Arian and understands her changeability.

In the bedroom: Sexually these two signs don't always ignite: the Arian is more prone to instant gratification and the Gemini is not noted for his sexual prowess. But if they take the time to fan the flames, they could ignite a fire that is hard to extinguish.

♊ Mr Gemini + Ms Taurus ♉

Sign	Gemini	Taurus
Symbol	Twins	Bull
Ruler	Mercury	Venus
Type	Mutable	Fixed
Element	Air	Earth

Fixed with mutable is not a good astrological mix. Ms Taurus is grounded, earthed, practical and sensible, which in the eyes of Mr Gemini is staid and boring. These two signs share no common ground. She has a serious disposition, and her love of order and practical application is poles apart from the Gemini guy, who loves constantly dynamic conditions.

Ms Taurus will see Mr Gemini as too fickle and inconsistent, flitting from place to place and with a superficial attitude to life. Geminis need to regularly move into new situations and be constantly stimulated, while Ms Taurus needs someone with their feet planted firmly on the ground. At times the bull may try to be more flexible and feels somewhat angry at herself that she can't respond quickly enough to the ambidextrous Mr Gemini, who will be far too quick-footed and elusive for her.

The Taurean female will drive her Gemini mate to distraction with her responsible and dutiful approach to life. His is an air sign, hence he is tuned in to his Mercurial mind, which is all about reason and logic and communication in words, whereas she is the silent type and delivers her passion through actions and deeds.

The outlook for this relationship isn't good. Ms Taurus is consistent in her behaviour within her relationships, unlike Mr Gemini, whose fickle tendencies are unlikely to bring out the positive side of the bull.

In the bedroom: Ms Taurus is an all-or-nothing kind of woman and expects the same from her lover. She'll want not only sexual fulfilment but emotional stability from her Gemini man and may become resentful when she thinks he's there only in a physical sense – which is probably the case since this air man often has his mind in the clouds.

♊ Mr Gemini + Ms Gemini ♊

Sign	Gemini	Gemini
Symbol	Twins	Twins
Ruler	Mercury	Mercury
Type	Mutable	Mutable
Element	Air	Air

These twins have a great deal in common and seek the same things from each other. They have a notorious flirtatious streak; neither can claim that they are making the other jealous. Both are daring, expressive individuals who seek to throw themselves enthusiastically into life. Equally, they are independent individuals who dislike any form of restriction. They value their freedom and will not try to control each other; on the contrary, they will encourage and support each other's interests. On most occasions, they will share a passion for the same activities and pursuits.

Both are adaptable personalities because Gemini is a mutable sign, and so will be more understanding of each other's need for freedom and flexibility. These two characters will always communicate their thoughts, an important feature of any successful relationship, and bring fun and frivolity into the union. However, this banter doesn't always lead to a solid union. Ms and Mr Gemini may not have the power to hang on because they both relate on a superficial level. So when the going gets tough, these two agile creatures might not want to work through the difficult times; they want fun instead of the hard work and commitment needed to sustain a relationship.

Sexually these two will ignite because they are drawn to the charm and elusive quality that each of them portrays. Air signs exude a detached persona, which can often incite emotional insecurity in the earth and water signs; however, it is a quality that really turns on Ms and Mr Gemini, and lends more of an unpredictable quality to the relationship, keeping it alive and challenging. This pair becomes bored if things are too predictable. They need emotional freedom and tend to become panicky if they feel trapped and stifled.

In the bedroom: The sexual escapades of two Gemini lovers have no limits. Since the changeability they each feel is reflected in the other, they will be able to satisfy each other's whims and double the magic of the occasion.

♊ Mr Gemini + Ms Cancer ♋

Sign	Gemini	Cancer
Symbol	Twins	Crab
Ruler	Mercury	Moon
Type	Mutable	Cardinal
Element	Air	Water

The Gemini guy has a playful, light-hearted, elusive charm that makes this crab feel alive and entertained. Her instinctive and nurturing ways give Mr Gemini a feeling of safety and warmth; however, her hard, protective shell will at times become too much of a barrier for the outgoing, social Gemini. He will also find it difficult to handle his Cancerian mate's vulnerable and moody disposition. The crab tends to protect but also needs protection and the Gemini man is too single-minded and selfish to understand the needs of this intuitive and sensitive creature.

While he instinctively endears himself to a wide variety to women, she is too cautious and self-protecting to take to the light-hearted approach Mr Gemini uses so readily. The difference between these two is that she means what she says but he doesn't, so they come from different moral standings. His truth changes at a whim and she is very much a woman who remembers and keeps track of the past. Ms Cancer could teach Mr Gemini a few things about appropriate behaviour; however, his charming ways often get him out of a tight spot so he thinks he doesn't need to heed the crab's wise words.

She is about family unity and he is about friendships far and wide so her nesting instincts are worlds apart from his. The Cancerian's 'I feel' approach to relationships versus the Gemini's 'I think' attitude sums up this union – she is an instinctive, feeling type of person and he is a more analytical soul with emotions close to the surface.

In the bedroom: Ms Cancer is forever trying to please her Gemini man but this trait might not spill over into the bedroom. When these two are expressing their physical connection, the penny might just drop for the sensitive and emotional Cancerian, whose magical Moon qualities might lure her Gemini man out of his head and fully into her bed.

♊ Mr Gemini + Ms Leo ♌

Sign	Gemini	Leo
Symbol	Twins	Lion
Ruler	Mercury	Sun
Type	Mutable	Fixed
Element	Air	Fire

Natural charm, flamboyancy and quick-wittedness are what attract the Gemini guy to this alluring lioness. Their combined communicative and social interactive skills are what bind these two together.

Mr Gemini can admire and encourage Ms Leo's talents when she seeks his approval, which she often does. Although they both like to be in the limelight, Mr Gemini will need to take the back seat at times to allow his star to have her way.

Ms Leo expects loyalty and faithfulness from her mate and will keep his philandering ways under control. This woman is strong and assertive – just what Mr Gemini needs. She thrives on competition and, because her Gemini guy is not fazed by this behaviour, he will tolerate her desire for success. They are both pleasure-seeking individuals and will always keep each other entertained. Since both are romantically inclined, given the right environment, they can make a wonderful love combination.

Geminis and Leos share similar interests, particularly a love of theatre since they are both natural-born actors, playing roles on and off the stage. If Ms Leo is willing to curb her overpowering need for Mr Gemini's constant approval, these two could have a lively and dynamic relationship. She might be just exciting enough to sustaining his attention long enough to create a lasting union.

In the bedroom: Since Geminis take everything much more lightly than other signs, including sex, he might well extinguish the lion's fiery passions with his casual and nonchalant attitude towards their lovemaking. This man will need to deepen his intensity if he wants to keep Ms Leo from wandering off to find a more demonstrative mate.

♊ Mr Gemini + Ms Virgo ♍

Sign	Gemini	Virgo
Symbol	Twins	Virgin
Ruler	Mercury	Mercury
Type	Mutable	Mutable
Element	Air	Earth

Mr Gemini and Ms Virgo will have a lively exchange of words because both are ruled by the planet Mercury. Theirs will be an easy flow of communication but the language each uses will be very different.

In their displays of affection for each other, the Gemini guy will err on the side of dishonesty, whereas his Virgoan mate will be totally truthful. He will often tell her what he thinks she wants to hear and be quite affronted with her critical and truthful analysis. Mr Gemini will find Ms Virgo's nit-picking and her attention to detail a turn-off; this scatter-brained man would prefer not to hear the truth about his lazy and untidy ways.

Domestically this couple are poles apart and in the long run will start to irritate each other. The air and earth components have a different way of seeing life, which signifies many challenges in a union. Mr Gemini, with his carefree, come-what-may approach to life, will find Ms Virgo too conservative and responsible. She needs to know where she is heading and he prefers the element of surprise. Since both are mutable signs they do have an ability to see each other's perspective but, regardless of their adaptability, rarely will they have the inclination to completely surrender to the other's needs. It's highly unlikely these two will be able to sustain a long-term relationship given their myriad different needs and expectations.

In the bedroom: The Virgoan woman will need to feel some degree of security with her Gemini lover if she's ever going to give of herself physically. This will be hard for the twin, who is as changeable as the wind. It's unlikely there'll be much sexual compatibility between this earth woman and her air man.

♊ Mr Gemini + Ms Libra ♎

Sign	Gemini	Libra
Symbol	Twins	Scales
Ruler	Mercury	Venus
Type	Mutable	Cardinal
Element	Air	Air

These charming critters pair up beautifully. Both air signs, the Gemini and Libran take a more superficial and light-hearted approach to their relationship, but that's not to say that they don't feel passion and intensity when connected. However, they don't bring too much heavy energy into their connection.

Both are good talkers and can spend endless hours discussing a range of topics. Socially these two are very adept at conversing with a wide cross-section of people and will admire, rather than feel jealous, of the other's ability to captivate a crowd. Mr Gemini will find Ms Libra's grace, charm and refinement alluring and she will find his intellect and mental dexterity particularly appealing.

Concerned with how they are perceived, this pair will always want to put their best foot forward, rarely allowing the other to drop their guard. If they can strip the veneer of superficiality from their personas, they will share a vulnerability that each understands. Mr Gemini will always benefit from the wise and balanced viewpoint that Ms Libra has to offer when he is so often split down the middle; in turn, he will, in an instant, help her jump off the fence and take a stand.

Astrologically these two air signs form a harmonious combination and if they can look seriously into one another's eyes and see each other's soul then it will be a romance made in heaven.

In the bedroom: The quest for pleasure rather than lustful fulfilment will fuel the fires of passion between these two air signs. Neither has raw, animal instincts in their makeup, so they will blend beautifully when they make slow, instinctive love.

♊ Mr Gemini + Ms Scorpio ♏

Sign	Gemini	Scorpio
Symbol	Twins	Scorpion
Ruler	Mercury	Pluto
Type	Mutable	Fixed
Element	Air	Water

The union of Mr Gemini and Ms Scorpio is not a match made in heaven. The energy these two exude is very different. The Scorpio expects commitment from her man which is something Mr Gemini struggles with. She tends to scare the boyish Gemini with her brooding and secretive disposition and he will never be able to handle her possessive and controlling ways.

This man abhors any female who wants to pin him down and her jealous streak will send him running into the arms of a more easy-going and fun-loving woman. Nothing scares a Gemini guy more than commitment and because Ms Scorpio needs guarantees, issues of trust will creep into the pairing process, forcing an impasse that will rarely see the two head down the road of love. This man is far too interested in himself to provide the deep and intuitive Ms Scorpio with a caring and sensitive partner. She, in turn, is security-conscious and manipulative and rarely will she fall prey to the wishy-washy, smooth-talking, charming ways of Mr Gemini.

Mr Gemini needs a woman who will share his thirst for knowledge, information and communication with people from all walks of life. Ms Scorpio is a far more self-contained and secretive soul who will become insanely jealously when she has to share her gregarious Gemini with the plethora of other women he claims are 'just friends'. These two are polarised in their needs and desires and Mr Gemini will soon tire of Ms Scorpio's need to try to contain his free-spirited soul.

In the bedroom: Mr Gemini is more likely to sink than swim when confronted with Ms Scorpio's deeply intense and passionate yearnings. She will be fascinated by the twin, desperate to prove her sexual prowess. But his wandering and detached spirit will eventually force this woman into the bed of a more sensual and passionate lover.

♊ Mr Gemini + Ms Sagittarius ♐

Sign	Gemini	Sagittarius
Symbol	Twins	Archer
Ruler	Mercury	Jupiter
Type	Mutable	Mutable
Element	Air	Fire

Sparks are likely to fly when Mr Gemini and Ms Sagittarius lay eyes on each other. Both mutable signs, their air and fire elements blend well together and both are freedom- and adventure-loving souls. Neither likes to keep the home fires burning and both prefer relationships free from boundaries and constraints.

These independent souls will enjoy a spontaneous and exciting relationship with excellent communication between them. Mr Gemini can often be insincere, plying a potential love partner with falsehoods in order to win her heart. But the secure and feisty Ms Sagittarius will rarely buy into this barrage of bulldust. Instead, if she can rely on what's revealed in his eyes, she will find the truth.

Jealousy will not be an issue for either sign, particularly for the archer, who like her Gemini mate has a huge collection of friends and acquaintances she likes to spend time with. Mr Gemini has much to gain from Ms Sagittarius, who has a strong thirst for knowledge and an equally strong desire to share it with those willing to learn.

Astrologically, these signs are in opposition to one another but this can ignite a magical pull between them. If Mr Gemini can evolve into a more caring and sympathetic soul, then his Sagittarian love might just be able to commit long term to this perennial player.

In the bedroom: These two have a tendency to use ploys to evoke jealousy in each other that often leads them to engage in plenty of makeup sex. Neither makes a particularly loyal partner because they are often attracted to new and exciting adventures. However, in the confines of the bedroom, they will be only too happy to give themselves one hundred per cent.

♊ Mr Gemini + Ms Capricorn ♑

Sign	Gemini	Capricorn
Symbol	Twins	Goat
Ruler	Mercury	Saturn
Type	Mutable	Cardinal
Element	Air	Earth

The hard-working, practical and tenacious Capricornian will rarely fuel the fires of passion within the freedom-loving, adventure-seeking Gemini. Mr Gemini hardly lets the dust settle beneath his feet before he leaps to his next conquest while Ms Capricorn rarely moves before she feels the security of solid earth beneath her.

Geminis and Capricornians have different needs and desires from a relationship: she'll want an emotionally secure and mature man while he'll be after a more flexible and freedom-loving woman. The Capricornian lass likes guarantees – certainly in everything she undertakes – so will need to believe her relationship is genuine and has a good chance of permanency before she commits entirely to the union with her Gemini beau. She seeks the truth while he struggles to reveal it. Mr Gemini usually shuns emotional stability but, ironically, while he may resent this very quality in his Capricornian love, it will be the very thing that lures him back to the union because some part of his psyche secretly harbours a need for security.

Ms Capricorn is hardworking and committed to every task she undertakes and a relationship is no exception so, despite the emotional highs and lows this relationship brings, she will try to make it work because to admit defeat is something she struggles with.

In the bedroom: Sexually this couple may not set the house on fire but, because both can be fairly independent, their lovemaking creates a strong but not all-consuming bond between them.

♊ Mr Gemini + Ms Aquarius ♒

Sign	Gemini	Aquarius
Symbol	Twins	Water bearer
Ruler	Mercury	Uranus
Type	Mutable	Fixed
Element	Air	Air

When two in-sync signs collide, it can be the start of a beautiful friendship that blossoms into an even more beautiful relationship. Mr Gemini will notice this zany and effervescent Aquarian enigma across a crowded room and she'll be equally enchanted to finally have met someone who truly understands her.

Although no relationship is perfect, the Gemini and Aquarian union will be close to harmonious compared with the other rocky relationships they have each weathered along the way. She is a true humanitarian who will have no qualms about being the more giving and tolerant partner in this union. She prides herself on her quest for the truth and is likely to become deeply annoyed at Mr Gemini's continuous ability to bend it. But the sharp-witted twin is quick to point out to his fellow air sign that while she speaks the truth, it's often not always at once.

Both love people and neither will have the slightest concern with the menagerie of various souls each gathers into their fold. In this relationship, both Mr Gemini and Ms Aquarius give as much as is needed and expected from their mate which results in satisfaction all round. Since these two value friendship above all else, they often sacrifice love in favour of it because it is less demanding and intense. But if they can weather the trials and tribulations of a love match – she understanding his need for freedom and he recognising and understanding her complexities – then this will be a pairing of soul mates.

In the bedroom: The Gemini and Aquarian understand each other's physical needs and can make beautiful music together. Both tend to favour expressing their love through mental exchanges rather than physical abandonment.

♊ Mr Gemini + Ms Pisces ♓

Sign	Gemini	Pisces
Symbol	Twins	Fish
Ruler	Mercury	Neptune
Type	Mutable	Mutable
Element	Air	Water

Mr Gemini's changeable attitudes and actions will be both attractive and abhorrent to the sensitive and intuitive Ms Pisces, who will be continually striving to understand what makes her man tick. Neither the air or water signs are particularly warm and demonstrative types, but their combined essence makes them value the need for freedom.

Mr Gemini and Ms Pisces are both elusive, imaginative types but she lives more in a fantasy world and will frustrate the twin who wants to know what's going on in her mind. She needs a deep and meaningful union to feel spiritually connected and at times will be frustrated by his flighty and fanciful ways. Ms Pisces often plays the role of the rescuer, sacrificing her own needs in order to sustain a relationship. She will tolerate the excesses of her Gemini guy because she will always want to see her partner as the perfect, ultimate mate. Even if he is not her King Neptune, she will continually make allowances in the union.

Pisces represents the 'I believe' motto of the zodiac so when this fish puts her trust in a relationship, she believes it will lasts forever. Mr Gemini is more interested in instant gratification than his Piscean companion, who is more emotional and needs to create the perfect mood before she can give herself completely. If this Gemini guy is willing to spend time on the relationship, looking into the depths of his love's deep Piscean soul, he will find many hidden delights in Neptune's treasure chest.

In the bedroom: These two can have a very fulfilling and sensual physical connection when they join as one. Their imaginations will take them to great heights of pleasure.

Celebrity Mr Gemini: Paul McCartney

Singer/songwriter, born 2.30 am 18 June 1942 in Liverpool, England

```
Personal planets: Sun in Gemini
                  Moon in Leo
                  Mercury in Gemini
                  Venus in Taurus
                  Mars in Leo
```

In the end the love you take is equal to the love you make. Love is all you need.

– Paul McCartney

Paul McCartney's chart is predominately air and fire, which creates an artistic and idealistic personality. He has a natural curiosity and is open to meeting new people. McCartney needs a partner who can share in his passion for learning and exchanging ideas. He is a man who enjoys social interactions and is off in all directions in his quest for gaining new insights and knowledge. His relationships are based on companionship and McCartney seems to be attracted to women who are not necessarily aesthetically beautiful but who are reliable and steadfast with a sharp mind and quick wit. He also needs a woman to be tuned into his sensual pleasures in and out of the bedroom.

His Mars in Leo makes him yearn for integrity and honesty and he has a great sense of pride in the women he chooses. McCartney has a committed and direct approach to his emotional relationships but also has a high degree of emotional intensity, which affects his interactions with people. He has a deep psychological awareness of what women want and this makes him work hard at making his unions a success.

McCartney's Moon in Leo makes him a boyish, playful and flamboyant partner but at times demanding of attention. He needs a positive, strong and dramatic type of women in his life. His Venus in Taurus sees McCartney love material possessions and desire an intimate sensual union. Ironically people born with this aspect in their chart usually have a predisposition to being able to sing, because Taurus rules the throat.

His first marriage to Linda Eastman had all the ingredients of success because her Libran Sun combined very favourably with his Sun in Gemini. The air combination lent this partnership openness; they had an easy flow of communication between them – often the key to a successful union. Linda also appealed to McCartney's Venus in Taurus instincts because she was an archetypical Mother Earth with whom he felt a great deal of kinship.

His second failed marriage to Heather Mills, who is a Capricorn and focused and driven in her quest to make a difference, was evidence that pragmatism of the earth perhaps didn't quite connect with the Gemini's need for a less serious and more playful partner.

CANCER (23 June-23 July)

Ruled by the Moon
Water sign
Cardinal
Feminine energy

In general ...

Cancer is the most emotional of the three water signs. Its ruler, the Moon, tends to reflect the changing moods of people born under this sign. Astrologically, the Moon rules our emotions and our nurturing instincts and the responses we desire from others. People who have a strong Cancerian theme in their chart are needy, sensitive and emotional beings. Additionally, they have a well-developed sense of intuition which often acts as a valuable guide in determining who the appropriate people are in their lives.

Like their Moon's tides, the emotions of these water personalities run deep, with the same high and low ebbs. Cancerians are particularly security conscious and need a stable and loyal mate to give them a sense of belonging. Family is of upmost importance to Cancerians, and they will uphold family values and traditions above all else. It follows that Cancerians need to be in a committed union and will prefer marriage to just living with their partner. They have a knack of sensing what their partner needs and will provide a secure family base with all the essential nurturing and comfort. This sign is a cardinal mode; hence Cancerians will take the initiative in the relationship if it 'feels' right.

Having a propensity to cling to their past, especially hanging on to perceived hurts, Cancerians will be unforgiving if they have been wronged. They have an extremely sensitive nervous system and will not take kindly to rejection so they take the time to invest in relationships before they commit. If you are in a hurry for some intimacy with a Cancerian, you will need to be patient. However, it is well worth the wait because, once the crab has been caught, they will be all yours forever. Rarely do they seek extra marital pursuits; they would rather concentrate on building on what is in their own back yard.

The exceedingly faithful and loyal Cancerian will be a great sounding board but, in turn, needs a mate who will be encouraging and supportive of their ambitions. Cancerians need to be known for what they do in a career sense and will strive for some recognition; very often they will present in careers on stage where they are very much in the limelight.

This public persona is different from their private world where they are happiest nestling in the arms of their beloved and can think of nothing better than spending quality, intimate time with them. Because both male and female Cancerians are protective of their feelings, they have a tendency to hide their emotions to avoid being hurt. Crabs need to allow people to penetrate their hard exterior shell on occasions so they can reveal their deep and compassionate inner souls.

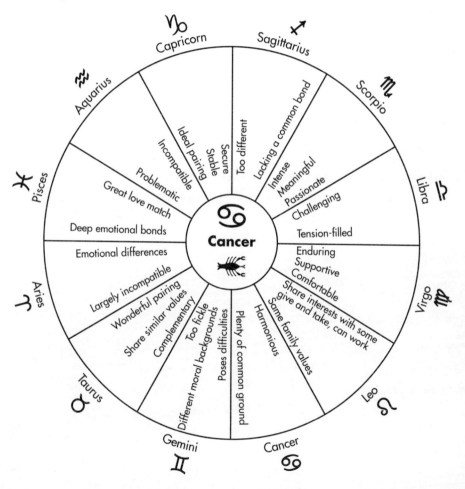

How a Cancerian personality might match up with other star signs

Ms Cancer - an overview

The female crab is an instinctive nurturer and will give you her all once she truly commits. But this can take some time because she is not as trusting and as confident as she pretends to be. She suffers from some emotional hang-ups and will feel highly vulnerable, particularly if she comes from a non-supportive background. Ms Cancer's childhood tends to shape her emotions; the more encouragement she has had, the more she is willing to give.

This woman is intensely passionate and will demand the same from her partner. Her needs are simple. She wants faithfulness, intimacy and security and a man who will allow her to find her own career path. Instinctively a wonderful home maker, Ms Cancer needs something more. She will eventually want to forge a fulfilling and stimulating career in an occupation where she can express her talents and creativity. Her mate will need to recognise her talents and support her endeavours to forge her own career path, otherwise she will clam up and develop a deep-seated resentment.

Family life is of upmost importance to Ms Cancer and she will want a partner on the same committed wavelength. She is suited to the gentler and more sensitive males of the zodiac – those born under earth or water signs – who will give her the nourishment she desires. Cancerian women make wonderful partners. Ms Cancer sees her primary role in life making her man and her family numero uno.

Famous Cancerian women

* Princess Diana
  (British royalty)
* Natalie Wood (actor)
* Ginger Rogers
  (dancer/actor)
* Camilla Parker-Bowles
  (British royalty)
* Helen Keller (writer)
* Jerry Hall (model)

Combinations

♋ Ms Cancer + Mr Aries ♈

Sign	Cancer	Aries
Symbol	Crab	Ram
Ruler	Moon	Mars
Type	Cardinal	Cardinal
Element	Water	Fire

Ms Cancer and Mr Aries don't have much in common. Her sensitivity, complexity and neediness make her very different from the forthright, insensitive and selfish Arian. Although often initially attracted to Ms Cancer's sensitive and silent energy, the independent Mr Aries finds her neediness becoming too overbearing.

Arians find it hard to commit to one person, let alone to the institution of marriage, whereas the Cancerian woman craves security and commitment. She can at times display her moody tendencies, which will only aggravate the Arian guy. He has neither the insight nor the patience to deal with her changeable emotions. And although Mr Aries' sense of fun and adventure appeals to Ms Cancer, she will find his childlike ways infuriating, which will frustrate her complex and emotional nature.

Cancer's motto is 'I feel' which is in stark contrast to the Aries' 'I am'. The Arian man is too unsophisticated for the complex, sensitive crab and her tendencies to bring unresolved issues into the relationship. He can neither fathom nor appreciate the complexities of Ms Cancer, and quite frankly would rather be spending time with someone more outgoing. In turn, she likes stability and gets somewhat agitated by the flighty nature of the freedom-loving Arian. Ms Cancer's over-protectiveness and clingy nature will turn this crab into a crab apple as far as Mr Aries is concerned.

In the bedroom: It's likely Ms Cancer will extinguish the fiery and passionate flames of Mr Aries because the watery crab's heavy-going energy will be a turn-off for the playful ram who likes to jump up and down and get excited in the sack.

♋ Ms Cancer + Mr Taurus ♉

Sign	Cancer	Taurus
Symbol	Crab	Bull
Ruler	Moon	Venus
Type	Cardinal	Fixed
Element	Water	Earth

This is a great match with these signs having a mutual rapport on an intimate level – earth and water are a good mix. Mr Taurus is a loving sort of guy, who really appreciates a sensitive woman, and Ms Cancer is a nurturer and giver. And because these two signs have a great capacity to nourish and support, they will bring out the best qualities in each other. They each have their own unique style and artistic streak, which can be reinforced and strengthened in their union.

The crab is ruled by the Moon, which can make Ms Cancer prone to mood swings and depression. Mr Taurus is just the man to provide the understanding and steadfastness she needs. In return for that extra care and support, she will provide him with the traditional family values and instinctive loving qualities he so longs for. The crab is a feeling sort of individual who understands her Taurean's outbursts of jealousy and possessiveness because she shares the same characteristics.

These two like predicability and don't like to venture to greener pastures once they have found their little plot and set up a safe and secure home. Both have strong family ideals and values, which will be an important ingredient in this relationship. Because of their record of longevity and commitment, rarely will Ms Cancer and Mr Taurus abandon their union until they have exhausted all possibilities. They have staying power and a sense of endurance.

Home life is an important feature of this combination and the Taurean guy will value his crab's input in creating a comfortable environment for him.

In the bedroom: Neither the Taurean nor Cancerian gives themselves completely unless they're truly, madly and deeply in love. This will be a physically loving union because each is able to nurture and support the other.

♋ Ms Cancer + Mr Gemini ♊

Sign	Cancer	Gemini
Symbol	Crab	Twins
Ruler	Moon	Mercury
Type	Cardinal	Mutable
Element	Water	Air

The Gemini male has a playful, light-hearted, elusive charm that makes this crab feel alive and entertained. In turn, her instinctive and nurturing ways give Mr Gemini a feeling of safety and warmth – although he might find her hard, protective shell too much of a barrier at times. The outgoing and sociable Mr Gemini will also find it difficult to handle Ms Cancer's vulnerable and moody disposition.

The crab tends to protect but also needs protection, and the Gemini man is too single-minded and selfish to understand the needs of this intuitive and sensitive creature. While he instinctively endears himself to a wide variety to women with his easy-going, light-hearted approach, she is too cautious and self-protecting to follow suit.

The difference between Cancerians and Geminis is that she means what she says but he doesn't; they come from different moral backgrounds. His truth changes at a whim, while she is very much a woman who remembers and keeps track of the past; in fact this Cancer girl could teach Mr Gemini a few things about appropriate behaviour. But his charming ways often get this guy out of a tight spot so he doesn't feel the need to take heed of the crab's wise words.

She is about family unity and he is about friendships far and wide, so her nesting instincts are worlds apart from his. The crab's 'I feel' approach to relationships verses the Gemini's 'I think' attitude sums up this relationship – she's an instinctive feeling type of person and he is a more analytical soul with emotions close to the surface.

In the bedroom: Ms Cancer is forever trying to guess how to please her Gemini man but this trait will not spill over into the bedroom. When these two are expressing their physical connection, the penny will drop for the sensitive and emotional Cancerian, who might just have the right Moon qualities to lure her Gemini man out of his head and fully into her bed!

♋ Ms Cancer + Mr Cancer ♋

Sign	Cancer	Cancer
Symbol	Crab	Crab
Ruler	Moon	Moon
Type	Cardinal	Cardinal
Element	Water	Water

Mr and Ms Cancer are warm, sensitive, emotional and vulnerable people who have a mutual rapport and understanding. They instinctively feel what the other wants, making this union particularly compatible. Cancerian males and females have a strong drive for security and acceptance and share a high level of emotional understanding. They find much comfort in each other's arms.

Ms Cancer is more inclined to be the giver and may at times resent her partner's complacency; however, being a cardinal sign she is extremely assertive and will not hold back if she needs to air her dissatisfaction. 'Shape up or ship out' is her motto although it rarely comes to that, as most Cancerians are reluctant to leave a union once firmly ensconced. Loyalty is of upmost importance. They are the homemakers and value family commitment above all else. They are devoted spouses and parents and will do their best to stay in a relationship for the kids, of whom they are fiercely protective.

Most Cancerian women are not as close to their mothers as their male counterparts but she will assume the motherly role for her partner. Both these signs are the 'I feel' types and that's exactly what they do. They feel their emotions on an instinctive level, which always stands them in good stead.

In the bedroom: Romance is the key to a gratifying sexual union for the male and female crab. Both deeply sensitive and needy of affection to set the mood, the crab coupling will be delicate and passionate, especially when there's a full moon. But beware of external worries that can inhibit performance and dampen the fires of love.

♋ Ms Cancer + Mr Leo ♌

Sign	Cancer	Leo
Symbol	Crab	Lion
Ruler	Moon	Sun
Type	Cardinal	Fixed
Element	Water	Fire

Ms Cancer will provide her Leo mate with a good dose of loyalty and respect, which is exactly what this man needs from a relationship. Both have strong family values, and will be interested in some form of commitment and stability. Ms Cancer is more low key and inclined to stay in the background but she possesses a great strength and reserve. So if her lion mate roars too loudly or becomes too arrogant, she has her own quiet way of dealing with him. He will love her genuine interest in his activities and he, in turn, will encourage her to fulfil her own desire for external pursuits. This pair is often attracted to the arts, theatre, film and other cultural activities, and this is often the glue that binds them.

Not often will fire and water click as well as these two signs. And if Mr Leo can moderate his temperament a little more and Ms Cancer can keep her emotions in check, these two could have a positive impact on each other. The important element here is water, which tends to dampen the fire's idealism and spirit. However, these two have a great need to please each other and have a tremendous capacity for sensual intimacy. The lion genuinely want to please his partner and will make his woman feel that she is the only girl in the world.

In the bedroom: The brash and bold Leo man will have to woo his way into the bedroom of Ms Cancer. He'll need to be caring and considerate if he wants to fall into the crab's open arms, and she'll have to learn not to be so sensitive and secretive if they are to set the room on fire.

♋ Ms Cancer + Mr Virgo ♍

Sign	Cancer	Virgo
Symbol	Crab	Virgin
Ruler	Moon	Mercury
Type	Cardinal	Mutable
Element	Water	Earth

The pairing of the virgin and the crab sounds ghastly but it will work if they can tolerate each other's individuality. Ms Cancer and Mr Virgo have the same understanding of commitment and both need loyalty and trust in their union. She is by far the more romantic of the two and her Virgoan mate will need to pull some passionate tricks out of his neat-and-tidy bag to turn on this emotional creature.

Both are nurturing in their own unique way – she in her desire to give of herself emotionally and physically, and he in his matter-of-fact, practical manner. Given the crab's and the virgin's insecurities, they will need to address this issue in their partnership. They have the ability to bring out each other's weaknesses to be examined and purged. His strong sense of commitment and her touchy, feely ways will give them both a reprieve from their otherwise moody dispositions, which will go a long way to settling the relationship. They have an uncanny way of knowing what the other needs from the union and so will work towards creating balance. If Mr Virgo can keep his nit-picking thoughts to himself and Ms Crab can curb her need for emotional excesses, this could wind up being an exceedingly harmonious pairing.

In the bedroom: The Cancerian woman will be like soothing and nourishing water for the Virgoan earth man. Together they will become one as they blend beautifully together in a sexual union. But beware of the Moon's powerful influence over this crab, which can turn her into a moody mistress on occasions.

♋ Ms Cancer + Mr Libra ♎

Sign	Cancer	Libra
Symbol	Crab	Scales
Ruler	Moon	Venus
Type	Cardinal	Cardinal
Element	Water	Air

Ms Cancer and Mr Libra will have an interesting relationship. She is the deeper and more sensitive of the two, and he appears to hide his true feelings and rely more on his superficial nature. If the Cancerian woman can dig below the surface of this charming Libran, she will tap into the deeper side of his nature. Although attractive to all star signs, the Libran man in particular will bring out the crab's more sensitive and emotional nature.

This couple has an artistic flair and will make their domestic life a feature of this union. Both are cardinal signs, suggesting they are initiators; however, Librans are renowned for their procrastination, a trait Ms Cancer will find frustrating at times. They both need partners but search for different things. Ms Cancer is more likely to look for deeper qualities in her mate; conversely, he will be happy with a pretty face and to judge the book by its cover, rather than opening pages and finding the mystique that lies waiting within.

If this Libran man is willing to expose his vulnerabilities and share his true emotions with his Cancerian mate, this might work; however, it is more likely she will see only ever the shallow quality of her mate. Sadly for Mr Libra, he will lose a deep passionate and nurturing partner, which is what he really needs.

In the bedroom: Sex between Mr Libra and Ms Cancer is like riding a seesaw – sometimes it's breathtaking, but at other times her mistrusting nature and his lack of depth can cause them to come crashing down to earth. But because they're both sentimental souls they'll be able to put their differences aside for a good dose of loving!

♋ Ms Cancer + Mr Scorpio ♏

Sign	Cancer	Scorpio
Symbol	Crab	Scorpion
Ruler	Moon	Pluto
Type	Cardinal	Fixed
Element	Water	Water

These water signs have a natural affinity. Ms Cancer and Mr Scorpio are both passionate creatures, which will result in them forming an intense relationship. They share a particularly sensual energy which tends to highlight their union. However, because Cancerians and Scorpios can overwhelm each other emotionally, they need to recognise that if they don't pull back on occasions, they will be drowned in a sea of emotions.

Because this pair has experienced some emotional discontentment in their early years, they can be guarded and self-protective in their relationships. The cardinal Cancerian, however, can initiate well and will be the instigator in trying to bring the secretive Scorpio out of his shell. Mr Scorpio is controlling because he is mistrusting of those close to him. But it will be Ms Cancer's gentle and non-aggressive approach that will coax him into being more open and honest with her.

Mr Scorpio's planetary ruler is Pluto; hence he needs to feel in control of his relationship. His behaviour and attitude will match the equally intense persona of his Cancerian partner. Although they have different ways of dealing with their emotions, she views his intensity as a reassurance of how he feels. This union has all the hallmarks of success, given their shared similarities.

In the bedroom: If this pair understands what each other needs, then there'll be no stopping the sexual heights they will reach in the bedroom. As long as there are no major ripples, they will float along together in a sea of satisfaction.

♋ Ms Cancer + Mr Sagittarius ♐

Sign	Cancer	Sagittarius
Symbol	Crab	Archer
Ruler	Moon	Jupiter
Type	Cardinal	Mutable
Element	Water	Fire

These two have fundamentally different natures. Mr Sagittarius is interested primarily in freedom, variety and greener pastures, and for him the journey is often the more meaningful part of his experiences. Ms Crab, on the other hand, needs guarantees and assurances, so she will not feel protected and nurtured by her archer man, whom she sees as too elusive and selfish. She tends to cling to her past and will always run back to the fold when she feels vulnerable, which will be very often if she finds herself with a Sagittarian man.

Her water elements, intensity and mood swings will not be readily understood or tolerated by the optimistic and expansive mind of the Sagittarian guy. He is a lover of the outdoors, nature and challenges, while she is more the domesticated creature with a flare for creating harmonious and nurturing environments. Ms Cancer will be too single-minded to allow her archer mate to have the space and freedom he requires in his relationships. He will only exacerbate her insecurities and sense of stability by the very essence of his hedonistic and insensitive nature.

This crab will be too rigid, staid and possessive for her Sagittarian guy, who will find her energy and disposition stifling and boring. The archer likes to shoot his arrow in many directions and this will ultimately be the undoing of this duo.

In the bedroom: 'Shoot that bow and arrow through my hear-ah-ah-art,' croons the crab. But the Saggy man might miss the mark with this woman; she wants deep and fulfilling passion from their sexual union and he's more after physical gratification.

♋ Ms Cancer + Mr Capricorn ♑

Sign	Cancer	Capricorn
Symbol	Crab	Goat
Ruler	Moon	Saturn
Type	Cardinal	Cardinal
Element	Water	Earth

These signs are steeped in tradition and family values. Mr Capricorn is ruled by Saturn, which represents hard work, responsibility and discipline, all of which he can bring into his relationship with Ms Crab. She respects his tenacity, admires his responsible attitude and enjoys the material benefits he can provide her with. Mr Capricorn is very much commitment oriented and will value his family life with the same degree of intensity as Ms Cancer, but he can project a cold, hard exterior at times.

He is a pragmatic soul and does not understand the emotional needs of his Cancerian partner, who is prone to mood swings that baffle the stoic and seemingly emotionless goat. His aloof attitude will at times create disharmony in their union because, by nature, Ms Cancer needs a tactile, demonstrative man – something the Capricornian is most definitely not.

All is not lost, however. Despite his lack of compassion and understanding, Mr Capricorn will be able to provide his Cancerian lover with the financial security and stability she seeks. In turn, she is well able to melt the icy bravado of her mountain goat.

In the bedroom: The Cancerian woman will take the Capricorn man to undiscovered heights of sexual pleasure. She does appreciate the commitment and loyalty he gives her, which will allow her to open up and really be herself.

♋ Ms Cancer + Mr Aquarius ♒

Sign	Cancer	Aquarius
Symbol	Crab	Water bearer
Ruler	Moon	Uranus
Type	Cardinal	Fixed
Element	Water	Air

This is not the ideal relationship pairing. Ms Cancer is all about family and home life; Mr Aquarius, on the other hand, is independent, freedom-loving and open to new ideas, which make him extremely unpredictable. Her need for conventionality is marred by his desire to explore different and untried territory. He thrives on change; she abhors it. She values tradition; he's unconventional.

The Aquarian male is detached and aloof in relationships, something Ms Cancer will interpret as a form of rejection, leaving her feeling unloved and unsupported. However, this will not worry the water bearer. He loves a challenge and the more the crab tries to hold him down, the more distant he will become. The Aquarian man will not want to be told what time he's expected home – possessiveness will stifle his need for freedom and self-expression. Another hurdle in this pairing is that Aquarians tend to intellectualise their feelings in comparison with Cancerians, who are more swayed by emotions. At times his behaviour might appear odd and reduce his crab to tears, but he probably won't even be aware of it.

These two seem to make a greater success of a friendship rather than an intimate union. Both are humanitarians, always fighting for the greater good and often using their creative talents for a good cause. In a work scenario, they will encourage each other's ideas and thoughts, pushing them to achieve greater heights.

In the bedroom: Sexually these two will share great passion. And Mr Aquarius, who never likes to be pinned down, will feel that he really has caught his own moonbeam, and love it.

♋ Ms Cancer + Mr Pisces ♓

Sign	Cancer	Pisces
Symbol	Crab	Fish
Ruler	Moon	Neptune
Type	Cardinal	Mutable
Element	Water	Water

There is a mutual rapport and empathy between these two water signs. Each can indulge the other and feed off their strengths and weaknesses. Ms Cancer will appreciate the depth, sensitivity and talents of her creative mate who, in turn, will share her interests in the arts and other aesthetic pursuits. She will have the strength and determination needed to help her Piscean mate to combat his excessive and needy qualities, and will ground his idealistic nature and delusional state of mind.

Water signs seem to have a flair for providing their mate with sentimentality and romance, and Mr Pisces will appreciate his crab's loyalty and protective nature. She, in turn, will feel needed and loved unconditionally. Because each is intuitive, this couple can pick up on the other's moods and overall disposition, making them ideally suited.

At times the more security-oriented crab will find her Piscean mate's elusive nature and lack of commitment and drive frustrating. In turn, he might find her too intense, stifling and protective.

In the bedroom: On the plus side, the crab and fish will have a very passionate relationship in the physical sense, which can fuse them together as one. Their shared sixth sense makes these two particularly sensitive to each other's thoughts, needs and desires – a dynamic combination in the bedroom.

Celebrity Ms Cancer: Jerry Hall

Model, born 2.30 pm 2 July 1956 in Gonzales, Texas, USA

```
Personal planets: Sun in Cancer
                  Moon in Aries or Taurus
                  Mercury in Gemini
                  Venus in Gemini
                  Mars in Pisces
```

Mick Jagger and I just really liked each other a lot. We talked all night. We had the same views on nuclear disarmament.

– Jerry Hall

Jerry Hall is a Cancerian with a strong fire element in her chart. Her Mars in Pisces combined with her Cancerian Sun displays emotional, intuitive and giving qualities. She is empathetic and receptive and her responses are based on feeling her emotions on an inner level. She is representative of the sign that is known for nurturing and sustaining relationships. Although Hall has a facade of needing the protection of a strong male, she uses her protective and nurturing attributes to encourage and foster the growth of her partner. Cancerians are known for 'hanging in there'. This is exaggerated in her case by the lack of earth elements, which makes her feel that she needs the security of material and emotional comforts, so she may stay in a relationship for the wrong reasons and compromise herself.

This woman has a predisposition towards needing a mate with whom she can exchange her ideas and also needs to respect his mental agility. Her Venus and Mercury in the sign of Gemini can make her fickle or impatient with a person who cannot keep up with her speed.

Hall's one-time attraction to singer Brian Ferry, a Libran, would have blended well with her Venus, which is in the air sign of Gemini, and their mental rapport would have been a big drawcard.

Her relationship with rocker Mick Jagger, which lasted a considerable amount of time, is indicative of her Mars in the sign of Pisces, which would have given her an interest in his artistic and musical creativity.

Since both have their Mercury in planets of communication – Hall's is in the sign of Gemini and Jagger's is in the sign of Virgo – they would have shared a strong communicative bond and could have talked about almost anything.

Jagger is a Leo, exemplified in his attraction to this statuesque, larger-than-life woman. His being a man who takes pride in having the absolutely perfect woman by his side, the refined Hall suited him admirably for many years before his wandering eye brought an end to the relationship. Hall, the more sensitive and potentially giving of the two, would have been the one to make the adjustments and keep the relationship on an even keel, even if at times her Cancerian senses were bombarded by the lion's roar.

Mr Cancer – an overview

The Cancerian male is a feeling and vulnerable person and, just like the tides of the ocean, will have mood changes surging from highs to lows depending on his state of mind; hence he needs to find a partner who is happy to swim alongside him in life. A Cancerian man will have a very close bond with his mother, which transfers to an instinctive understanding of what his partner needs. In turn, his partner will have to maintain some connection or rapport with his mother because she will always be an important part of his life.

If you are the jealous type, forget it because you don't stand a chance – learn to let go and accept. Go with the flow and you will not be sorry because this gentle man has strong sensual qualities. He is a giver but will expect something in return. Being a water sign makes him the sort of man who needs a responsive partner, one who will encourage and support him in all endeavours. She will have to be a strong, independent-thinking woman who doesn't buy into his somewhat negative predisposition. In turn, Mr Cancer with his strong family values will be a caring and loving companion.

Although they don't always verbalise their inner thoughts and emotions, Cancerian men are very demonstrative in a physical sense, whether in the bedroom or helping around the home. He makes a great homemaker; he is interested in creating a sanctuary for his partner and can often be found whipping up a storm in the kitchen. This gives him a sense of acceptance and security and will validate the relationship for him. If you are into smooching and love cuddles, then this is the man for you.

Famous Cancerian men

* Tom Cruise (actor)
* George Orwell (writer)
* Georgio Armani (fashion designer)
* John Glenn (astronaut)
* Dalai Lama XIV (religious leader)
* Ringo Starr (musician)

Combinations

♋ Mr Cancer + Ms Aries ♈

Sign	Cancer	Aries
Symbol	Crab	Ram
Ruler	Moon	Mars
Type	Cardinal	Cardinal
Element	Water	Fire

Think of the two most incompatible energies and you can't go past this union. Mr Cancer's sensitivity, complexity and neediness make him somewhat of a wet blanket for the forthright Ms Aries. His usually strong bond with his mother can be a cause of resentment for his Arian mate, who wants to be number one in his life.

Not particularly adventurous, with home and family life his priorities, this crab will be a bit of a killjoy for someone who craves excitement and fun, like Ms Aries. Cancer's motto is 'I feel', which is in stark contrast to the Arian's 'I am'. She is too unsophisticated for the complex, sensitive crab, which often brings unresolved issues into their relationship. Additionally, she cannot unravel the mysteries of this Cancerian male and quite frankly would rather be spending time with someone more upbeat and dynamic. He, in turn, likes stability and can become somewhat agitated by the flighty nature of the freedom-loving Arian woman.

Initially, Ms Aries will be drawn to Mr Crab's gentle nature, but as time moves on, she will become frustrated and bored with him. Unless he meets Ms Aries at the end of her journey through the zodiac, he will find her ultimate rejection heartbreaking.

In the bedroom: It's likely the watery crab will extinguish the fiery flames of the passionate Ms Aries, because his heavy-going energy will be a turn-off for the playful ram, who likes to jump up and down and get excited in the sack.

♋ Mr Cancer + Ms Taurus ♉

Sign	Cancer	Taurus
Symbol	Crab	Bull
Ruler	Moon	Venus
Type	Cardinal	Fixed
Element	Water	Earth

This connection is a match made in heaven because these two are particularly suited, sharing similar goals and visions. Ms Taurus is an earth sign and her loyal, practical approach to life will be greatly appreciated by Mr Cancer, who needs shelter, nurturing, stability and above all else security, all of which are in ample supply from Ms Taurus. He, in turn, can give her the respect and appreciation she desires. The Cancerian man also is prone to emotional highs and lows, which is where Ms Taurus will come into her own – always a positive support and with an innate understanding of what her crab needs. Because they share the traits of sympathy and protectiveness, each knows how to make their mate feel 100 per cent secure.

When Mr Cancer feels like retreating from the outside world, the home fires will always be burning for him and the warm chicken soup for the soul is in good supply. This relationship carries a lot of depth – it is not based on any of the superficial trappings of lust, greed and ego – and has all the ingredients of a very loving and lasting union. The Cancerian guy and his Taurean love will provide each other with the loyalty and commitment each so desperately seeks and, with both craving a happy and loving home environment for their families, they thrive on domestic bliss.

In the bedroom: Sexually . . . wow – this is a very powerful union as the lovemaking will be an extension of the friendship they have cemented.

♋ Mr Cancer + Ms Gemini ♊

Sign	Cancer	Gemini
Symbol	Crab	Twins
Ruler	Moon	Mercury
Type	Cardinal	Mutable
Element	Water	Air

Ms Gemini tends to fall in love with men who are mentally agile and can stimulate her mind. She is a great conversationalist and will always be attracted to a man who has a lot to say. Alas, Mr Cancer is too introverted, serious and sensitive for the restless Ms Gemini, whose short attention span causes her to constantly seek new adventures.

She doesn't have the understanding required for the intuitive and emotionally sensitive crab, who is far more of a feeling type of guy. And they come from different perspectives. Mr Cancer will only start to communicate his feelings when he feels sure and trusting of the relationship – security is an important ingredient for this male – whereas Ms Gemini will profess love in an instant only to change her mind the next day, leaving the confused crab feeling even more insecure.

These two have a different approach to relationships. She will always verbalise how she feels and, because he doesn't have the same dexterity with words, he remains silent, instead demonstrating his feelings through actions that show great sensitivity and depth – ways not so easily understood by Ms Gemini.

At first the silent crab will mystify Ms Gemini; she will see his brooding quality as a sign of significant sensuality. However, the fickleness that Ms Gemini so often displays will create much tension in this relationship. Mr Cancer's desperation for security will drive a wedge between them, and Ms Gemini will feel too trapped and stifled by what she interprets as clingy and somewhat controlling behaviour.

In the bedroom: The sex life of this couple will be surprisingly good. He's perceptive enough to go with the flow when she changes her mind about what turns her on; and she'll appreciate his warm and caring approach to sex and feel safe from the world in his arms.

♋ Mr Cancer + Ms Cancer ♋

Sign	Cancer	Cancer
Symbol	Crab	Crab
Ruler	Moon	Moon
Type	Cardinal	Cardinal
Element	Water	Water

Both Mr and Ms Cancer are warm, sensitive, emotional and vulnerable people who have a mutual rapport and understanding. They will find much comfort in each other's arms. They know instinctively what the other wants and needs, resulting in a union that is particularly compatible. Cancerian women are usually not as close to their mothers as their male counterparts but she will assume the motherly role for her partner. Because both male and female Cancerians have a strong drive for security and acceptance, they are able to give each other a great deal of emotional understanding.

Ms Cancer will be more inclined to be the giver in the relationship and may at times resent her mate's complacency. However, being a cardinal sign, she is exceptionally assertive and, if necessary, will not hold back in airing her dissatisfaction. 'Shape up or ship out' is her motto, although it rarely comes to that as most Cancerians are reluctant to leave a union once firmly ensconced. They are the homemakers and value family commitment above all else. Loyalty is of upmost importance to this pair. Both are devoted individuals who will stay in a relationship for the kids, whom they will both do anything to protect. With both in the relationship 'I feel' types, that's exactly what they do. They feel their emotions on an instinctive level, which always stands them in good stead.

In the bedroom: Romance is the key to a gratifying sexual union for the male and female crab. Both deeply sensitive and needing affection to set the mood, the crab coupling will be delicate and passionate, especially when there's a full Moon. But beware of external worries that can inhibit performance and dampen the fires of love.

♋ Mr Cancer + Ms Leo ♌

Sign	Cancer	Leo
Symbol	Crab	Lion
Ruler	Moon	Sun
Type	Cardinal	Fixed
Element	Water	Fire

When Mr Cancer meets Ms Leo he will be captivated by her charm and beauty. Not domineering by nature, he will allow the lioness to get her own way – at least this is what she thinks is happening most of the time. The crab will be a loyal, caring and gentle partner, but in a subtle way he's also very much in control of situations and their outcomes.

Ms Leo will be delighted that she's finally found someone who truly understands her and allows her to shine. However, it may take some time for her to realise that while she can freely engage in activities and pursuits that make her happy, her sensitive crab will usually have the final say. This Moon (Cancer) and Sun (Leo) combination have the wonderful ability to reflect and enjoy the qualities they admire in each other. On a physical level, this pairing can take the crab and lion out of their comfort zones into an amazingly satisfying realm of pleasure. It will be a fresh and exciting experience for both, which breaks free from previous boundaries they have known in former relationships.

Since Mr Cancer likes guarantees and certainty and Ms Leo wants to be numero uno in her man's life, it's likely these two will settle down long term with each other. He will encourage his talented lioness to pursue a career where she can shine and lead: otherwise she has a tendency to want to dominate, which can lead to discontentment all round.

In the bedroom: Trying a little bit of tenderness is exactly what the Cancerian man and his lioness need to do to enjoy a passionate, physical relationship. Both can retreat if either feels slighted or hurt, but if she turns up the heat with her emotional warmth and he digs deep into his pit of emotions, then there will be no stopping the chemistry between these two.

♋ Mr Cancer + Ms Virgo ♍

Sign	Cancer	Virgo
Symbol	Crab	Virgin
Ruler	Moon	Mercury
Type	Cardinal	Mutable
Element	Water	Earth

Mr Cancer and Ms Virgo need loyal and sympathetic partners in their love relationships. The nurturing virgin can have a calming and comforting effect on Mr Crab, whose sensitive soul is not always immune to the criticism of others. Her practical, no-nonsense approach to life is like a breath of fresh air to Mr Cancer, and she seems to be able to cope quite well with his moodiness and occasional withdrawal.

The crab can be quite bossy and demanding of his partners but Ms Virgo seems to be able to take this in her stride, happy to accept what he says if it sits comfortably with her. She will admire the business acumen of her crab, but if he's one of the insecure Cancerians whose frequent dark moods make him err on the side of negativity, he will find Ms Virgo's intolerant, critical tones strong enough to create a wedge between them. She doesn't believe in emotional excesses and he doesn't take well to criticism, regardless of whether or not it was well intended. But the crab's intuition and the virgin's analytical nature should be sharp enough to allow them to detect and avoid any bumps in the road ahead.

In the bedroom: On the surface Ms Virgo can appear cool, reserved and undemonstrative, but the sensitive, gentle crab has just the right touch to awaken deep feelings of passion within Ms Virgo, which can lead them to share a fulfilling sexual union.

♋ Mr Cancer + Ms Libra ♎

Sign	Cancer	Libra
Symbol	Crab	Scales
Ruler	Moon	Venus
Type	Cardinal	Cardinal
Element	Water	Air

Like most in the zodiac, Mr Cancer will fall for the beautiful, charming and graceful Ms Libra. Her Venusian qualities will be so enchanting to the sensitive crab that he will find her irresistible. She in turn will be captivated by the crab's sensitivity, compassion and warmth. He is likely to make her feel safe and secure like none of her lovers have before.

Because both can be moody at times, they will understand each other's changeable natures, although the crab has difficulty in expressing his true emotions, which can create some divisions. Mr Cancer likes security and guarantees and, although his ultimate relationship pinnacle is marriage, he is more likely to tread cautiously before making this final commitment. It's not that he doesn't love the idea of the security and comfort it can offer; he's more concerned with being able to fulfil his partner's needs on an emotional and financial level. Ms Libra can interpret this hesitation as rejection and can resort to jealous game-playing to try to cajole her crab down the aisle. He may become moody and irritated by such behaviour but, once Ms Libra senses she's losing her grip, she can turn on the charm as quick as a flash to woo her lover back.

In the bedroom: In the bedroom is where Mr Cancer lets down his guard and his true feelings and emotions shine through. Ms Libra will bring an abundance of TLC into the union, but often the differences between these two will only be temporarily allayed through sex.

♋ Mr Cancer + Ms Scorpio ♏

Sign	Cancer	Scorpio
Symbol	Crab	Scorpion
Ruler	Moon	Pluto
Type	Cardinal	Fixed
Element	Water	Water

When Mr Cancer and Ms Scorpio come together in love, there is an amazing transformative energy force that will allow them to form a deep and intense union. They both have a tremendous ability to survive the most arduous and tough encounters in their lives. Not for nothing are they known as the survivors of the zodiac. In fact, on most occasions they will grow stronger from these testing and traumatic experiences.

Although both are initially reticent when comes to love, and protective of their secrets and their souls, when the crab initiates and the scorpion responds it will be a fulfilling and enduring relationship. Because both are water signs and family-oriented, they need partners who are highly responsive. Neither treats their relationship lightly, which can lead to jealous tendencies. However, the mutual understanding between them eliminates much of this fear and anxiety.

Mr Cancer has strong ties with his mother, endowing him with an understanding of women and their vulnerabilities, so he can indulge Ms Scorpio in her constant desire for attention. They hide their aggressive tendencies well but if either one is under threat they will stop at nothing to protect each other. And because they are both complex characters who suffer mood swings, they will be tolerant of each other's occasional outbursts.

Mr Cancer and Ms Scorpio are both people who need time out and crave a certain amount of privacy and solitude to re-engerise themselves.

In the bedroom: A very powerful sexual force exists between the crab and the scorpion. It will be a blending of their bodies and minds when these two water signs play bedroom games.

♋ Mr Cancer + Ms Sagittarius ♐

Sign	Cancer	Sagittarius
Symbol	Crab	Archer
Ruler	Moon	Jupiter
Type	Cardinal	Mutable
Element	Water	Fire

Mr Cancer will be far too introverted for the outgoing, adventurous Ms Sagittarius, who prefers a relationship that allows her plenty of freedom and space. Most of the astrological signs respect and admire the Sagittarian energy, and Mr Cancer is no exception. He will find this girl uplifting and positive; and she will rarely display the same intensity and moodiness that afflicts him.

These signs have very different needs from a relationship. The sensitive crab will seek a mate who can give him security, loyalty and an inner sense of peace, whereas the zany Sagittarian 'foot-in-mouth' gal will be too loud, brash and tactless for him. He relishes home delights and would much rather snuggle up than take up her offer of any boisterous or daring escapades. Although of a gentle nature, he is not so timid that he can't rise to a challenge.

But it is her inability to commit that frustrates this man more than anything else. He likes certainties and guarantees and, because he is ruled by the Moon, he is an exceptionally nurturing partner. On the other hand, Ms Sagittarius is ruled by the planet Jupiter, which makes her crave experiences in abundance. Even though Mr Cancer might find a relationship with this happy-go-lucky, fun girl rather exciting at the outset, ultimately he will be too possessive to make a permanent go of this union.

In the bedroom: If blended correctly, water and fire can create a simmering sexual union. The crab will be enchanted by his fiery, physical lover and she will be equally captivated by her deep and mysterious man.

♋ Mr Cancer + Ms Capricorn ♑

Sign	Cancer	Capricorn
Symbol	Crab	Goat
Ruler	Moon	Saturn
Type	Cardinal	Cardinal
Element	Water	Earth

These two are very similar in their desire for security and financial independence. Mr Crab will admire the Capricornian girl's managerial abilities and commitment to achieving her goals. She is a pragmatic soul and gets on with her life with minimal fuss and few hang-ups. This woman is on mission to succeed, which will embrace all areas of her life. Failure is not a word she relates to and she will aim to give her all in a relationship.

Although their life goals appear to be the same, by their very nature Cancerians and Capricornians get to where they want via different approaches. Mr Cancer displays a more emotional and needy vulnerability in relationships, which is not always understood by the more stoical Capricornian. In turn, her lack of warmth and affection will at times cause some dissension in the union. He's a tactile creature who needs physical responsiveness from his mate, so he may have to teach his Capricornian girl to be a bit more touchy-feely.

Mr Cancer's worrying nature can be tempered by Ms Capricorn's no-fuss and solution-oriented personality, which can help keep the intense emotions of her man on a more grounded and balanced level. If the Capricornian can modify her desire for professional success and spend more time with her Cancerian mate, this union will be very workable and can be a prosperous for both parties.

In the bedroom: The crab and the goat take lovemaking just as seriously as they do other aspects of their lives. He will draw out the sensuality of this woman and will take her to heights of intimacy that will surprise and thrill her.

♋ Mr Cancer + Ms Aquarius ♒

Sign	Cancer	Aquarius
Symbol	Crab	Water bearer
Ruler	Moon	Uranus
Type	Cardinal	Fixed
Element	Water	Air

The Cancerian man and the Aquarian woman will share some great intellectual times together and are really better suited to a friendship or business relationship than a love match. Ms Aquarius's strong independent streak, her elusive manner and cool disposition do not give Mr Cancer the validity he needs to embark on the emotional relationship he desires.

The Aquarian woman's strong drive for independence will always leave her mate struggling to possess this girl, especially a Cancerian male who is after a woman who will stand by his side and be there for him in every situation. Ms Aquarius finds it hard to commit to a relationship because she is a lover of humanity and shares her life with many. Her life's journey is to spread her altruistic message to all who wish to listen and, although she has a kind heart, Mr Cancer rarely gets to see it because she does not know how to show emotional depth the same way he does. All air signs seem to have this inability to give themselves completely to a relationship; often their detached and impersonal attitude is misinterpreted as a lack of desire and love.

Mr Cancer needs someone who will openly display affection and be committed to the union. He is the clingy type and his jealous streak will drive Ms Aquarius away because she doesn't have his same possessive or needy disposition. Variety for her is the spice of life, but for Mr Cancer it is finding true love.

In the bedroom: Mr Crab can pull out all his sexual trickery and, as long as he keeps it bright and bubbly and loaded with fun, his Aquarian lover will be only to happy to join the party. However, if Mr Cancer is longing for a long and languid romp with lots of foreplay, he'll be walking sideways in the wrong direction.

♋ Mr Cancer + Ms Pisces ♓

Sign	Cancer	Pisces
Symbol	Crab	Fish
Ruler	Moon	Neptune
Type	Cardinal	Mutable
Element	Water	Water

Mr Cancer can be very attracted to the sensuous, passionate and mysterious Ms Pisces. He immediately senses this woman shares his compassionate, intuitive and nurturing instincts. Cancerians and Pisceans are in touch with their feelings and will share a give-and-take approach in their relationships.

Mr Cancer will delight in Ms Pisces' rescuing qualities and she will thrive on his support. She is, at the same time, a dreamer, who has high expectations of a relationship, and will adore her crab mate, who can fulfil her fantasies. There are plenty of romantic and passionate exchanges between these two. The combined energy of Cancer's ruling planet, the Moon, and Pisces' rulers – Jupiter and Neptune – creates an easy and dynamic flow. Mr Cancer's Moon shines brightly on Neptune's great oceans and, like a mirror at night, will reflect the alluring qualities of his Piscean lover.

This pair will be perceptive enough to see each other's positive qualities and she in particular will recognise the long-term potential of this caring and gallant man, who shares a mutual interest in the arts and has the same value system.

In the bedroom: There will be no denying the deep and passionate attraction between these two signs and it will be in the bedroom where the crab and fish give themselves completely. This will not be a hurried affair; more a languid process that will see them float on a wave of pleasure.

Celebrity Mr Cancer: Tom Cruise

Actor, born 2.30 pm 3 July 1962 in Syracuse, New York, USA

```
Personal planets: Sun in Cancer
                  Moon in Leo
                  Mercury in Gemini
                  Venus in Leo
                  Mars in Taurus
```

I always look for a challenge and something that's different.

– Tom Cruise

Tom Cruise's chart shows that he has two strong yet different components to his personality. His Cancerian Sun reflects a warm, sensitive and nurturing quality that is indicative of a man who lives his life with great purpose and intensity, and seeks emotional closeness and security; on the other hand, he has a strong fixed component, which can make him controlling, manipulative and stubborn.

His natural instinct is to be protective of his loved ones and to foster mutual growth, and consideration, yet he is not always open and honest with his true feelings and, just like a typically cold-blooded crab, will retreat into his shell when he is emotionally injured.

Cruise has a tendency to be clingy and possessive in his relationships and loves to 'mother' his beloved but he lacks a certain ability to recognise that his partner may not appreciate his enthusiastic, nurturing and protective approach. If she has different ideas or values from him, then she might find this over-protective quality particularly stifling.

The predominance of fire elements in his chart gives him a sense of pride and admiration for his lady. He needs to feel he has a prized possession by his side and will always treat her with the utmost respect.

Cruise has both maturity and a child-like quality, so he likes to have fun and can be very playful. He has a predisposition to confuse love with lust and has a weakness for physical passion which may get him into a spot of bother at times, since a pretty face is not always the answer to a fulfilling union.

This man is extraordinarily creative and uses his intuitive understanding to figure out what his partner needs, so he will always be able to keep her satisfied. Cruise has a strong sensuality coupled with a strong restlessness and wilfulness that leads him into wanting it all his own way, so the challenge for him is to learn how to balance his need for freedom and excitement with his responsibilities.

He has been attracted to air qualities in his relationships with, first, actor Mimi Rogers, who is an Aquarian and, then, actor Nicole Kidman, a Gemini. Both these women would have appealed to Cruise's Mercury in Gemini – the planet of communication. He needs a partner who is stimulating and has a sharp mind and a quick wit.

His new love, actor Katie Holmes, is a Sagittarian and a fire sign, which is in sync with the abundance of fire elements in his chart. This playful couple have a strong affinity in and out of the bedroom as well as shared passion for having fun, and bringing out the child in each other.

Holmes has the ability to rise to a level where Cruise's more controlling side doesn't faze her. She will not allow his domineering nature to impede her own development. Both have their own sense of individuality and need independence, so each will have the insight to allow the other the space and freedom to explore their own potential and interests.

LEO (24 July–23 August)

℧

Ruled by the sun
Fire sign
Fixed
Masculine energy

In general ...

The planetary ruler of Leo is the Sun, which means it is a fundamental desire of Leos to shine as brightly as they can. Lions want to be the kings of their domain and are seen to be forthright personalities with the courage of their convictions. They are also the dramatists of the zodiac, and their youthful exuberance, combined with their flair and brilliance, makes them extremely attractive to the opposite sex. This is highly appealing to Leos, who crave recognition and acknowledgment. In love, they have a strong need to feel respected and admired and want their partners to feel the same. They have a strong vitality and natural enthusiasm.

Lions are happiest when they have someone hanging off their arm they can show off. Loyalty features very strongly in the Leo persona and both sexes take fidelity seriously. Leos fall very hard when they meet the 'right' one and will be generous in their displays of affection. Being a fixed sign means Leos have a tendency to dominate their partners and override their wishes. This intensity is typical of all the fire signs – Sagittarius, Leo and Aries – who all like to feel as if they are in control.

Leos need to find an outlet for their creative expression to allow them to reach their potential, otherwise they can be demanding, stubborn and needy, and dump their frustrations on their partners. Like the lion, Leos love to roar when they're protecting their pride, but they can also have a 'pussy cat' side to their natures and can be overwhelmingly generous when it suits. With Leos, what you see is what you get – there are no hidden agendas when it comes to their relationships – and people gravitate to their warm, energetic glow, adding to their feelings of self-worth and security. Although they make great partners in love, relationships are only one facet of what Leos need to feel complete.

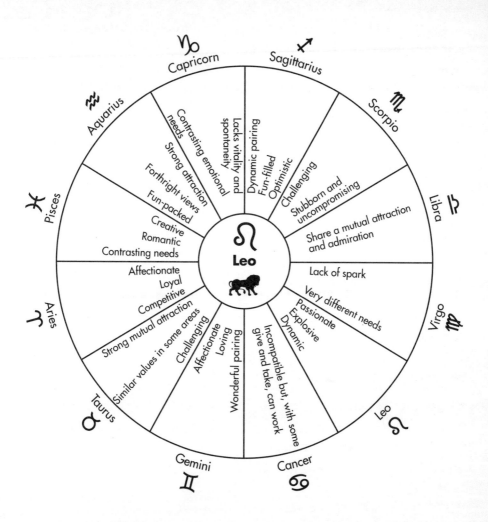

How a Leo personality might match up with other star signs

Ms Leo - an overview

Leo women radiate a regal air and command respect, recognition and attention in all areas of their lives. These fiery women have a magnetism and sparkle that can attract an equally gallant partner to share their limelight. Many men will find Ms Leo's extroverted personality and air of confidence appealing and alluring, and their beauty, grace and charm will sweep most men off their feet.

In relationships, Ms Leo will never be dominated, because she likes to be in the driver's seat. Highly opinionated, she might very well scare off some of the more submissive types who seek a more genteel and passive partner. Ms Leo needs a lot of romance to sustain a relationship, which means her mate will have to be particularly attentive and generous, and share her passion for the arts and other cultural interests. In turn, this woman will be an excellent homemaker and a supportive and faithful partner who will back her man to the hilt in his career.

As with her male counterpart, Ms Leo's father plays an important role in shaping her needs and desires in a relationship. She will be looking for a knight in shining armour to rescue her. Ironically, however, she will ultimately need to be in control. At times this male influence can make her strive for the perfect partner and, because she can be a harsh judge of character, she may not always find what she 'thinks' she's looking for. On the career front, her father's influence can be seen in her constant need for approval and respect.

Famous Leo women

* Madonna (singer)
* Emily Bronte (writer)
* Jacqueline Kennedy Onassis
  (former US first lady)
* Mae West (actor)
* Lucille Ball (comedian)
* Coco Chanel
  (fashion designer)

Combinations

♌ Ms Leo + Mr Aries ♈

Sign	Leo	Aries
Symbol	Lion	Ram
Ruler	Sun	Mars
Type	Fixed	Cardinal
Element	Fire	Fire

This combination is a particularly compatible one and these signs can bring some wonderful energy to the table. The charismatic and sociable Ms Leo will sweep Mr Aries off his feet. Finally he has met the charming and expressive self-confident woman who can share in his enthusiasm for life. Both fire signs, their need for approval is very strong, so each will encourage the other all the way. This highly idealistic combination shares similar interests and hobbies and will be out to have fun. The lioness seems to be more mature than her Arian guy, and understands the importance of compromise and tolerance in a relationship. She is loyal and committed and will give Mr Aries the acknowledgment and support he is after.

Both enjoy socialising and are drawn to creative pursuits. While most lions enjoy being the centre of attention, they are happy to share the spotlight with their attention-seeking ram partners. This is a happy union where partners respect and enjoy each other's qualities. The father figure played an important role in the early lives of both these signs, with the result that their standards, ethics, morals and codes of behaviour are very similar. Respect features strongly in this union, which seems to be the basis for a strong and committed relationship.

Both Arians and Leos require a certain degree of strength and solidarity from their partners. Even though Mr Aries is more emotionally idealistic than his intellectual Leo, they both carry a strong sense of loyalty and commitment to each other. Providing they don't overshadow each other and keep their egos in check, this will be a lasting and exciting relationship.

In the bedroom: Not only will these two light one another's fires, an added insatiable thirst for sexual gratification mixed with a strong need for tenderness will make this a lasting and satisfying union for them both.

♌ Ms Leo + Mr Taurus ♉

Sign	Leo	Taurus
Symbol	Lion	Bull
Ruler	Sun	Venus
Type	Fixed	Fixed
Element	Fire	Earth

The glamorous and generous-spirited Ms Leo will be a natural drawcard for the Taurean man. Her appealing looks and vivaciousness will charm this man off his feet. However, she is not one to commit as easily as he would like, which means this match could take time to get off the ground.

If the relationship is taken to a new level, these two will need to keep their controlling natures in check because both are fixed signs with the same stubborn streak. The flamboyant Ms Leo will be expressive in her needs and desires, all of which Mr Taurus can readily provide. However, this lioness is too elusive – she is owned by the world – and her Taurean mate's possessiveness will need to be tempered if he wants to keep his girl. Mr Taurus is looking for constancy and needs a mate to keep the home fires burning but, alas, Ms Leo wants to be on stage, her name up there flashing in neon lights.

Mr Taurus is inclined to see Ms Leo as his possession – his pride and joy – and although she will appreciate his overwhelming generosity and loyalty, she needs a partner who shares her outgoing and broad-minded outlook. Despite her strong ego, Ms Leo does respond to her mate in a loving and committed way, which can be a positive contribution to this match. Mr Taurus, however, is likely to be too needy because his sense of security is based on ownership. This is not what Ms Leo is about. She is too regal and too 'out there' for the more stay-at-home, play-at-home bull.

In the bedroom: Mr Taurus is a man who enjoys the sensual pleasures of life. His lioness lover will turn him on with her passion and beauty, and these two will share a fulfilling love life. But Ms Leo must temper her ego if she wants to linger forever in the loving embrace of her earthly man.

♌ Ms Leo + Mr Gemini ♊

Sign	Leo	Gemini
Symbol	Lion	Twins
Ruler	Sun	Mercury
Type	Fixed	Mutable
Element	Fire	Air

Natural charm, flamboyancy and quick-wittedness are what attract the Gemini male to this alluring lioness, and their shared communication and social interaction will bind them together. Mr Gemini will need to encourage and admire Ms Leo's talents often, because she constantly seeks his approval. Although both like to be in the limelight, he will need to be prepared to take the back seat at times to allow his star lioness to have her way.

Ms Leo expects loyalty and faithfulness from her mate and will keep Mr Gemini's philandering ways under control. She is strong, assertive and competitive – the type of woman every Gemini needs. Not having the same drive to succeed, he will tolerate his mate's desire to keep climbing the ladder to fame and fortune.

They share similar interests, particularly a love of theatre, because they are natural-born actors, playing roles on and off the stage. If Ms Leo is willing to curb her overpowering need for Mr Gemini's constant approval, these two could have a lively and dynamic relationship. She might be just exciting enough to sustain his attention long enough to create a lasting union.

In the bedroom: Pleasure-seeking individuals, Ms Leo and Mr Gemini will always entertain each other. And since both are romantics in the right environment, they can make a wonderful love combination, dancing and romancing the night away.

♌ Ms Leo + Mr Cancer ♋

Sign	Leo	Cancer
Symbol	Lion	Crab
Ruler	Sun	Moon
Type	Fixed	Cardinal
Element	Fire	Water

When Mr Cancer meets Ms Leo, he will be captivated by her charm and beauty and, because he is not domineering by nature, will allow the lioness to have her own way – at least this is what she thinks is happening most of the time. The crab will be a loyal, caring and gentle partner, but in a subtle way he's also very much in control of situations and their outcomes. Ms Leo will be delighted to finally find someone who truly understands her and allows her to shine and, although it might take some time for her to realise it, she will come to learn that her sensitive crab usually has the final say.

This Sun (Leo) and Moon (Cancer) combination has the wonderful ability to reflect on and enjoy the qualities they admire in each other. On a physical level, this pairing can take the crab and lion out of their comfort zones into an amazingly satisfying realm of pleasure. It will be like a new, fresh and exciting experience for both, which breaks free from previous boundaries they have both known in former relationships.

Since Mr Cancer likes guarantees and certainty and Ms Leo wants to be numero uno in her man's life, it's quite likely these two will marry. The Cancerian will always encourage his talented lioness to pursue a career in which she can shine and lead: otherwise she might see herself as the leader in their relationship, which can lead to discontentment on his part.

In the bedroom: Trying a bit of tenderness is exactly what the Cancerian man and his lioness need to do to enjoy a passionate, physical relationship. If either feels slighted or hurt, they will beat a hasty retreat, but if she turns up the heat with her emotional warmth and he digs deep into his emotions then there's no stopping the chemistry between these two.

♌ Ms Leo + Mr Leo ♌

Sign	Leo	Leo
Symbol	Lion	Lion
Ruler	Sun	Sun
Type	Fixed	Fixed
Element	Fire	Fire

Ms Leo and Mr Leo have healthy egos, which is part of their mutual attraction. They seem to command attention in most situations; however, they have a tendency to override each other, if that's at all possible given their dominating personalities. Both need their fair share of attention and regular stroking of egos, which can lead to problems in the relationship. But if either is willing to take the back seat occasionally, they can have a great time playing together. This combination has a strong affinity and, if they can curb their somewhat overpowering temperaments, they will be a highly compatible match.

Leos are affectionate and demonstrative and love the pleasures life has to offer. Their dynamic and colourful personalities act as a magnet, with each drawn to the other's charisma. And their loyal and committed nature is such that they are trusting and protective in the relationship. Additionally, they have a similar values system, which means the way they conduct their lives is very much in sync.

Leo women are very liberated and, with a no-nonsense approach, will stand up to their Leo mate; they will also be the first to pull him down a peg or two if he becomes too arrogant or narcissistic.

In the bedroom: This fiery duo share the same vitality and gregariousness, which can result in a physically passionate union. When he croons, 'Come on baby light my fire', she'll respond with 'Give it to me one more time'.

♌ Ms Leo + Mr Virgo ♍

Sign	Leo	Virgo
Symbol	Lion	Virgin
Ruler	Sun	Mercury
Type	Fixed	Mutable
Element	Fire	Earth

Ms Leo and Mr Virgo have equally strong needs; however, they are very different personalities. Mr Virgo is more down-to-earth and practical than his lioness, and will be on the lookout for a partner who needs him. The colourful and vibrant Ms Leo wants to be in the limelight with little thought about the consequences, whereas Mr Virgo has a tendency to dampen her flamboyant spirit with his over-analysis and scrutiny of her actions. This constant nit-picking falls on deaf ears because Ms Leo is such a 'know-it-all'. She is a fixed sign so even the constructive suggestions Mr Virgo throws her way will never be acknowledged.

Ms Leo's spontaneity and flamboyancy will grate on the more industrious Virgoan guy. But his methodical and structured approach to life could really suit the lioness, who sometimes throws herself into the deep end before really weighing up the consequences. On the other hand, the eternal worrier Mr Virgo could well do with a dose of Ms Leo's frivolity and bravado to lighten his load. More often than not, the earth signs, which include Virgo, seem to lack the *joie de vivre* displayed by the more spirited fire signs. Ultimately, the lioness will rarely be able to temper her passion and enthusiasm despite Mr Virgo's inclination to drag her down.

In the bedroom: The sexual rapport between Ms Leo and Mr Virgo will need plenty of nourishment to flourish because they can't relax in each other's arms, fundamentally because they feel misunderstood. Mr Virgo might find he is too analytical for the lioness, wounding her pride with his critical comments and thus dashing any hope he harbours of passionate lovemaking.

♌ Ms Leo + Mr Libra ♎

Sign	Leo	Libra
Symbol	Lion	Scales
Ruler	Sun	Venus
Type	Fixed	Cardinal
Element	Fire	Air

Ms Leo and Mr Libra have a strong social connection because they both enjoy involving other people in their lives. Her attractiveness and colourful personality will be admired by her Libran mate, and she will find that he will put her up on a pedestal where she feels most comfortable.

Mr Libra, by nature, likes balance and harmony in his life so when his lioness roars too loudly on occasions – she is prone to temper tantrums – he will turn a blind eye. They share a love of beauty and both have a strong creative ability, which includes an eye for design and colour. Given their many similarities in this sphere, Ms Leo and Mr Libra will come to appreciate and admire each other's talents.

The Libran man will be happy to provide his lioness with the respect and loyalty she insists upon in a relationship; as well, he will allow her to strut her stuff rather than cramping her style. Since Leos and Librans both stand out in a crowd, it will be hard for them not to be drawn to each other's magnetic and alluring personalities. They are traditionalists, so when they decide the union is working, they'll be more inclined to agree to marry rather than simply coasting along. It is a great combination if Mr Libra doesn't get too miffed at Ms Leo's constant need to be the centre of attention.

In the bedroom: Fire and air are usually a good match since both are the romantics of the zodiac and enjoy the fuss they make of each other. Ms Leo will be turned on by her charming Libran lover, who enjoys lengthy foreplay.

♌ Ms Leo + Mr Scorpio ♏

Sign	Leo	Scorpio
Symbol	Lion	Scorpion
Ruler	Sun	Pluto
Type	Fixed	Fixed
Element	Fire	Water

Challenging aspects in this union doom this pair to constant power struggles. Ms Leo is a fire sign, which surfaces in her strong, freedom-loving and idealistic streak. This girl doesn't like to be controlled and Mr Scorpio will try to manipulate her into following his preferred course of action. Because Leo and Scorpio are both fixed signs, both are stubborn and neither is likely to compromise or readily give in to the other.

The planetary ruler of Ms Leo is the Sun, giving her an open, generous and brightly shining demeanour. This is in opposition to Mr Scorpio's Plutonic energy, which makes him more secretive, jealous and manipulative, and is exhibited in his intense and controlling manner. The lioness wants to be free and independent, and her constant string of admirers will cause her Scorpio mate much grief.

Mr Scorpio's energy will be too dark and draining for the lioness, who much prefers to be out and about lapping up attention from the masses rather than being stuck in a relationship with a brooding, control-freak. Because Ms Leo can be egotistical at times and needs constant admiration and respect from people around her, her Scorpio mate will fight a losing battle against his lover's incessant need to hog the limelight.

In the bedroom: Initially, an intense, physical attraction can ignite these two but Mr Scorpio's overwhelming need to possess her will stifle Ms Leo's self-expression in the bedroom. None of the trickery Mr Scorpio uses so successfully on other women of the zodiac will work on the lioness, who is rarely tempted out of the den because she can see through his slippery and sneaky facade.

♌ Ms Leo + Mr Sagittarius ♐

Sign	Leo	Sagittarius
Symbol	Lion	Archer
Ruler	Sun	Jupiter
Type	Fixed	Mutable
Element	Fire	Fire

Ms Leo and Mr Sagittarius make a dynamic duo. The element of fire fuels this union with intensity, passion, idealism and a sense of adventure. This couple plays well together, each encouraging the other to pursue their own interests, yet will always show a unified front.

Ms Leo will ground the impulsive Mr Sagittarius and, in turn, he will encourage her to broaden her outlook and help whet her appetite for adventure. They are both free-thinking, independent, energetic individuals who share a passion for life. Both have tremendous self-confidence and rather dominating egos and never buy into the negative aspects of each other's personalities.

The lioness and the archer have a healthy perspective on life and rarely harbour hidden agendas – what you see is what you get. Each has an optimistic attitude towards life and together can merge their creative and insightful attitudes into a partnership that is destined for success. Rarely will they make their partner feel jealous; they allow each other the other space to enjoy friendships outside their relationship. These fire signs are larger than life and participate in a variety of pursuits, so they can bring a lot of this external stimulus into the union and will learn much from each other.

In the bedroom: Sexually these two are highly compatible: they don't have to prove themselves and can relax and have fun. Their playful expression is the key to keeping these two on their sexual toes. But sometimes the honesty and frankness of the archer may wound the high and mighty lioness, who likes to hear only praise of her positive traits. Overall this duo's physical passion is intense but there's plenty of fun along the way.

♌ Ms Leo + Mr Capricorn ♑

Sign	Leo	Capricorn
Symbol	Lion	Goat
Ruler	Sun	Saturn
Type	Fixed	Cardinal
Element	Fire	Earth

Ms Leo has much to gain from the steady, reliable and stable Mr Capricorn, however, these qualities don't always excite the lioness. She gains her security by participating in life, whereas he gains his from financial success. And she likes to live in a world of colour, vitality and excitement – needing to express her creativity through whatever turns her on; Mr Capricorn is far too reserved and earthed for that.

And although both need recognition, it comes from different sources. For her it's a platform where she can strut her stuff, which is an area where he will not want to compete. He is more interested in receiving accolades for his ability to accumulate money.

On a relationship level, the Capricornian guy prefers a one-to-one intimate connection and is inclined to become quite possessive and jealous of his Leo girl, who has no shortage of adoring males waiting to make their move. She is much more gregarious and outgoing than her Capricornian mate, who will turn his back on anything he considers shallow and frivolous.

In the bedroom: Capricornian men crave success in all their undertakings and their performance in the bedroom is no exception. He will be an attentive and persistent lover because he wants to please his partner and teach her a thing or two, but he might very well become frustrated that Ms Leo's hedonistic attitude dominates all areas of her life.

♌ Ms Leo + Mr Aquarius ♒

Sign	Leo	Aquarius
Symbol	Lion	Water bearer
Ruler	Sun	Uranus
Type	Fixed	Fixed
Element	Fire	Air

Both Ms Leo and Mr Aquarius have an air of flamboyancy and attract excitement into their lives. She is drawn to the spontaneity and unexpected treats that her Aquarian mate seems to hand out regularly. The lioness is a fun-loving individual and will relish her partner's last-minute surprises, which might require her to pack her bags on a minute's notice – destination unknown.

Both are fixed signs and know their own minds well, and both are involved in world pursuits: Ms Leo wants to be on stage – she loves the entertainment industry and wants her name up in lights, whereas Mr Aquarius is passionate about humanitarian affairs. Both are likely to have careers that involve public recognition. They are well-respected and well-liked individuals who make friends easily.

On the relationship front, these two don't muck around; they like to get to the core of what they want and can be quite forthright when asking for it. Ms Leo will give her Aquarian mate the space he needs but will still be able to pull the reins when she needs to tame him. If he is willing to be a little more demonstrative in his affections, these two can sustain a fun-packed life filled with great variety, fun and spontaneity.

In the bedroom: Mr Aquarius can teach his lioness a few tricks in the bedroom; he is an experimental and experienced lover and anything goes in this relationship. However, it's more a physical exchange than a sensual experience for these two.

♌ Ms Leo + Mr Pisces ♓

Sign	Leo	Pisces
Symbol	Lion	Fish
Ruler	Sun	Neptune
Type	Fixed	Mutable
Element	Fire	Water

Mr Pisces' tendency to appear helpless and in need of direction will appeal to Ms Leo, who likes to take charge and be acknowledged for her strengths and capabilities. She seems to take on responsibility particularly keenly, so she will feel she's well in command of this union.

The Piscean man is self-sacrificing and instinctively knows what turns this lioness on. She, in turn, will be flattered by his constant attention. However, the fish also has a predisposition to retreating periodically and this introspective quality will be seen as a weakness by a confused Ms Leo, who will interpret his actions as submissive. She will be left out in the cold wondering what this personality change is all about. Leo is a fixed sign; she thrives on consistency and needs to know where she stands at all times. Mr Pisces is known for his escapist tendencies and will disappoint Ms Leo with his changeability. If he can stay focused and balanced somewhere between his intensity and detachment, this fish might be able to keep Ms Leo's flame burning – or at least flickering.

The lioness and the fish sound like an unusual pair but if they can find their way into each other's hearts, she will discover a gentle, sensitive and inspiring man; he, in turn, will find her confident and bold persona inspiring. Both romantic idealists, they are attracted to artistic or musical pursuits, which can give them much in common.

In the bedroom: Sexually speaking, this duo might miss the mark: the Piscean is a spiritual being whereas the lion is more focused on the physical. The fish will want to swim upstream, away from what he perceives to be an overbearing, dogmatic lover who is more about physical gratification than emotional fulfilment.

Celebrity Ms Leo: Madonna

Singer, born 7.05 am 16 August 1958 in Bay City, Michigan, USA

```
Personal planets: Sun in Leo
                  Moon in Virgo
                  Mercury in Virgo
                  Venus in Leo
                  Mars in Taurus
```

To be brave is to love someone unconditionally, without expecting anything in return – to just give. That takes courage because we don't want to fall on our faces or leave ourselves open to hurt.

– Madonna

Madonna exemplifies a strong, bold personality and her Leo Sun symbolises an energy that craves approval and attention. As a Leo woman, her father's influence resulted in her need to throw her talents into a profession where she would command respect and admiration. She consistently strives for perfection due to the predominance of earth planets in her chart, which makes her self-critical and will always mean she feels there is room for improvement. Her desire to be in the limelight and her responsiveness to attention, praise and recognition will also be reflected in her personal relationships.

As a Leo, she is incredibly romantic; however, she can also be strong and controlling. She needs a partner who can diffuse her single-mindedness and be equally strong and commanding in his own right. In love, Madonna is fiercely loyal and has a strong moral code. With her Moon in Virgo, she is discriminating in her choice of men and seeks a mate who is mentally challenging. Madonna is far from superficial and is attracted to the intellect of her partner, rather than his physical appearance. She thrives on intensity and needs a deep connection with her mate. With five fixed modes of expression in her chart, she is very stubborn and single-minded and tends to know what she wants. This aspect of her chart makes her want her own way – often!

Madonna has an idealised view of her relationships and looks for the 'perfect' union, which might lead to disillusionment, and she needs to look beyond the human love connection into a more spiritual plane.

Madonna's early attraction to actor Sean Penn, a fellow Leo, would have had its ups and downs. A relationship involving two Leos can work very well; however, they both need to keep their egos in check because two public personalities can clash.

Madonna and husband Guy Ritchie's relationship has the makings of a strong and committed bond. He is a Virgo and Madonna has a strong Virgo theme in her chart, with her Moon and Mercury making a fundamental connection to Ritchie's Virgo Sun. Both professionally and romantically, their need for commitment, support and loyalty will be a strong feature of this union. Although Madonna has a need for excitement and challenge, Ritchie's Sun and Pluto connection would give him the strength to stand up to his equally powerful and commanding partner. Additionally, Ritchie's Libra in Venus endows him with an ability to relate well, which can give his relationship with Madonna a sense of balance and harmony.

Mr Leo – an overview

A father plays an important role in shaping the moral and ethical codes of young Mr Leo. Some Leo men will grow up to value and respect their relationships while others will be domineering and somewhat controlling. Generally speaking, Leo men exude a charm and strong presence that makes them attractive to the opposite sex. Courage and strength seem to emanate from this man; he wants to be king of his castle but is equally delighted to share his kingdom with a woman who engenders feelings of pride in him.

Mr Leo is a mixture of youth and maturity; he has a well-developed inner child making him playful and fun-loving yet responsible at the same time. Even though he displays a confident and strong demeanour, this man has his vulnerabilities and needs to feel admired and encouraged to help maintain his sense of dignity.

Leo is a fixed sign; hence the lion is firmly entrenched in his beliefs and opinions, and can be dominating and at times overbearing in his relationships. This man needs a woman who admires and humours him along the way, yet still has the courage to stand up to him occasionally. He takes great pride in his conquests and, even though he relishes being the centre of attention, he likes to be able to show off his partner. To get the best out of a relationship with the lion, you will need to value and appreciate his qualities. In turn, he will make you the queen of his castle, bestowing flowers, gifts and compliments upon you at every turn.

Famous Leo men

* Bill Clinton
  (former US president)
* George Bernard Shaw
  (writer)
* Alfred Hitchcock
  (film director)
* Mick Jagger (musician)
* Napoleon Bonaparte
  (French emperor)
* Fidel Castro
  (Cuban political leader)

Combinations

♌ Mr Leo + Ms Aries ♈

Sign	Leo	Aries
Symbol	Lion	Ram
Ruler	Sun	Mars
Type	Fixed	Cardinal
Element	Fire	Fire

Charming, charismatic and sociable, Mr Leo will sweep Ms Aries off her feet. Finally she's met her knight in shining armour, who has all the right moves and even more of the right lines for this needy, idealistic ram. At last – someone she can have some fun with!

Leos enjoy socialising and are drawn to creative pursuits. While most lions enjoy being the centre of attention, they are happy to share the spotlight with their attention-seeking ram partner. This is a happy union where both partners respect and enjoy each other's qualities.

The father figure played an important role in the early lives of both Leos and Arians. Accordingly, both need a certain degree of strength and solidarity from their partners. Even though Ms Aries is more emotionally idealistic than her intellectual Leo, they both carry a strong sense of loyalty and commitment to each other.

Because both are constantly seeking approval, it makes them understand and recognise this need in others. Providing they don't try to overshadow each other and keep their idealistic natures in balance with the practical side of life, these two signs will continue on a journey of passion throughout their relationship.

In the bedroom: When fire meets fire, the flames of love will spark a competitive love match in the bedroom. Ms Aries and Mr Leo are highly sexually charged and both will last the distance.

♌ Mr Leo + Ms Taurus ♉

Sign	Leo	Taurus
Symbol	Lion	Bull
Ruler	Sun	Venus
Type	Fixed	Fixed
Element	Fire	Earth

These two signs are in a difficult astrological aspect with each other, which equates to challenges and competitiveness. The conflict between this pair is a result of their both having fixed modes of expression, which makes them stubborn and uncompromising. However, if Mr Leo and Ms Taurus are willing to put aside their egos, they can share some common goals.

They are attracted to similar interests, share the same values system and have high moral standards. Their sense of fairness, justice and loyalty is also on the same footing, but their intrinsic personalities are too polarised. The obstinate bull will never bow to the bold, proud lion, who will always need to take the limelight in the relationship. But if Ms Taurus is willing to search for a pussycat among the pride, she might find a docile, domesticated pet more to her liking.

Being of an earth sign, Ms Taurus will always be attracted to the colourful, flamboyant fire-sign personalities because they can lift her out of her life's predictability. But the speed at which Mr Leo moves and the adulation he needs from other admirers tends to bring the Taurean woman's insecurities to the surface.

Who's the boss here? This is a tricky question since both Mr Leo and Ms Taurus will continually fight for domination in the relationship. And since both find it difficult to compromise and can be somewhat obstinate, it is likely they will reach an impasse and be unable to move forward from that point on.

In the bedroom: The makeup sex between this pair will be right up there with the best Ms Taurus has ever had. Actions speak louder than words as far as she is concerned so she'll lap up the lion's passionate lovemaking, which will make him feel like the king he thinks he is.

♌ Mr Leo + Ms Gemini ♊

Sign	Leo	Gemini
Symbol	Lion	Twins
Ruler	Sun	Mercury
Type	Fixed	Mutable
Element	Fire	Air

The mental agility and desire to have fun and constant stimulation will herald this partnership a success, both in and out of the bedroom. Mr Leo errs more on the side of commitment and will want to have Ms Gemini by his side to show her off and, as long as he loosens the reins on occasions and gives her enough leeway to be herself, this relationship has the makings of a wonderful pairing.

Ms Gemini will be attracted to the lion's sense of adventure and has the power to control his arrogance and temper his desire to be in the spotlight. She has a way of cutting Mr Leo down to size and he seems to be able to take instructions rather readily from Ms Gemini, who will always critique his actions with typically frank explanations.

Both love to be involved in myriad activities: the constant variety is highly appealing to Ms Gemini. A successful union between these two is all about being able to provide enough stimulation for this flighty female. Mr Leo has a way of clipping his Gemini mate's wings, but without her knowledge. The Sun-ruled Leo has great aspirations and his Gemini mate will use her air qualities to inspire her man to bigger and better things. This pair will walk side by side in their eternal search for stimulation, variety and excitement, all of which, happily, they can give each other.

In the bedroom: The twin might put out the fires of passion burning deep within her Leo guy with her cool and detached approach to sex. The proud lion likes to be king – even in the bedroom – and might feel insecure if he thinks he's not satisfying his changeable Gemini lover. She'll need to be more in 'bed' than in her 'head' if she wants a compatible sexual union with this man.

♌ Mr Leo + Ms Cancer ♋

Sign	Leo	Cancer
Symbol	Lion	Crab
Ruler	Sun	Moon
Type	Fixed	Cardinal
Element	Fire	Water

The Cancerian woman will provide her Leo mate with a good dose of loyalty and respect, which is exactly what this man needs from a relationship. Both have strong family values and will be interested in some form of commitment and stability.

Ms Cancer will be inclined to keep in the background but has a great strength and reserve so, if her lion mate roars too loudly or becomes too arrogant, she has her own quiet way of dealing with him. He will love her genuine interest in, and support of, his activities and, in turn, will encourage her hankering for external pursuits. Both the lion and crab are attracted to the arts and other cultural activities, which is what often bonds these two lovebirds.

Not often will fire and water click as well as in this relationship and, if Mr Leo can keep his temperament a little more low-key and Ms Cancer can keep her emotions under control, these two could have a really positive impact on each other. A Leo man genuinely wants to please his partner and can make her feel as if she is the only girl in the world. The important element in this coupling is that water tends to dampen the fire's idealism and spirit; however, these two have a great need to please each other and, in the intimacy of their sexual life, have a tremendous capacity for sensual closeness.

In the bedroom: The brash and bold Leo man will have to woo his way into the bedroom of Ms Crab. He'll need to be caring and considerate if he wants to fall into her open arms and she'll have to learn not to be so sensitive and secretive with her lion if they want to set the room on fire.

♌ Mr Leo + Ms Leo ♌

Sign	Leo	Leo
Symbol	Lion	Lion
Ruler	Sun	Sun
Type	Fixed	Fixed
Element	Fire	Fire

This charming duo will be at loggerheads as to who will grab the spotlight and shine more brightly. Male and female Leos exemplify a certain style and razzamatazz and, although they understand each other very well, there may be a push as to who gets into the front seat first. Mr Leo will automatically be attracted to the style, glamour and strength Ms Leo represents and there is an automatic pride ignited when he links arms with this woman. His love of her magnificence is what will make his heart flutter and his attentiveness and openness will turn her on.

Mr and Ms Leo have a flair for the dramatic; they will embrace their lives with the same sense of purpose and need for variety. Romance is a high priority for both and each will bring their own creative spark into the union. They are passionate, idealistic and, above all, generous in nature; they will spoil each other, not only with material comforts, but also with their time.

Because Mr and Ms Leo share a fixed sign, a degree of rigidity and stubbornness can creep into their relationship. These two know themselves well and have a strong sense of conviction and purpose in their lives. Respect and loyalty are both virtues that these two hold in high regard and, with both having had strong male influences in their early lives, they are likely to have a well-balanced and healthy outlook. Direct in their dealings, Mr and Ms Leo will know where they stand in their relationship. This connection will lead to a very satisfying sexual chemistry between them.

In the bedroom: This fiery duo share the same vitality and gregariousness, which can result in a physically passionate union. Both will have an abundance of energy and enjoy plenty of playful sexual exchanges in their private den.

♌ Mr Leo + Ms Virgo ♍

Sign	Leo	Virgo
Symbol	Lion	Virgin
Ruler	Sun	Mercury
Type	Fixed	Mutable
Element	Fire	Earth

The Leo man and Virgoan woman seem to be at odds with one another because he wants to be the centre of his world and she will always have to work around his universe. The core of this relationship is that he will be the taker and she will be the giver. Unfortunately, Ms Virgo will always want Mr Leo to show her a certain sense of gratitude he might find difficult to verbalise. Mr Leo's outgoing yet demanding nature will push Ms Virgo to her limit.

This combination has contrasting temperaments: his is flamboyant, attention seeking and exuberant, whereas hers is more retiring, shy and pragmatic. This Leo man needs an outgoing, charming and vivacious lady and, although Ms Virgo has many virtues, she is a woman who likes to scrutinise and analyse her man. It is only when she feels truly confident that the relationship is rock solid that she will relax and feel comfortable in the union. Mr Leo is a man of spontaneity and a risk taker. Because Ms Virgo seems so reticent, Mr Leo's sense of self-confidence will start to wane because he will feel unappreciated. Mr Leo needs a warm, optimistic mate who also has an air of self-confidence. However, Ms Virgo seems to be too self-critical and lacks the spontaneity to excite this man.

Mr Leo will be drawn to Ms Virgo's intellectualism but she won't understand his dramatic nature. Leo can't get from cool, reserved Virgo the sexual responsiveness he demands. She is practical and prudent; he is extravagant and a spendthrift. He likes to live life in a really big way, but she is conservative, frugal and a nit-picker, which puts a dampener on his high spirits. Ms Virgo won't be dominated either. The Leo guy needs lots of flattery, but Ms Virgo tends to puncture inflated egos. They should both look elsewhere.

In the bedroom: Ms Virgo will be too busy analysing the relationship instead of enjoying it, which will cause Mr Leo to become frustrated and lead to feelings that his sexual advances have been rebuffed. Not much to roar about in this bedroom!

♌ Mr Leo + Ms Libra ♎

Sign	Leo	Libra
Symbol	Lion	Scales
Ruler	Sun	Venus
Type	Fixed	Cardinal
Element	Fire	Air

This stylish, well-balanced woman will catch Mr Leo's eye, and his fire energy – combining ambition, generosity and a zest for life – will likewise attract her. These two signs have a keen eye for beauty and glamour and, with both having these qualities in abundance, they will hold one another in high esteem. Mr Leo's need for admiration and Ms Libra's desire to be noticed will put them on common ground. The zodiac sign of Leo is ruled by the Sun, which sits harmoniously with Ms Libra's ruling planet Venus.

His creativity and artistic flare and her Venusian, romantic and idealistic nature will ignite their passion. Ms Libra has a penchant for putting her men up on pedestals and Mr Leo will love nothing better than being held up to be admired and adored. These lovers have a mutual understanding of what is needed to create a passionate interlude. The lion will be starry-eyed over his Libran mate, who exudes an ethereal beauty. Both Mr Leo and Ms Libra value beauty and need to feel that their world is surrounded by colour and love.

In the bedroom: Mr Leo and Ms Libra have great chemistry together and their lovemaking is more about quality than quantity. The lion will be lustier in the bedroom than his image-conscious partner, who is more focused on ensuring that her partner finds her alluring.

♌ Mr Leo + Ms Scorpio ♏

Sign	Leo	Scorpio
Symbol	Lion	Scorpion
Ruler	Sun	Pluto
Type	Fixed	Fixed
Element	Fire	Water

These two are both passionate and intense in their desire to have a relationship but compromise is always an important aspect of it. In many ways they share similar personalities: both are control freaks and have a tendency to want to take the dominant role in the relationship. However, their tactics are different. Mr Leo is open, vocal and demonstrative and says it how it is, which can cut Ms Scorpio to the quick. While she might know where she stands with him, more often than not he won't with her, because of her secretive nature and her suspicion of his bravado and his need for public adoration.

Her sting will ultimately be more lethal than his roar and Mr Leo will wind up being the one to make more sacrifices in this relationship. As a fire sign, Mr Leo likes a woman who is direct and honest in her feelings but Ms Scorpio is distrusting of most men until they prove their worth. Mr Leo is too proud to play games he has no chance of winning. The scorpion is too demanding and far too jealous for the lion, who usually has a string of admirers waiting in the wings.

In the bedroom: With both being fixed signs, these two are equally self-contained and need to feel emotionally secure before they will reveal themselves sexually to a partner. Both will be the initiators and want to have sexual dominance over the other – a passionate mix if one plays a more submissive role in their union. Bring on the cat-and-mouse games!

♌ Mr Leo + Ms Sagittarius ♐

Sign	Leo	Sagittarius
Symbol	Lion	Archer
Ruler	Sun	Jupiter
Type	Fixed	Mutable
Element	Fire	Fire

The planetary rulers of Leo and Sagittarius – the Sun and Jupiter – are all about living life to the full. The two fire signs crave excitement and will stop at nothing to expand their horizons and fulfil their need to express their fiery, dynamic energies. Fire signs need an outlet for their overflowing creative and passionate energy, and this can come in the form of an inspiring relationship where two people can express their mutual desires without compromising their individuality.

Mr Leo and Ms Sagittarius are exceptionally physical beings; he's highly masculine, and she will always find a strong, well-built and confident man appealing. The lion in turn will find an athletic physique and shapely thighs a huge turn-on.

Ms Sagittarius is a woman who needs to respect her partner and feel protected, and the proud and regal Mr Leo will be an ideal mate for her. But his sometimes controlling and demanding demeanour can irritate the freedom-loving Ms Sagittarius, who values her independence and will fight fiercely to hang on to it. But if the archer is too independent, her lion will become disheartened with her perceived lack of attention and commitment to him. Even though these fire signs have a natural affinity, they also have a competitive streak, which can dampen the Sagittarian's enthusiasm for her Leo lover.

In the bedroom: These two will enjoy a good romp under the covers! Both possess a strong physical energy and can play around for hours.

♌ Mr Leo + Ms Capricorn ♑

Sign	Leo	Capricorn
Symbol	Lion	Goat
Ruler	Sun	Saturn
Type	Fixed	Cardinal
Element	Fire	Earth

Both Mr Leo and Ms Capricorn have a desire to make it in a worldly sense. Respect and commitment tie these two together; however, more in a commercial than romantic sense. A less passionate Leo male might be aroused by the managerial and organisational skills of this woman, but the true lionhearted spirit of fun, frivolity and adventure isn't compatible with this distant and aloof Capricornian. She projects a serious and responsible disposition which does not attract Mr Leo, who needs a woman who can enhance his sense of status.

Mr Leo's fire is infectious and volatile, and Ms Capricorn will see him as superficial and lacking in commitment. He needs an open-minded and fun-loving woman with whom he can laugh but, alas, the goat is more focused on climbing her mountain and reaching the pinnacle than letting her hair down.

Ms Capricorn is often attracted to partners who can speed her rise to prominence and will often marry someone who is above her station. The motto 'I use' is about the Capricornian's ability to utilise the talents and abilities of others to move forward. Mr Leo is too opinionated and caught up with his own rise to fame to have the inclination to help her along that path.

In the bedroom: Sexually these signs don't really gel. Ms Capricorn's drive is not so much in the bedroom as in the boardroom. And the lion will be far too concerned with pleasing himself to worry about pleasing his goat as well.

♌ Mr Leo + Ms Aquarius ♒

Sign	Leo	Aquarius
Symbol	Lion	Water bearer
Ruler	Sun	Uranus
Type	Fixed	Fixed
Element	Fire	Air

The fire and air elements of this combination create a good rapport between Mr Leo and the zany Ms Aquarius, but only if he can play down his domineering persona. Leo men like a partner who can support them and help them shine so he may be a little disappointed that his Aquarian women is off saving the world instead of doting on him and pandering to his needs.

Both might find themselves in the public arena; however, she's more likely to be involved in a humanitarian cause and he'll be in the latest Broadway production. They will admire and respect each other's capabilities and share a great passion for collecting and surrounding themselves with a menagerie of people from all walks of life.

Ms Aquarius will not be the least bit flustered or jealous of her lion's string of adoring female fans. She's more likely to join in the praise for her wonderful, creative and talented man instead of wondering about the motives behind the female flattery. Mr Leo, in turn, will be in awe of Ms Aquarius's amazing mind and intellect and the two will be kept entertained for hours chatting about world peace, politics or what the Martians really look like.

In the bedroom: Ms Aquarius may be a little detached and aloof for the voracious Mr Leo, who is much more tactile and demonstrative. But if she truly admires and respects him, she can soon turn into a passionate playmate for her lion.

♌ Mr Leo + Ms Pisces ♓

Sign	Leo	Pisces
Symbol	Lion	Fish
Ruler	Sun	Neptune
Type	Fixed	Mutable
Element	Fire	Water

The watery Piscean is too evasive, dreamy and slippery when it comes to a relationship with Mr Leo. The lion needs to know he's being acknowledged and respected; however, Ms Pisces seems to be too distant and wrapped up in her own dreamy world.

She is a woman who needs to retreat and regroup to become revitalised, which will leave her Leo mate feeling left out in the cold, not really understanding what makes this deep and soulful creature tick. Mr Leo often lacks the depth and spirituality to make a fulfilling partner for Ms Pisces. She will unnerve the Leo man with her intuitive abilities and he will be unsettled when she can read his mind and know his motives.

Although these two are both romantics, they have unrealistic expectations of one another. Mr Leo may see this giving, vulnerable woman as a victim rather than his equal and won't have the patience or inclination to nurture and be compassionate enough to understand her vulnerabilities. His roar is much too loud for the demure and gentle fish, who would rather swim upstream in search of someone who understands her. Dreamy Ms Pisces prefers to be in a relationship where she can nurture her man and envelop him with her compassionate nature, but Mr Leo is too arrogant and self-centred to appreciate her martyr-like qualities.

In the bedroom: The watery nature of the fish tends to cause the Leo's fire to fizzle. The lion will need to be a mind-reader to know what will turn on his sensitive and secretive lover. The fish has a tendency to slip far too easily in and out of the sheets, keeping her lion on his paws!

Celebrity Mr Leo: Bill Clinton

Former US president, born 8.51 am 19 August 1946 in Hope, Arkansas, USA

```
Personal planets:  Sun in Leo
                   Moon in Taurus
                   Mercury in Leo
                   Venus in Libra
                   Mars in Libra
```

I may not have been the greatest president, but I've had the most fun in eight years.

– Bill Clinton

Bill Clinton's bold and prominent Leo personality is tempered by his abundance of planets in the sign of Libra, which gives him a strong desire for harmony and balance in his love relationships. His chart indicates that he is rather idealistic in life and his naivety often leads him romantically because he has a strong capacity for self-delusion. He has a tendency to be confused about what he really wants from a relationship. He is a true romantic and puts his women on pedestals and can become very disappointed when his expectations are not met.

His Moon in Taurus gives him a preference for stability in his relationships and he also a natural flair for providing his mate with the comforts and pleasures of life. Clinton has a strong air component in his chart, suggesting that his need for mental stimulation in a relationship makes him a communicative partner. He has a strong presence, yet he has a gentle and soft disposition and can sometimes be taken advantage of.

Clinton and former lover Monica Lewinsky, also a Leo, share the same Sun and Moon signs and also the same ascendant (rising sign), giving them a connection. Like Clinton, Lewinsky has a highly romantic and imaginative mind and strong capacity for spiritualising her relationship but does not always have a realistic perspective.

Clinton's wife, Hillary, is a Scorpio with her Moon in the sign of Pisces, causing her to be a deep, compassionate and feeling woman with a selfless attitude to life. Although she is a passionate and intuitive person, she carries the typical traits of the Scorpio demeanour and will need to feel secure in her relationships before she can entrust her feeling and thoughts to another. Conversely, the lack of water in Clinton's chart gives him the desire to experience a great intensity in his emotional life, causing him to be more open and vulnerable.

The connection between these two is a strong Leo influence in Hillary's chart. Her Mars in Leo makes her want a man she can admire, respect and compete with. His earth Moon and her water Moon will make for a caring, nurturing and supportive union. Because the Moon is a crucial component of a person's emotional needs, this couple can co-operate with each other. And with both having an underlying empathy with each other, they will have an ability to transcend difficulties that arise in their relationship.

VIRGO (24 August–23 September)

ℳ

Ruled by the planet Mercury
Earth sign
Mutable
Feminine energy

In general ...

Virgos, both male and female, will always be more confident and positive about themselves when they feel they are well regarded and productive. They need relationships that are deep and meaningful and will always be scrutinising and analysing situations to make any improvements. Mercury is the planetary ruler of Virgo, which means that communication is a driving-force in their bonding with others.

People born under this sign are service-orientated and are an employer's dream, because the Virgoan will always give more than is required – a characteristic that also flows into the relationship arena. Their fastidious attention to hygiene, cleanliness and order in their life will either attract a mate or send him packing. Virgos have a tendency to be reserved, holding back their emotions in case of rejection; they need to give a relationship plenty of time to develop to feel safe and secure. However, once they meet their 'perfect' partner they will be loyal and fully committed.

Virgos will try to please their partners in most circumstances; however, their critical nature can at times create friction with their mate. They are constantly searching for perfection, which includes looking for the perfect relationship. This Virgo tendency towards criticism stems from their own feeling of inadequacy because they tend to judge themselves too harshly. Because of this they have a tendency to seek out a partner who can reassure them and understand that their criticisms are well meaning and designed to be constructive rather than undermining.

Virgo is an earth sign, which indicates they are practical by nature and physically active, and they are likely to seek a partner who can keep up with their sexual energy. Most Virgos are not in a rush to tie the knot, perhaps because their discriminating nature makes it difficult for them to find the right mate. As Virgos mature, they become more comfortable with themselves and might even recognise their nit-picking and critical behaviour is often counterproductive.

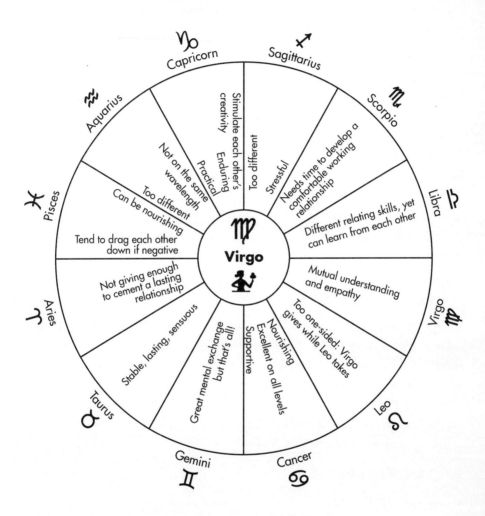

How a Virgo personality might match up with other star signs

Ms Virgo — an overview

Ms Virgo is obsessive by nature and, although accommodating in relationships, will always try to improve the quality of the union. She sets herself high goals and standards, expectations her partner often feels he has to live up to. Because Virgo is a mutable sign, this woman finds it easy to adapt to her partner's needs. However, given Virgo's analytical and enquiring mind, she is best suited to a mate with whom she can have a meaningful mental exchange.

Ms Virgo is a great contradiction: on one hand she is a true romantic and idealistic about what she needs from her partner; on the other she has a very practical, grounded and critical nature. She is often misunderstood because her constant need to be discriminatory can make her appear ruthless. Her relationship is fundamentally about duty, commitment and fulfilling her obligations. Her emotional responses may be interpreted as cool and distant, yet this girl has a warm heart and will give you the shirt off her back if necessary. Ms Virgo needs to feel appreciated in a relationship and will steer clear of any confrontations. Although she can enjoy and feel content in a satisfying union, she will never compromise herself if it fails to live up to her expectations. This girl is too self-sufficient and practical to be in a negative relationship and has the means to live her life without a partner's support.

As a lover, Ms Virgo has this part of her life down to a fine art. Her need to please her partner is very obvious and her lovemaking is sensual, selfless and uninhibited. Her desire for perfection spills into the bedroom and she becomes a passionate seductress. A mate who can crack this ice-maiden's heart will be an individual who knows his own mind well, is self-confident and can communicate his needs and desires.

Famous Virgoan women

* Raquel Welch (actor)
* Mother Teresa (humanitarian)
* Agatha Christie (writer)
* Lauren Bacall (actor)
* Claudia Schiffer (model)
* Sophia Loren (actor)

Combinations

♍ Ms Virgo + Mr Aries ♈

Sign	Virgo	Aries
Symbol	Virgin	Ram
Ruler	Mercury	Mars
Type	Mutable	Cardinal
Element	Earth	Fire

The personalities of these two don't mix well, making a love relationship more of a battlefield than a loving union. The sensitive, nervous and critical nature of the Ms Virgo will often be tried and tested by the blunt and brash Mr Aries.

Both Arians and Virgos are honest in their feelings, which sometimes can be the basis for long-term disharmony. Ms Virgo's critical nature can wear down Mr Aries, who needs constant adulation, support and encouragement. Instead of interpreting her analytical comments as the constructive criticisms she intended, he will view them as personal attacks he can live without. Since both signs seem to have an underlying lack of self-confidence, their differing natures don't give them the ability to make the other feel their worth. This can lead to feelings of rejection and insecurity on both sides.

Mr Aries is too impulsive for Ms Virgo, who likes to weigh up the pros and cons of a situation rather than diving straight in. She will find she plays servant to the demanding and headstrong Mr Aries. On the other hand, as both have a predisposition to physical activities – the Virgo more in her dietary needs and the Aries in his sporting prowess – they can find some common ground to express their interests in outdoor pursuits and health.

In the long term, however, although the self-controlled and self-contained nature of Ms Virgo will be initially attractive, this earth sign will be too grounded and practical to hold a long-term attraction for the fiery, quick-fix and non-committal Aries man.

In the bedroom: If Mr Aries can be patient with Ms Virgo, who may not share the same sexual stamina as him, then he will be rewarded with a caring and loving partner. She will also need to take care and not criticise his techniques in the bedroom!

♍ Ms Virgo + Mr Taurus ♉

Sign	Virgo	Taurus
Symbol	Virgin	Bull
Ruler	Mercury	Venus
Type	Mutable	Fixed
Element	Earth	Earth

These two earth signs are very comfortable with each other. They share a strong need for the physical and both are ready to please their partner. Ms Virgo is loyal, supportive and practical and will be seduced by the generosity of her Taurean man. As long as Ms Virgo can keep her critical nature under control, this pair will have a mutual respect and an underlying empathy for each other.

Mr Taurus's requirements from a relationship are simple – honesty, loyalty, integrity and commitment, which is what Ms Virgo also requires. Hence, this is a union in which the partners share many common ideals and values.

Mr Taurus and Ms Virgo have personal issues with security that can affect their relationship. She is too critical of herself and he sometimes tries too hard to accumulate money and possessions. Ms Virgo is the one who will always be accommodating in the relationship because she is a mutable sign, and will bend to allow her fixed bull to think that he is in control. But little does he know that beneath this seemingly passive-natured woman lies a tower of strength. The ice-maiden doesn't get her nickname for nothing.

In the bedroom: Sexually, both are sensual and will be highly compatible when it comes to lovemaking. Ms Virgo is a perfectionist and will always want to be seen in her best light, so she has a tendency to give it her best shot, which her Taurean lover will appreciate.

♍ Ms Virgo + Mr Gemini ♊

Sign	Virgo	Gemini
Symbol	Virgin	Twins
Ruler	Mercury	Mercury
Type	Mutable	Mutable
Element	Earth	Air

Ms Virgo and Mr Gemini will have a lively exchange of words because both are ruled by the planet Mercury. Theirs will be an easy flow of communication but the language each uses will be very different.

In their displays of affection for each other, the Gemini guy will err on the side of dishonesty, whereas his Virgoan mate will be totally truthful. He will often tell her what he thinks she wants to hear and be quite affronted with her critical and truthful analysis. Mr Gemini will find Ms Virgo's nit-picking and her attention to detail a turn-off; this scatter-brained man would prefer not to hear the truth about his lazy and untidy ways.

Domestically this couple are poles apart and in the long run will start to irritate each other. The air and earth components have a different way of seeing life which signifies many challenges in a union. Mr Gemini, with his carefree, come-what-may approach to life, will find Ms Virgo too conservative and responsible. She needs to know where she is heading and he prefers the element of surprise. Since both are mutable signs, they do have an ability to see each other's perspective but, regardless of their adaptability, rarely will they have the inclination to completely surrender to the other's needs. It's highly unlikely these two will be able to sustain a long-term relationship given their myriad different needs and expectations.

In the bedroom: The Virgo woman will need to feel some degree of security with her Gemini lover if she's ever going to give of herself physically. This will be hard for the twin, who is as changeable as the wind. It's unlikely there'll be much sexual compatibility between this earth woman and her air man.

♍ Ms Virgo + Mr Cancer ♋

Sign	Virgo	Cancer
Symbol	Virgin	Crab
Ruler	Mercury	Moon
Type	Mutable	Cardinal
Element	Earth	Water

Ms Virgo and Mr Cancer require loyal and sympathetic partners in their love relationships. The nurturing virgin can have a calming and comforting effect on Mr Crab, whose sensitive soul is not always immune to the criticism of others. Her practical, no-nonsense approach to life has a calming effect on the crab and she seems to be able to cope quite well with his moodiness and occasional withdrawal. Mr Cancer can be quite bossy and demanding with his partners but Ms Virgo seems to be able to take this in her stride, not hesitating for a moment to accept what he says if it sits comfortably with her.

Ms Virgo will admire the business acumen of Mr Crab, but if he's one of the insecure Cancerians whose frequent dark moods make him err on the side of negativity, he'll find Ms Virgo's intolerant, critical tones strong enough to create a big wedge between them. She doesn't believe in emotional excessiveness and he doesn't take well to criticism – regardless of whether or not it was well intended. But the crab's intuition and the virgin's analytical nature should be sharp enough to allow them to detect and avoid any bumps in the road ahead.

In the bedroom: On the surface Ms Virgo can appear cool, reserved and undemonstrative, but the sensitive, gentle crab has just the right touch to awaken deep feelings of passion within Ms Virgo which can lead them to share a fulfilling sexual union.

♍ Ms Virgo + Mr Leo ♌

Sign	Virgo	Leo
Symbol	Virgin	Lion
Ruler	Mercury	Sun
Type	Mutable	Fixed
Element	Earth	Fire

The Leo man and Virgoan woman seem to be at odds with one another because he wants to be the centre of his world and she will always have to work around his universe. The core of this relationship is that he will be the taker and she will be the giver. Unfortunately, Ms Virgo will always want Mr Leo to show her a certain sense of gratitude that he might find difficult to verbalise. Mr Leo's outgoing yet demanding nature will push Ms Virgo to her limits.

Both have contrasting temperaments: his is flamboyant, attention seeking and exuberant, whereas hers is more retiring, shy and pragmatic. This Leo man needs an outgoing, charming and vivacious lady and, although Ms Virgo has many virtues, she is a girl who likes to scrutinise and analyse her man. It is only when she feels truly confident that the relationship is rock solid that she will relax and feel comfortable in the union. Mr Leo is a man of spontaneity and a risk taker. Because Ms Virgo seems so reticent, Mr Leo's sense of self-confidence will start to wane because he will feel unappreciated. Mr Leo requires a warm, optimistic mate, who also has an air of self-confidence. However, Ms Virgo seems to be too self-critical and lacks the spontaneity that excites this man.

Mr Leo will be drawn to Ms Virgo's intellectualism but she won't understand his dramatic nature. Leo can't get from cool, reserved Virgo the sexual responsiveness he demands. She is practical and prudent; he is extravagant and a spendthrift. He likes to live life in a really big way, but she is conservative, frugal and a nit-picker, which puts a dampener on his high spirits. Ms Virgo won't be dominated either. Leo needs lots of flattery, but Ms Virgo tends to puncture inflated egos. Both should look elsewhere.

In the bedroom: Ms Virgo will be too busy analysing the relationship instead of enjoying it, which will cause Mr Leo to become frustrated and lead to feelings that his sexual advances have been rebuffed. Not much to roar about in this bedroom!

♍ Ms Virgo + Mr Virgo ♍

Sign	Virgo	Virgo
Symbol	Virgin	Virgin
Ruler	Mercury	Mercury
Type	Mutable	Mutable
Element	Earth	Earth

The planet Mercury rules Virgo, which means this pair will share a similar outlook and be able to communicate freely. They will be giving in their relationship and, with both being practically minded people, will work well together as a team, sharing similar interests particularly as far as their lifestyles are concerned. With them both having an analytical, discriminating nature, they will accept criticisms and see them more as constructive comments rather than slights on their personalities.

Virgos tend to be mother-dominated so there is a tendency to act out their mother's personality – usually one of service and commitment. Ms Virgo always gives her mate more than is required in the relationship and his feminine side means he'll be appreciative and supportive of the role she plays in his life.

Their shared drive for perfection will make them a dynamic duo and, hopefully, they will both be finicky in the same areas. Because they are so alike, they will share the same negative traits, but with both striving for perfection, they will be aware of their shortcomings and reduce any friction that might arise.

In the bedroom: Virgoans are not spontaneous by nature but, if they can lighten up a bit, it will add a certain spark to their romantic union. They will both be committed in the bedroom and will be very keen to please each other. They take their lovemaking as seriously as any other aspect of their lives.

♍ ♈ Ms Virgo + Mr Libra ♎

Sign	Virgo	Libra
Symbol	Virgin	Scales
Ruler	Mercury	Venus
Type	Mutable	Cardinal
Element	Earth	Air

In their own way, Ms Virgo and Mr Libra have a desire for perfection. The virgin thrives in an environment where there is order and harmony. She likes her life to be neat and tidy and will make improvements if she feels they are necessary. Mr Libra also relishes an orderly domain and both will work together to create balance. But where these two differ is that Ms Virgo is much more of a hands-on worker whereas Mr Libra is more likely to want to give orders rather than pitching in and getting his hands dirty.

He is much more of a charming, sweet-talker who never likes to get to the point, preferring instead to keep everyone happy, but Ms Virgo – who always gives 100 per cent in her relationships – will have no qualms about speaking the truth, so she may be too blunt and critical for this passive fence-sitter. Mr Libra will never want to rock the boat and is likely to suffer in silence if something is bothering him.

Because commitment is a top priority for these two, if they do end up in a long-term union, it will take a lot for either one to end the relationship if things aren't working out.

In the bedroom: Virgoans are fairly practical even when it comes to sex but the right encouragement and nurturing from her Venusian man might be just enough to awaken a strong sensual side to her nature. She may even throw caution to the wind and surprise her man with her sexual spontaneity.

♍ Ms Virgo + Mr Scorpio ♏

Sign	Virgo	Scorpio
Symbol	Virgin	Scorpion
Ruler	Mercury	Pluto
Type	Mutable	Fixed
Element	Earth	Water

Both Ms Virgo and Mr Scorpio have sharp tongues and will not hold back on finding fault or criticising each other. This attitude can have a negative effect on their relationship. He seems to undermine her self-confidence and, in turn, he is too insecure to be able to handle her nit-picking and criticisms. These two are too uptight for each other and the fixed energy of Mr Scorpio will rarely give into the demands of Ms Virgo.

There's a judgmental quality to this union that tends to put pressure on the relationship from time to time. Although they are both fiercely loyal and committed individuals, Ms Virgo can feel that the over-protective, possessive and controlling attitude of Mr Scorpio is too demeaning.

She, however, is an open book and will always be upfront in her dealings with people. He is sly and secretive and, although he might claim he is not dishonest, that is open to interpretation. As far as Ms Virgo is concerned, holding back information is a form of dishonesty.

In the bedroom: Their sexual connection will rarely get off the ground: Mr Scorpio's persistent approach will be rebuffed and Ms Virgo will find him too intense. Love for this pair is no express train. They prefer a slower road to romance.

♍ Ms Virgo + Mr Sagittarius ♐

Sign	Virgo	Sagittarius
Symbol	Virgin	Archer
Ruler	Mercury	Jupiter
Type	Mutable	Mutable
Element	Earth	Fire

These two have a mutual interest in the outdoors. They love adventure and can engage in a lively exchange of ideas, yet have different natures. Truth and honesty are paramount to their relationship. Ms Virgo will be attracted to her honest and, at times, too blunt Sagittarian man because she also calls a spade a spade.

In this relationship, Ms Virgo will learn a lot about tolerance and patience and how to develop a sense of humour. Mr Sagittarius does everything in a big way because his ruling planet, Jupiter, is the planet of expansion, enthusiasm and abundance. Ms Virgo, on the other hand, is more cautious and conservative, preferring to analyse a situation before throwing herself in at the deep end like her archer mate.

Being a fire sign, Mr Sagittarius is idealistic in life and love and, since he is the eternal optimist, his energy and drive for new frontiers will be a little bit overwhelming for the discriminating Ms Virgo. Mr Sagittarius will find the virgin's nagging nature a drain on his free-spirited outlook. But she's only complaining because she likes to keep things orderly, especially at home, and can become annoyed with her Sagittarian man's messy and scattered energies.

In the bedroom: Ms Virgo is a loyal and committed lover, unlike her philandering Sagittarian mate who can be quite promiscuous. These two can learn from each other and have a lustful connection, but a long-term romantic relationship is unlikely to be on the cards.

♍ Ms Virgo + Mr Capricorn ♑

Sign	Virgo	Capricorn
Symbol	Virgin	Goat
Ruler	Mercury	Saturn
Type	Mutable	Cardinal
Element	Earth	Earth

These two earth signs have a mutual respect for each other; they share the same virtues, which seem to be an important ingredient for stability and longevity. Ms Virgo and Mr Capricorn have a practical and pragmatic approach to life – a no-fuss, get-on-with-it attitude. Their hardworking energies lead to success in business and combine to build a happy relationship together. Ms Virgo will appreciate Mr Capricorn's commitment, his stable persona and his logical mind.

Trust is a strong link between this pair. It brings Ms Virgo and Mr Capricorn closer together and allows them to 'open up' and share their expectations and intimacies. Ms Virgo will take comfort in her loyal, Capricornian mate, who not only can provide a consistent and stable environment, but be her devoted protector as well.

This couple's driving force is that they share the same vision for the future: they are builders and yet can encourage one another to learn to relax a little and take time out to smell the roses.

In the bedroom: The sexual attraction between Mr Capricorn and Ms Virgo will grow from strength to strength as they learn to respect and appreciate each other's values. Both can harbour feelings of sexual inadequacy, but this is a relationship based on mutual trust, so it won't be long before both are enjoying a romp in the hay.

♍ Ms Virgo + Mr Aquarius ♒

Sign	Virgo	Aquarius
Symbol	Virgin	Water bearer
Ruler	Mercury	Uranus
Type	Mutable	Fixed
Element	Earth	Air

The initial attraction in this relationship is a meeting of the minds. Ms Virgo will find Mr Aquarius exciting, independent and informative. He will find not only a stimulating muse but someone who shares his vision to create a better world. The relationship between these two will be more in the mind than on a physical level, and they will spend many hours conversing. She will discuss her need to be of service in a personal sense while Mr Aquarius will be more visionary, looking at how he can improve the universe.

But Ms Virgo is too reserved and insular for the Aquarian male, who is known for his unusual and off-beat ideas and interests and his collections of friends from all walks of life. She will be much more discerning in her choice of friends and won't understand his need to be in the company of many, especially since she is such a discriminating, committed and devoted lover.

Ms Virgo is an extremely loyal partner and Mr Aquarius can often take advantage of this self-sacrificing woman. He is likely to neglect her while he is out searching for rainbows and she will be annoyed if he doesn't include her in some of his outlandish pursuits.

Ms Virgo has the physical drive and the mental dexterity to face any challenge that the water bearer throws at her and she will be only too willing to show him that he needs a woman like her, who can keep him on the straight and narrow and organise him when his life – with its many commitments – becomes too challenging. Her success only adds to her confidence and self-esteem and this can only have productive consequences. Mr Aquarius just needs to show this virgin some patience and he will be in for a surprise or two when he least expects it.

In the bedroom: Sexually, there may be a few surprises in store for Ms Virgo as far as Mr Aquarius's tendency to throw an element of shock into the mix. She'll be intrigued by her mysterious Uranian man and passion will not be lacking between the practical earth girl and her wacky lover.

♍ Ms Virgo + Mr Pisces ♓

Sign	Virgo	Pisces
Symbol	Virgin	Fish
Ruler	Mercury	Neptune
Type	Mutable	Mutable
Element	Earth	Water

This union typifies the ideal give-and-take relationship because each will try to make adjustments to accommodate the other. Mr Pisces will be delighted to find a mate who listens to him and Ms Virgo will find the lure of the fish extremely seductive. On some levels they have a mutual understanding and both are extremely compassionate beings, but Ms Virgo will find she'll need to be the director of the relationship, as her watery man has a way of occasionally swimming up the wrong stream and she'll often have to throw him a lifeline.

He'll be frivolous with his money and she will be overly cautious and protective of hers. Sensitive Mr Pisces won't be able to handle Ms Virgo's constant nagging, especially since the sensitive fish will feel he must have let her down in some way. He is a dreamy, romantic visionary and is often spaced out after too many wines (maybe just to escape her constant criticisms), while she is a practical, level-headed, commonsense woman who won't tolerate such wayward behaviour.

Ms Virgo will also become extremely worried if she feels her Piscean lover is hiding secrets, especially since she is such an up-front girl. If these two can communicate their concerns and worries to each other – and find resolutions – they just might become a caring and compassionate couple.

In the bedroom: Neither is selfish, especially when it comes to sex, which they will consider an extension of their love for each other. The delicate and sensual touch of the fish will be a big turn on for the earthy virgin.

Celebrity Ms Virgo: Agatha Christie

Crime writer, born 4 am, 15 September 1890 in Torquay, England

```
Personal planets: Sun in Virgo
                  Moon in Libra
                  Mercury in Libra
                  Venus in Scorpio
                  Mars in Libra
```

I married an archaeologist because the older I grow, the more he appreciates me.

– Agatha Christie

Agatha Christie was a passionate woman whose mind was actively engaged in all forms of communication. Her Virgo Sun sign gave her an incredible, analytical mind, which resulted in her becoming a prolific writer of dozens of crime novels. In her chart we can see the strength of air, which resulted in her need to communicate with a variety of people on different levels, making her a diverse and stimulating companion. Christie sought mental stimulation from her relationships and that was the bond that cemented her marriages. True to Virgoan form, Christie served as nurse during World War I before she became a famous author. Her chart shows a need to have balance and harmony; her Moon and Mercury were in the sign of Libra, which gave her the ability to always see two sides to any situation.

Her first marriage to Colonel Archibald Christie fell apart when he became involved with a younger woman. The writer's Venus in the sign of Scorpio made it difficult for her to relinquish control and, to have the ultimate say in their marriage, she staged her own disappearance, which only added fuel to an already fiery relationship.

Her second marriage to Sir Max Mallowan, an eminent archaeologist, was harmonious because both were Earth signs – his was Taurus – giving them an interest in the same things. Both enjoyed digging in the dirt so to speak! In fact, Christie met her second husband at an archaeological site in Ur and later assisted him at his digs by cleaning and photographing artefacts.

Mallowan was 14 years her junior, typifying the Virgoan woman's attraction to youthful energy. Her Mars in the sign of Sagittarius and his Venus in sign of Aries would have sparked an immediate attraction between them and given them a sense of comfort and understanding of each other. This is a very favourable aspect for a compatible marriage. Both would have enjoyed freedom and welcomed challenges in their lives.

Christie's Mars in the freedom-loving sign of Sagittarius also gave her the impetus to travel and kept her mind open to new ideas and concepts for her writing and her relationships.

Mr Virgo - an overview

Like his female counterpart, Mr Virgo is analytical and discerning in his relationships. He will hold back and wait until he feels the timing is right to make his moves, as he is insecure and afraid of rejection. Mr Virgo is interested in women who can live up to his expectations, as he is a person who strives for perfection in himself and in others. Unfortunately, this can see some potentially good relationships never get off the ground because of his quick-to-judge attitude.

If you give Mr Virgo encouragement, you will see a softer, more gentle side shine through his rather aloof, somewhat cool exterior. Mr Virgo is not a romantic and is rarely charming, however, when the chips are down, he will be by your side providing comfort and support in every possible way.

Good communication is a necessity for Mr Virgo and he will be attracted to a partner who can keep pace with his need for mental stimulation. He is often attracted to a partner who is more outgoing and vivacious than him, but this can backfire because he can be too critical and judgemental of those who displays these characteristics.

As an earth sign, the Virgoan man is very practical. He can be a wonderful home maker, as he is not averse to plunging headlong into domestic chores or whipping up some tasty treats for his beloved. This is a man committed to keeping fit and healthy, which also spills over into physical intimacy with his partner. His consideration and skill, both in and out of the bedroom, is the glue that helps keep the relationship alive.

Famous Virgoan men

* Lyndon B Johnson
  (former US president)
* Hugh Grant (actor)
* Arnold Palmer (golfer)
* D H Lawrence (writer)
* Shane Warne (cricketer)
* Roald Dahl (writer)

Combinations

♍ Mr Virgo + Ms Aries ♈

Sign	Virgo	Aries
Symbol	Virgin	Ram
Ruler	Mercury	Mars
Type	Mutable	Cardinal
Element	Earth	Fire

The personal habits and instinctive emotional responses that define these two signs make their union fraught with ups and downs. The sensitive, nervous nature of the Virgoan male will often be tried and tested by the blunt and brash Arian female.

Although both Mr Virgo and Ms Aries strive for the unadulterated truth in all situations, there are some basic differences in their makeup that can make them uncomfortable with each other. Ms Aries tends to act on a whim, which can rattle poor Mr Virgo, who likes to weigh up the pros and cons of a situation rather than diving straight in. Mr Virgo will discover he plays servant to the demanding and headstrong Ms Aries, who can find the perfectionism and over-critical nature of her mate hard to take. Both of these signs will need to make a lot of adjustments to make their relationship work.

On the other hand, because both Mr Virgo and Ms Aries have a predisposition to physical activities – the Virgoan more in his dietary needs and the Aries in her sporting prowess – they can find common ground to express their interests in outdoor pursuits and health.

In the bedroom: The self-controlled nature of Mr Virgo will initially attract Ms Aries but again this earth sign will be too grounded and practical to hold a long-term sexual attraction for the fiery, quick-fix Aries woman.

♍ Mr Virgo + Ms Taurus ♉

Sign	Virgo	Taurus
Symbol	Virgin	Bull
Ruler	Mercury	Venus
Type	Mutable	Fixed
Element	Earth	Earth

Mr Virgo and Ms Taurus can support one another on many levels. The Virgoan shares similar interests and hobbies with her Taurean mate – both earth signs like practical pursuits. Ms Taurus will appreciate Mr Virgo's attention to detail and the extra effort and energy he puts into the relationship. He is skilled at catering to her every whim and, in turn, will value the loyalty and security his Taurean mate provides.

These two are both particularly faithful when it comes to love, and it will take a long time for them to give up on each other. However, their strong desire to please people does not always lead to an equally strong understanding of what each other needs on an emotional front.

Ms Taurus will provide an excellent home environment for her mate; she'll cook the gourmet meal while he'll do the washing up. Although this pair will do well in most aspects of their lives together, their main challenge will be communicating, because people born under these signs tend to lose themselves in their own world by focusing on the practicalities of life.

Since both Taurus and Virgo are earth signs, they can be practical and self-sufficient, and neither will need to exploit one another's generosity and good nature. On the downside, Virgoans can be quite critical, and their constant nagging might frustrate Taureans, who will soon tire of the analysis of their actions. Likewise the methodical and somewhat slow energy of Ms Taurus will bother the energetic and alert Mr Virgo. Ultimately these two can have a lasting union if they don't get too bogged down in the functionality of life.

In the bedroom: Silent sex is probably the best way to describe these two in bed. Taureans prefer to get down to the business of making love rather than talking about it and Mr Virgo is simply not a man who's into talking dirty. Mr Virgo will be most concerned about pleasing his lover and Ms Taurus will be the eager recipient of such TLC!

♍ Mr Virgo + Ms Gemini ♊

Sign	Virgo	Gemini
Symbol	Virgin	Twins
Ruler	Mercury	Mercury
Type	Mutable	Mutable
Element	Earth	Air

Gemini and Virgo are ruled by the planet Mercury; hence they both feel the need to communicate despite coming from different angles. Although they need to feel mentally stimulated, Mr Virgo is more practical and down to earth than Ms Gemini, who tends to talk fast and doesn't really think before she opens her mouth.

She is too impractical and messy for the discriminating and analysing Virgo, who likes routine and order. He is a germ freak and, with her being no domestic goddess, there won't be time for the dust settle on this relationship. Domestically they are poles apart and, in the long run, will start to irritate one another.

Any initial attraction will not be long lasting because these two have very different needs in a relationship. Ms Gemini is a restless individual, full of enthusiasm and who likes to roam freely, which annoys the serious, heavy-going Mr Virgo. His constant disapproval and criticism leaves Ms Gemini feeling unhappy, meaning she won't stick around for long.

Earth and air don't seem to mix well. Mr Virgo likes to spend his time plodding away at various projects until they're completed systematically, while Ms Gemini finds it hard to concentrate on one thing for any sustained period of time with the result that boredom usually prompts her on to move on to the next pursuit.

In the bedroom: Sexually speaking, Mr Virgo is unlikely to set the bed of Ms Gemini on fire. He is not prone to sexual abandonment but given that Ms Gemini is light and airy in her approach to sex, it might just work.

♍ Mr Virgo + Ms Cancer ♋

Sign	Virgo	Cancer
Symbol	Virgin	Crab
Ruler	Mercury	Moon
Type	Mutable	Cardinal
Element	Earth	Water

The pairing of the virgin and the crab sounds ghastly but it will work if they can tolerate each other's individuality. Ms Cancer and Mr Virgo have the same understanding of commitment and both need loyalty and trust in their union. She is by far the more romantic of the two and her Virgoan mate will need to pull some passionate tricks out of his neat-and-tidy bag to turn on this emotional creature.

Both are nurturing in their own unique way – she in her desire to give of herself emotionally and physically, and he in his matter-of-fact, practical manner. Given the crab's and the virgin's insecurities, they will need to address this issue in their partnership. They have the ability to bring out each other's weaknesses to be examined and purged.

His strong sense of commitment and her touchy, feely ways will give them both a reprieve from their otherwise moody dispositions, which will go a long way to settling the relationship. They have an uncanny way of knowing what the other needs from the union and so will work towards creating balance. If Mr Virgo can keep his nit-picking thoughts to himself and Ms Cancer can curb her need for emotional excesses, this could wind up being an exceedingly harmonious pairing.

In the bedroom: The Cancerian woman will be like soothing and nourishing water for the Virgoan earth man. Together they will become one as they blend beautifully together in a sexual union. But beware of the Moon's powerful influence over this crab, which can turn her into a moody mistress on occasions.

♍ Mr Virgo + Ms Leo ♌

Sign	Virgo	Leo
Symbol	Virgin	Lion
Ruler	Mercury	Sun
Type	Mutable	Fixed
Element	Earth	Fire

Mr Virgo and Ms Leo have equally strong needs; however, they are very different personalities. Mr Virgo is more down-to-earth and practical than his lioness, and will be on the lookout for a partner who needs him. The colourful and vibrant Ms Leo wants to be in the limelight with little thought about the consequences, whereas Mr Virgo has a tendency to dampen her flamboyant spirit with his over-analysis and scrutiny of her actions. This constant nit-picking falls on deaf ears because Ms Leo is such a 'know-it-all'. She is a fixed sign, so even the constructive suggestions Mr Virgo throws her way will never be acknowledged.

Ms Leo's spontaneity and flamboyancy will grate on the more industrious Virgo guy. But his methodical and structured approach to life could really suit the lioness, who sometimes throws herself into the deep end before really weighing up the consequences. On the other hand, the eternal worrier Mr Virgo could well do with a dose of Ms Leo's frivolity and bravado to lighten his load. More often than not, the earth signs, which include Virgo, seem to lack the *joie de vivre* displayed by the more spirited fire signs. Ultimately, the lioness will rarely be able to temper her passion and enthusiasm, despite Mr Virgo's inclination to drag her down.

In the bedroom: The sexual rapport between Ms Leo and Mr Virgo will need plenty of nourishment to flourish because they can't relax in each other's arms, fundamentally because they feel misunderstood. Mr Virgo might find he is too analytical for the lioness, wounding her pride with his critical comments and thus dashing any hope he harbours of passionate lovemaking.

♍ Mr Virgo + Ms Virgo ♍

Sign	Virgo	Virgo
Symbol	Virgin	Virgin
Ruler	Mercury	Mercury
Type	Mutable	Mutable
Element	Earth	Earth

The planet Mercury rules Virgo so this pair will share similar outlooks and communicate freely. They will be giving in their relationship and, with both being practically minded people, they will share similar interests, particularly as far as their lifestyles are concerned. This pair shares an analytical, discriminating nature so they will understand one another's criticisms and consider them as constructive comments.

Virgos tend to be mother-dominated so there is a tendency to act out their mother's personality, which is one of service and commitment. Ms Virgo always gives her mate more than is required in the relationship and he, too, has a strong feminine side, so will be appreciative and supportive of the role she plays in his life.

They have a drive for perfection which can be the makings of a dynamic duo. Hopefully they will be finicky in the same areas! When people are so similar, they often don't like the negative traits that are mirrored in each other.

In the bedroom: Virgoan are not spontaneous by nature but if they can lighten up a bit it will add a certain spark to their romantic union. Both will be committed in the bedroom and will be very keen to please each other. They take their lovemaking as seriously as any other aspect of their lives.

♍ Mr Virgo + Ms Libra ♎

Sign	Virgo	Libra
Symbol	Virgin	Scales
Ruler	Mercury	Venus
Type	Mutable	Cardinal
Element	Earth	Air

Who could not be attracted to this physically appealing woman with a gentle and balanced mind? The Virgoan man will often wish that he too could have a dose of her charm and an ability to relate to people on all levels, especially since he has a flaw in this area. Because Ms Libra seems to have an ability to scrutinise, yet diplomatically convey her thoughts – and sometimes dissatisfactions – to Mr Virgo, he finds her most appealing.

Both are discriminating in their own ways: Mr Virgo will be touched and encouraged by this female, and her need for harmony and balance will rub off in return. He will be attracted to the enormous amount of energy she puts into the relationship, especially as she is always willing to make the adjustments required. He will find this union a breath of fresh air because he is usually the one who puts the extra time and effort into his partnerships.

The big difference between these two is how they make decisions: Mr Virgo is decisive and does not have time for procrastination and, when he makes up his mind, it is instant. It may drive him to distraction that Ms Libra seems to waste a lot of time on the decision-making process.

Each has their own insecurities: Mr Virgo can be too hard on himself because he has high self-expectations, and Ms Libra has high expectations of her relationships, so they might need to come to some compromise. Both care about their physical appearance; Mr Virgo like to work out in the gym and Ms Libra is a natural beauty, so they make a particularly attractive pair.

In the bedroom: This pair bring a special quality into the bedroom as both want to be seen to be giving it their best shot in whatever task they undertake, yet a strong connection occurs when these two unite. Mr Virgo must remember not to be too loose-tongued, because the slightest criticism could upset the carefully balanced scales of Ms Libra – and they won't tip in his favour!

♍ Mr Virgo + Ms Scorpio ♏

Sign	Virgo	Scorpio
Symbol	Virgin	Scorpion
Ruler	Mercury	Pluto
Type	Mutable	Fixed
Element	Earth	Water

Mr Virgo is not compatible with the suspicious Ms Scorpio, whom he finds too closed and secretive. He is an open book and will always communicate his feelings, often at times too bluntly and honestly, but Ms Scorpio is not a trusting soul and will keep her man in the dark. For some males this can be a turn on, as Ms Scorpio has an air of mystique and an alluring quality that is often interpreted as a strong sexual energy.

Mr Virgo is not a man who thrives on challenges and he needs his sense of self-confidence boosted rather than being undermined. Both he and Ms Scorpio have issues regarding tolerance: they don't like weakness, and tend to be judgemental of each other. This couple has a strong sense of commitment and will be supportive of each other if a connection is made, but Mr Virgo is too 'straight' to buy into the complexities of the watery Scorpio who needs constant reassurance about her position in the relationship.

He will find Ms Scorpio's tendency to be jealous frustrating because he considers himself to be a trusting and loyal mate, and doesn't take to her undermining approach easily. If these two can get past first base, Ms Scorpio can provide enough water to make Mr Virgo's earthy qualities flourish.

In the bedroom: Sexually, there won't be an easy connection between these two because neither gives themselves completely in this union. Their key to sexual compatibility is for both to let go of their fears and throw themselves into it when the lights go out.

♍ Mr Virgo + Ms Sagittarius ♐

Sign	Virgo	Sagittarius
Symbol	Virgin	Archer
Ruler	Mercury	Jupiter
Type	Mutable	Mutable
Element	Earth	Fire

To begin with, this union can seem quite compatible because the Virgoan man and Sagittarian woman share mutual interests – especially a desire for sport and outdoor pursuits. However, Mr Virgo is a perfectionist, so it won't be good enough for him to throw the tent in the backseat and head off to unknown adventures. He would rather spend time on making sure the pegs and other attachments are neatly packed into their box. That seems to sum up the fundamental difference between these two. Mr Virgo is a man who uses his discriminatory powers to the letter and near enough is not good enough for him. Ms Sagittarius, however, has already moved on to the next adventure, not bothering to count the number of pegs in the box.

She is an idealist and he a realist who defines his world in neat compartments. Conversely, Ms Sagittarius will always have a Utopian view of her universe and will be disappointed by this man's analytical and, at times, critical nature. For her the journey is often more exciting than arriving at her destination and the more opportunities she has to fill her mind with the wonders of the world, the happier she will be. Mr Virgo will find this energy too frenetic and unsettling, despite the fact that he is an active participant in life. Everything he does needs to be checked out beforehand so rarely will they be at the same place at the same time.

In the bedroom: Ms Sagittarius may be too spontaneous and boisterous for this methodical and practical earthy man. Sadly, there might not be much room for any 'hanky panky'.

♍ Mr Virgo + Ms Capricorn ♑

Sign	Virgo	Capricorn
Symbol	Virgin	Goat
Ruler	Mercury	Saturn
Type	Mutable	Cardinal
Element	Earth	Earth

The Virgoan man will enjoy this woman because he sees in her a steady and practical mate who can participate and work systematically towards their mutual goals. Two earth signs might seem a little lacklustre because their focus is often work-orientated and each seems to bring out a strong work ethos in the other.

Capricornians and Virgoans are two signs in the zodiac that can be compared with a good wine. They mature and ripen well with age. Because they are committed to pleasing each other, the virgin and the goat will always have a lively sexual rapport. Although slow movers initially, once Mr Virgo has trapped his mountain goat, they both will ascend to higher ground in this union. Both are very grounded and have high expectations of themselves so neither will find this disconcerting.

The element of earth that runs through this pair's veins is about reality and practicality, so each will give 100 per cent commitment to this relationship. There will be no hidden agendas to contend with. What you see is what you get. These earthy guys will create a solid base where they can play house and service one another's needs. Both are slow to connect but it will be Ms Capricorn's cardinal energy that will initiate a connection and Mr Virgo will keep the ball rolling.

In the bedroom: Earth signs usually make very compatible sexual partners. Sex will solidify their already strong connection. Both are much better expressing themselves on a physical level.

♍ Mr Virgo + Ms Aquarius ♒

Sign	Virgo	Aquarius
Symbol	Virgin	Water bearer
Ruler	Mercury	Uranus
Type	Mutable	Fixed
Element	Earth	Air

These two signs have some mutual connection because both have sharp and intelligent minds and will be initially attracted to each other's mental agility and ideas. The main difference, however, is that Mr Virgo is far less tolerant and open minded than this Aquarian lady, who lives her life with no holds barred and with a mind open to the quirky and different. Like his female counterpart, Mr Virgo can be kind to his partner when he feels she deserves some tender loving care, but with this airy girl he feels a little out of his depth and will struggle to find a secure position in this union.

Mr Virgo is too practical and lacks the vision this Uranian girl needs. She is often seeking out various humanitarian pursuits that will take her far and wide, whereas Mr Virgo is too focused on his immediate environment. He perhaps has a secret admiration for this independent and highly intelligent woman: when it comes to communications, these two signs do click. But Mr Virgo lacks the tolerance to handle the Aquarian woman's detached and impersonal manner. In turn, she doesn't take kindly to any restraint and will not be curtailed by this man's constant nagging.

This pair is more suited to friendship than to a romantic union. Ms Aquarius collects friends from all walks of life and will always want to retain a friendship – even with past lovers. Earth and air signs don't blend well: the solid and grounded Virgoan man needs a partner he can fuse with and remain close to, but the airy Aquarian girl walks around with her head in the clouds and won't be hemmed in under any circumstance. But if Ms Aquarius can take the time to look a little deeper at this man, she will find a highly responsive mate: one that can keep up with her many antics.

In the bedroom: It's difficult for their bodies to connect as Mr Virgo analyses everything, and this spills into the bedroom. On the other hand, Ms Aquarius is a 'wham bam thank you m'am' kind of girl who won't stick around for a post mortem.

♍ Mr Virgo + Ms Pisces ♓

Sign	Virgo	Pisces
Symbol	Virgin	Fish
Ruler	Mercury	Neptune
Type	Mutable	Mutable
Element	Earth	Water

Water and earth are an ideal combination. Both Mr Virgo and Ms Pisces are feeling people with deep emotions and share a reputation for being compassionate and caring individuals. As polar opposites in astrological terms, they can bring about the best and worst in each other. Mr Virgo is attracted to Ms Pisces' responsiveness and she is turned on by his encouragement and support. He will be intrigued by her intuitive nature and secretly wish he could understand the deeper meaning of life and be more spiritual like her. However, his non-nonsense, pragmatic approach will never allow him to explore his mystical side.

Ms Pisces has strong escapist tendencies, which Mr Virgo can curtail. He will be able to ground her by keeping her on the straight and narrow and tempering her addictions. Mr Virgo has an appreciation for life's aesthetic pleasures, an interest that his Pisces partner will nourish because she too loves the arts and creative pursuits.

Although both have high expectations from their relationships, Mr Virgo has a better grasp of reality than his dreamy Piscean mate, who can be delusional and idealistic in love. They both have plenty of similarities on which to build a strong relationship.

In the bedroom: Sexually, there will be fireworks between Mr Virgo and Ms Pisces – mainly because they share a deep trust and understanding that allows them to be open and honest with their emotions. Since these two are at times unsure of themselves and self-critical, this union will provide a comforting blend of the elements as the watery woman nourishes her earthy man.

Celebrity Mr Virgo: Hugh Grant

Actor, born 9 September 1960 in London, England

```
Personal planets: Sun in Virgo
                  Moon in Taurus
                  Mercury in Virgo
                  Venus in Libra
                  Mars in Gemini
```

Women are frightening. If you get to 41 as a man, you're quite battle-scarred.

– Hugh Grant

Grant's chart has an abundance of earth planets that gives him a stubborn and grounded approach to his relationships and, as much as he enjoys having a partner, he will never compromise himself if it is not working the way it pleases him. His Virgoan quality makes him discriminating and sometimes judgmental, yet this is more reflective of his own inadequacies rather than his partners'. As with most Virgoans, he seems to have difficulty in relating, yet his need to be emotionally involved and his desire to participate in all facets of his relationships give him an understanding of what women are about.

His Venus in the sign of Libra makes him desire a love relationship that has all the ingredients of balance and harmony. There is an inclination for him to be in love with the idea of love and he is highly idealistic when it comes to the women in his life. His Moon in Taurus makes him needy of a mate with the same desire for financial and emotional security. She would also have to be intensely loyal because his Moon shows he needs a nurturing woman who can tend to his physical and emotional needs. Grant's six mutable modes of expression enable him to be particularly adaptable to his partner's needs, which might seem appealing; however, he will need to address his own personal fulfilment in the relationship instead of idolising his women. He has unrealistic expectations of his relationships and may need to look at his true motivations and desires.

Grant's relationship with actor Elizabeth Hurley, a Gemini, was dominated by the planet Mercury, which rules both their Sun signs. This attraction was based on a need to exchange ideas and siphon information and growth through learning. His Venus in Gemini would have attracted him to her unpredictable nature where he was kept on his toes, not allowing the relationship to get into a 'rut'.

The relationship Grant has with London socialite Jemima Khan is also based on an intellectual rapport and a strong friendship. Jemima is an Aquarian and has both the Sun and Moon in this freedom-loving sign. Her requirements are very simple: she needs to be with a man who allows her the freedom and space to explore the strong humanitarian side of her nature. She is a woman who seeks physical and emotional independence, yet thrives on a partnership where her mate also values the work she is involved with. This girl will always be committed and faithful in her relationship as she is very serious about love and will not enter into a union unless her man is committed, loyal and steadfast and has a strong moral code. This partnership is about growth and versatility. Both can bring their inspiring and encouraging qualities into this relationship.

LIBRA (24 September–23 October)

Ruled by the planet Venus
Air sign
Cardinal
Masculine energy

In general ...

Libra is ruled by Venus, the planet of love, and is associated with love and relationships. Librans are happiest when they are with someone. They crave a partnership; their balance will be upset when they are on their own. They want someone to share their lives with and are miserable alone. Out of all the astrological signs Librans need a mate the most.

Libran men and women are looking for peace, harmony and balance in their lives and their ideal mate is someone who can understand their desire for calmness and tranquillity and wants to share all of themselves in the union. However, it seems the harder Librans try to achieve this equilibrium and find the perfect mate, the more it seems to elude them in their lives. This is because, as an air sign, there is a degree of superficiality associated with them. Both sexes seem be drawn to a person's physical beauty, judging the 'book by its cover', rather than gaining a deeper understanding of what makes them tick, resulting in disappointment time and time again. Librans are attracted to beauty, style and refinement. They are extremely attractive themselves, and where they might lack physical beauty they make up for it with their charm and graciousness. Be warned, however, there does lurk a shadowy side to this persona. Librans' desire to keep everything perfect and 'nice' on the surface can frustrate them inwardly. Maintaining a constant pretence can take its toll, at which times their gloomy and depressive nature can emerge, which may come to quite a shock for their unsuspecting partner.

Librans, both men and women, are not so passionate in a physical sense. They are more into communication, which is what really turns them on. If they can find a mate they can talk to, this can be a real aphrodisiac. Librans are into romancing their partners and will be far more at home sipping a chardonnay under the stars and discussing their relationship than romping under the covers. That's not to say that sex won't happen, but all in good time, as their foreplay is to set the perfect romantic scene, with all the trimmings.

Because Librans' desire for harmony and social acceptance is so great, many will stay in difficult relationships and marriages, not wanting to upset the applecart. They tend to put up and shut up for the sake of peace and quiet, which can result in built-up resentment and internal anger.

Librans are noted procrastinators, which can prove frustrating for some of the more decisive signs, so don't offer them any choice, otherwise you could be in for a long wait. On the plus side, justice and diplomacy are strong Libran characteristics. They will always be a wonderful sounding board to help others get their relationships on track; however, rarely can they voice their own needs.

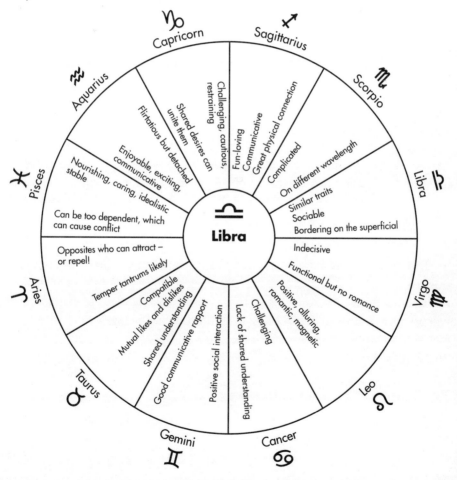

How a Libran personality might match up with other star signs

Ms Libra - an overview

The Libran woman is a breed of her own. She is attractive, charming and gracious, and is often referred to as the beauty of the zodiac. Ms Libra is a head-turner and will always have a string of admirers ready to catch her eye. This might sound appealing yet Ms Libra can have her share of disappointments. Highly idealistic and a true romantic, she has a tendency to be flattered easily and gets most upset when her knight in shining armour turns out to be a mere mortal with the usual flaws. Her tendency to keep things on the surface, rather than explore the depth of her union, can result in accusations of being cold and distant levelled at her. The more emotional water signs, in particular, appear to feel a lack of commitment from this woman.

Being an air sign, Ms Libra enjoys social interaction and requires a partner with whom she can communicate and discuss a wide variety of subjects. She is happiest when she is sharing her life with a mate. She loves to be joined at the hip, so to speak, and will usually prefer to be married rather than just living together. Her drive for finding her ideal partner is very strong yet she is also considerate of what her mate needs and requires. With fairness and justice high on her list of virtues, she will always consider her mate's opinion. Librans like to include their partners in their decision making, with the term 'we' rather than 'I' used more often in their vocabulary.

But don't let this pretty face fool you, because most Libran women also possess a sharp intellect, which can belie their appearance. Soft and fluffy she may seem, yet beneath the surface is an extremely capable woman who will be more than a match for any man. Beauty and brains – how much luckier can any woman get or, for that matter, any man that can capture this goddess's heart.

Famous Libran women

* Julie Andrews
  (singer/actor)
* Margot Fontaine
  (ballerina)
* Martina Navratilova
  (tennis player)
* Margaret Thatcher
  (British prime minister)
* Brigitte Bardot
  (actor/animal rights
  activist)
* Sarah Bernhardt (actor)

Combinations

♎ Ms Libra + Mr Aries ♈

Sign	Libra	Aries
Symbol	Scales	Ram
Ruler	Venus	Mars
Type	Cardinal	Cardinal
Element	Air	Fire

Opposites attract but, by the same token, the differences might become too great in a long-term relationship between these two. Ms Libra needs to have a relationship and will go to great lengths to have a union. Initially she will be attracted to the impulsive, innocent and charming Mr Aries but his overbearing nature and bossiness will eventually become a turn-off. She will put him up on a pedestal but will learn as time goes by that he won't fit the mould of the perfect, doting husband. His hot-tempered Arian nature will be too much for the Libran lass, who craves peace and harmony in her love relationships.

Idealistic and always looking at the world through rose-coloured glasses, Ms Libra will become frustrated with the somewhat unromantic Mr Aries, who'd rather be climbing mountains than sitting at a fine restaurant. He, in turn, will become irritated with Ms Libra's indecision and superficiality. While Ms Libra's natural good looks and refinement will charm him, his bossiness and demands will make her very unhappy because she needs peace and balance in her life – not an altogether ideal recipe for a perfect union.

And although Ms Libra might exemplify the perfect woman in charm and looks, underlying her perfect exterior is a very strong and demanding personality. When tested, she can become highly volatile, which is likely to prompt Mr Aries to end the relationship.

In the bedroom: Ms Libra should let her ram take the lead in the bedroom. He is headstrong and likes to lead the way. But being a woman of great charm and diplomacy, she will let her man take charge and sit back and enjoy herself.

♎ Ms Libra + Mr Taurus ♉

Sign	Libra	Taurus
Symbol	Scales	Bull
Ruler	Venus	Venus
Type	Cardinal	Fixed
Element	Air	Earth

This is a good match and can be a very workable arrangement because both are ruled by the planet Venus and share an appreciation of the finer things of life. Mr Taurus can secure the material benefits that allow Ms Libra to show off her style.

Ms Libra represents the goddess of love, and her beauty, style and charm captivate all the signs, especially the Taurean male, who has an eye for beautiful objects. Although they are both ruled by Venus, each has an individual approach to what they need in their relationships. The Taurean relates more to what makes him feel comfortable and secure in terms of physical belongings, while the Libran is more into finding comfort from her relationship rather than possessions. This can create an ideal union because Mr Taurus shows his love by providing the physical pleasures his Libran mate desires, and she in turn expresses her love and desire through words and actions.

Sharing the same ruling planet allows Ms Libra and Mr Taurus to feel comfortable in each other's space, as both have similar needs. Harmony, refinement and co-operation feature strongly in this union.

Both need a partner who can share their lives and be ready to please the other and give of themselves. The Taurean male will adore his Libran woman and is impressed by her grace and tact; in turn, his strong and supportive energy will be a turn-on for her.

In the bedroom: Ms Libra and Mr Taurus are both hopeless romantics who together can make mind-blowing love. Both are very physical and will be able to fulfil each other's wildest fantasies.

♎ Ms Libra + Mr Gemini ♊

Sign	Libra	Gemini
Symbol	Scales	Twins
Ruler	Venus	Mercury
Type	Cardinal	Mutable
Element	Air	Air

These charming critters pair up beautifully. Both air signs, the Gemini and Libran take a more superficial and light-hearted approach to their relationship, but that's not to say that they don't feel passion and intensity when connected. However, they don't bring too much heavy energy into their connection.

Both are good talkers and can spend endless hours discussing a range of topics. Socially these two are very adept at conversing with a wide cross-section of people and will admire, rather than feel jealous, of the other's ability to captivate a crowd. Mr Gemini will find Ms Libra's grace, charm and refinement alluring, and equally she will find his intellect and mental dexterity highly appealing. Concerned with how they are perceived, they will always want to put their best foot forward, rarely allowing each other to drop their guard. If they can strip the veneer of superficiality from their personas, they will share a vulnerability that is understood by the other.

Mr Gemini will always benefit from the wise and balanced viewpoint that Ms Libra has to offer him when he is so often split down the middle on decisions; in turn, he will help her jump off the fence in an instant and take a stand. Astrologically these two air signs form a harmonious combination and, if they can look seriously into one another's eyes and see each other's soul, then it will be a romance made in heaven.

In the bedroom: The quest for pleasure and not lustful fulfilment will fuel the fires of passion between these two air signs. Neither has raw, animal instincts in their makeup, so they will blend beautifully when they make slow, instinctive love.

♎ Ms Libra + Mr Cancer ♋

Sign	Libra	Cancer
Symbol	Scales	Crab
Ruler	Venus	Moon
Type	Cardinal	Cardinal
Element	Air	Water

Like most in the zodiac, Mr Cancer will fall for the beautiful, charming and graceful Ms Libra. Her Venusian qualities will be so enchanting to the sensitive crab that he will find her irresistible. She too will be captivated by the crab's sensitivity, compassion and warmth. He is likely to make her feel secure and safe like no other lover has before.

Because both can be moody at times, they will understand each other's changeable natures. Mr Crab likes security and guarantees and, although his ultimate relationship pinnacle is marriage, he is more likely to tread cautiously before making this final commitment. It's not that he doesn't love the idea of the security and comfort it can offer; he's more concerned with being able to fulfil his partner's needs on an emotional and financial level.

Ms Libra can interpret this hesitation as rejection and can resort to jealous game playing to try to cajole her crab down the aisle. He may become moody and irritated by such behaviour but, once Ms Libra senses she's losing her grip on Mr Crab, she can turn on the charm as quick as a flash to woo her lover back. However, the crab has difficulty in expressing his true emotions, which can create a division between these two.

In the bedroom: In the bedroom is where Mr Cancer lets down his guard and his true feelings and emotions shine through. Ms Libra will bring an abundance of TLC into the union, but often the differences between these two will only be temporarily allayed through sex.

♎ Ms Libra + Mr Leo ♌

Sign	Libra	Leo
Symbol	Scales	Lion
Ruler	Venus	Sun
Type	Cardinal	Fixed
Element	Air	Fire

This stylish, well-balanced woman will take Mr Leo's eye, and his fire energy – combining ambition, generosity and a zest for life – will likewise attract her. These two signs have a keen eye for beauty and glamour and, with both having this quality in abundance, they will hold one another in high esteem.

Mr Leo's need for admiration and Ms Libra's desire to be noticed will put them on common ground. The zodiac sign of Leo is ruled by the Sun, which sits harmoniously with Ms Libra's ruling planet Venus.

His creativity and artistic flare and her Venusian, romantic and idealistic nature will ignite the passion between them. Ms Libra has a penchant for putting her men up on pedestals and Mr Leo will love nothing better than being held up to be admired and adored.

These star-crossed lovers have a mutual understanding of what is needed to create a passionate interlude. The lion will be starry-eyed over his Libran mate because she can exude an ethereal beauty. Both Mr Leo and Ms Libra value beauty and need to feel that their world is surrounded by colour and love.

In the bedroom: Mr Leo and Ms Libra have great chemistry together and their lovemaking is more about quality than quantity. The lion will be lustier in the bedroom than his image-conscious partner, who is more focused on ensuring that her partner finds her alluring.

♎ Ms Libra + Mr Virgo ♍

Sign	Libra	Virgo
Symbol	Scales	Virgin
Ruler	Venus	Mercury
Type	Cardinal	Mutable
Element	Air	Earth

Who could not be attracted to this physically appealing woman with a gentle and balanced mind? The Virgoan man will often wish that he too could have a dose of her charm and an ability to relate to people on all levels, especially since he has a flaw in this area. Because Ms Libra seems to have an ability to scrutinise, yet diplomatically convey her thoughts – and sometimes dissatisfactions – to Mr Virgo, he finds her most appealing.

Both are discriminating in their own ways: Mr Virgo will be touched and encouraged by this female, and her need for harmony and balance will rub off in return. He will be attracted to the enormous amount of energy she puts into the relationship, especially as she is always willing to make the adjustments required. He will find this union a breath of fresh air because he is usually the one who puts the extra time and effort into his partnerships.

The big difference between these two is how they make decisions: Mr Virgo is decisive and does not have time for procrastination and, when he makes up his mind, it is instant. It may drive him to distraction that Ms Libra seems to waste a lot of time on the decision-making process.

Each has their own insecurities: Mr Virgo can be too hard on himself because he has high self-expectations, and Ms Libra has high expectations of her relationships, so they might need to come to some compromise. Both care about their physical appearance; Mr Virgo like to work out in the gym and Ms Libra is a natural beauty, so they make a particularly attractive pair.

In the bedroom: This pair bring a special quality into the bedroom as both want to be seen to be giving it their best shot in whatever task they undertake, yet a strong connection occurs when these two unite. Mr Virgo must remember not to be too loose-tongued because the slightest criticism could upset the carefully balanced scales of Ms Libra – and they won't tip in his favour!

♎ Ms Libra + Mr Libra ♎

Sign	Libra	Libra
Symbol	Scales	Scales
Ruler	Venus	Venus
Type	Cardinal	Cardinal
Element	Air	Air

The potential problem with this union is working out who will make the decisions. At least they will be able to laugh and not become too frustrated with their constant weighing up of this and that. This pair is into beauty, harmony, justice, peace – the list goes on. It truly can be a match that has the makings of perfection. Ms Libra and Mr Libra are into physical beauty and so will be tolerant of the time the other spends on preening themselves, with a touch of narcissism thrown into the equation.

Ms and Mr Libra's similar desire to surround themselves with aesthetic beauty and physical comforts will give them a sense of contentment in their relationship. Their mutual need for harmony and balance will see them in constant communication as to how to improve and perfect what they already have. Because they value fairness and equality and are both so passionate about contributing equally, this combination will be hard to fault. The Libran couple will feel very comfortable with each other. Both can be a little detached and cool, hence they will not require an abundance of emotional intimacy. Yet they will enjoy each other's need to be in a committed relationship.

They seem to gain an air of confidence when doing things together and can lend each other plenty of support and encouragement. Neither party likes to be alone, so these two can acknowledge their insecurities without feeling intimidated. They will be drawn to each other like bees to honey and share a relationship the envy of many. When you think of the ideal Libran couple, you can go no further than US actor Michael Douglas and his stunning Welsh actor wife Catherine Zeta Jones.

In the bedroom: 'Do you want the lights on or off tonight, darling?' says Ms Libra to her man. 'You decide, dear.' 'No, you. I can't make up my mind.' Some hours later, the loving might begin and then it will be a very steamy affair.

♎ Ms Libra + Mr Scorpio ♏

Sign	Libra	Scorpio
Symbol	Scales	Scorpion
Ruler	Venus	Pluto
Type	Cardinal	Fixed
Element	Air	Water

This combination will have all the typical conflicts that occur in a union between an air girl and her water man. She wants things to be light and uncomplicated and, above all, to have a strong line of communication with her partner. However, this deeply intense, complicated and secretive man will be too moody for Ms Libra. Her physical beauty and alluring personality will dazzle him, but will also intensify his insecurities and bring out his jealous streak.

Ms Libra thrives on verbal exchanges and needs an open, trusting and honest man. Mr Scorpio seems to have a problem opening up to her. He feels he is relinquishing control, so he will leave Ms Libra in the dark, which she will see as being totally unfair.

The passionate Mr Scorpio's water is deep and he needs constant reassurance, while his airy lady love seems too detached and emotionally cool for him. This couple come from different emotional planes and will not fit well together. She will always want to keep the peace and pretend all is well, but Mr Scorpio's penetrating mind will deduce this is not the case, and so more complications will set in.

In the bedroom: This man is known for his sexuality and has the capacity to turn on most women. Ms Libra is no exception. However, sex for Mr Scorpio needs to combine the physical act with emotional intimacy, which is a problem for his Libran. She will be too detached for this intense and deep man, who will always be able to satisfy her, yet will have the feeling that the scales are tipped more in her favour.

♎ Ms Libra + Mr Sagittarius ♐

Sign	Libra	Sagittarius
Symbol	Scales	Archer
Ruler	Venus	Jupiter
Type	Cardinal	Mutable
Element	Air	Fire

The magic of air and fire will always send sparks flying and this pair will have an immense attraction for one another. Mr Sagittarius and Ms Libra seem to have an easy time in life and will be attracted to each other's uncomplicated style. She is drawn to his optimistic and fun-loving nature and he is lured by her physical beauty. But, more importantly, and more appealing, for this archer, is his Libran love's ability to communicate and freely express herself. Ms Libra is interested in mental exploration and has a highly developed mind. Like her archer mate, she values learning and education, leading this pair to spend plenty of time in pursuit of excitement and social interaction.

Ms Libra and her archer share the same values and will be keen to encourage each other's talents and interests. Her refined manner and social appeal may at first be a little overwhelming for this basic, laid-back guy, who would rather hang out in his sports gear than don a tuxedo. Yet they seem to have a good flow of communication and a willingness to please each other so there will be compromises along the way. She might get her man to wear a tie on the odd occasion and he might convince her that she looks just as stunning in her tracksuit as in her 'glammed-up' gear.

Ms Libra will be happy to give this man room to move, which will be much appreciated by Mr Sagittarius, whose 'don't fence me in' attitude is typical of this star sign.

In the bedroom: Physical intimacy for Ms Libra and her archer is one of sheer joy. These two have plenty of fun together, combining humour and passion when the lights go out.

♎ Ms Libra + Mr Capricorn ♑

Sign	Libra	Capricorn
Symbol	Scales	Goat
Ruler	Venus	Saturn
Type	Cardinal	Cardinal
Element	Air	Earth

The Libran energy is particularly attractive to Mr Capricorn, who will admire the social skills and controlled personality of this woman. He is preoccupied with status and is often attracted to a partner who can elevate him socially. And Ms Libra is adaptable to most social situations and relates well to people, qualities the mountain goat aspires to. She will admire his business acumen, and his focus on achieving and knowing his own mind so well.

These signs can learn much from each other yet, sadly, the negatives seem to outweigh the positives, which leaves Ms Libra feeling uncomfortable because the scales are not perfectly balanced. The goat will be too critical of her need to surround herself with life's little luxuries and comforts, which can lead to some friction in the camp. She is a communicator and needs to talk about everything – especially feelings and relationships. He is a private person and too reserved, and will often appear too detached for the romantic Ms Libra.

Both signs are emotionally cool: fundamentally they both will feel in the dark as to where they stand with each other. The air sign girl might appear too superficial for the stoic, pragmatic goat, and he will be far too grounded for her.

Ms Libra and Mr Capricorn have conventional leanings and can be caught up with what they see as an appropriate form of behaviour. They will always favour a socially accepted marriage over living together, and so might end up married for convention's sake rather than for lust and romance.

In the bedroom: The intimate side of this relationship can make or break it. If it works, it will be sustaining and will heat up an otherwise lukewarm bond.

♎ Ms Libra + Mr Aquarius ♒

Sign	Libra	Aquarius
Symbol	Scales	Water bearer
Ruler	Venus	Uranus
Type	Cardinal	Fixed
Element	Air	Air

These two make great friends as well as lovers because both gravitate towards people and will always maintain a connection, even if their romantic relationship ends. Because both are air signs, they share a mutual passion for mental and physical exploration, and will encourage each other to experience as much texture and diversity as they can fit into their lives. They will give each other room to move in the relationship. Although Ms Libra will want to keep her Aquarian man in tow – her need for commitment is more strongly developed than his – her sense of fair play will allow him the periods of freedom he needs to stay happy.

Ms Libra and Ms Aquarius will always keep their channels of communication open. They come from an intellectual perspective and need to share knowledge and be intellectually stimulated. The only difficulty these two might have is on the occasions that Aquarian instincts lead this guy to indulge in off-beat and unconventional behaviour, which is when Ms Libra might need to keep the peace by dropping her airs and graces and letting it all hang out.

Air signs seem to lack in the feeling department and this relationship will be based more on a mental connection than instinctive feelings, which means the old 'you don't understand me' phrase is less likely to pop up. Both have a tendency to repress or disguise their emotions on an intimate level. However, when it comes to social justice, human rights and equality, they are both on the same wavelength – deeply committed to such causes. They both have a strong social conscience and a sense of fair play, which further strengthens their bonds.

In the bedroom: These two make great bedfellows because they both enjoy and take pride in the art of lovemaking. The open Mr Aquarius will pull a few tricks out of his bag to tantalise his Libran love and she will always express her appreciation in ways he has only dreamed of.

♎ Ms Libra + Mr Pisces ♓

Sign	Libra	Pisces
Symbol	Scales	Fish
Ruler	Venus	Neptune
Type	Cardinal	Mutable
Element	Air	Water

Ms Libra and Mr Pisces are both romantic and creative individuals who share a strange mix of positive and negative energy. They have the same unrealistic expectations of what they need and desire from a relationship and will always want to seek a perfect mate who fulfils their wildest dreams and fantasies.

Mr Pisces is a man who seeks perfection and Ms Libra – his dream woman – will be high on his agenda. This is the best water and air mix of the signs: both crave harmony and peace, and both will make some compromises if the union turns out less than ideal. However, the fish might be too emotional and needy for the controlled Libran woman who is not comfortable with having to confront her feelings. She would rather analyse how she feels in a more detached way. He is the more emotional of the two and will wear his heart on his sleeve. His water element allows him to be swept up in a sea of emotions, which can make the cool Ms Libra rather uncomfortable. She is more selfish and narcissistic than the self-sacrificing fish, who will swim whichever way his lady wants, yet will never mind that he is the one making all the compromises.

On a romantic level, however, this pair can feel very much at one with each other. Ms Libra likes nothing more than having her man tell her how passionate he is about her – the more often the better – and Mr Pisces is a genius at this.

In the bedroom: Ms Libra and her Piscean lover will take great delight in seducing each other with skill. He will take her to depths of emotion that she has never experienced and to mystical places she will never want to leave.

Celebrity Ms Libra: Martina Navratilova

Tennis player, born 4.40 pm 18 October 1956 in Prague, Czechoslovakia

```
Personal planets: Sun in Libra
                  Moon in Aries
                  Mercury in Libra
                  Venus in Virgo
                  Mars in Pisces
```

I came to live in a country I love. Some people call me a defector. I have loved men and women in my life. I have been labelled the bisexual defector in print. Want to know another secret? I'm even ambidextrous. I don't like labels. Just call me Martina.

– Martina Navratilova

Navratilova is a true Libran personality. Above all she values equality and fairness and her courteous disposition as a top professional tennis player has earned her the respect of both her peers and sports fans worldwide. Her personal life has made headlines in the media and she has had to defend herself many times from some harsh remarks, but has always done so in a gracious and non-combative way.

As Navratilova's quote implies, she is a lover of people and will always be happiest in a relationship. Librans are fulfilled when they can share their life with another. Her chart reflects the typical characteristics of a Libra Sun. She has a strongly developed sense of fairness, and will always be on hand to defend the people she cares about. She is also aware of the feelings and needs of her partner. Her Libran Sun is also connected to the planet Neptune, adding a self-delusional quality to her spiritual and humanitarian nature. Because she doesn't always have a clear perspective of herself, she often needs feedback from others. This can cause relationship problems because she lacks the ability to discriminate in her intimate life and has been taken advantage of as a consequence.

Navratilova has a yearning for ideal love and seeks a truly romantic union, sometimes becoming disillusioned when the reality of everyday life sets in. Librans are so romantic they forget people are mortal after all. Her Mars in the sign of Pisces gives her only one water element, adding to her need for intensity and passion from her relationships, but also showing that love and passion will be a strong outlet for her self-expression and escapism.

Her love affair with American writer and social activist Rita Brown, a Sagittarian, is reflective of Navratilova's natural attraction to people who are creative and artistic. This Libra–Sagittarian combination – a union interested in social justice and reforms – is another pointer to a long-term and satisfying relationship.

Mr Libra – an overview

The Libran male can best be described as a truly charming and physically handsome beast, but he can also have some beastly qualities beneath his glossy veneer. He has a way with words that will have the female of the species eating out of his hand. This man has a predisposition toward women. He has a string of female friends, not only lovers, but those seeking his words of advice and wisdom. He is a born mediator and has a knack for sorting out problems and difficulties for other people. His tactful and considerate demeanour wins him special favours with the girls and he will never be short of women to call upon.

He is a man who loves to be 'in love' and needs to have a woman to share his life with. He knows only too well how to woo his lady. A true romantic, Mr Libra will be prepared to indulge his lady love and can satisfy her every whim if she remains attentive to him. He likes to create the proper social image where everything appears perfectly balanced; however, appearances often belie the facts, with turmoil and frustration hidden just below the surface of this smooth operator.

Mr Libra tends to fall in love with a pretty face rather than finding out the true depth of a woman's nature, and is often disappointed when she is not the woman of his dreams because of his unrealistic expectations. He requires a peaceful non-confronting union where the line of least resistance is the most comfortable. His best attributes will be on show if he is in a peaceful and harmonious environment. The Libran man needs his mate to share his life on all levels, so if you are a independently minded woman this is not the man for you. He values communication above all else and has a need to discuss his relationship with her from all angles.

This man's biggest vice is his inability to make decisions, so you cannot give him a choice about anything because he will sit on the proverbial fence and deliberate for hours, driving his more decisive partner to distraction. However, he can be a wonderful companion and lover who will treat his lady love as if she is the only girl in the world.

Famous Libran men

* Michael Douglas (actor)
* Groucho Marx (comedian)
* John Lennon (musician)
* Oscar Wilde (writer)

* Bob Geldolf (singer/activist)
* Truman Capote (writer)

Combinations

♎ Mr Libra + Ms Aries ♈

Sign	Libra	Aries
Symbol	Scales	Ram
Ruler	Venus	Mars
Type	Cardinal	Cardinal
Element	Air	Fire

Sparks will fly at the initial meeting between Ms Aries and Mr Libra. Although opposites attract, the differences will prove too great in a long-term relationship.

Mr Libra will crave the closeness an intimate relationship provides. He will be concerned with society's expectations and will always want to be seen to follow traditional standards. Mr Libra will put Ms Aries on a pedestal but ultimately she won't fit the mould of the perfect, doting wife.

Idealistic and always looking at the world through rose-coloured glasses, Mr Libra will become frustrated with messy Ms Aries, who'd rather be outdoors climbing mountains than sitting at home playing house. She, in turn, will become irritated with Mr Libra. His indecisiveness and inability to make quick decisions will drive her crazy, along with his laziness. While his airs and graces will be quite charming to Ms Aries, once he's won her heart, he will have a hard time keeping it.

Libra is the sign of balance and harmony and he will always want to please his mate. But on this occasion the scales will rarely tip in his favour. Once again, Ms Aries, as in many of her other unions, will be in the driver's seat of the relationship and will soon tire of the fence-sitting Mr Libra.

In the bedroom: Air will fuel the flames of passion bursting in Ms Aries. These two will have a good sexual union because he can sweet talk the ram into bed and knows exactly how to please her.

♎ Mr Libra + Ms Taurus ♉

Sign	Libra	Taurus
Symbol	Scales	Bull
Ruler	Venus	Venus
Type	Cardinal	Fixed
Element	Air	Earth

Venus, the planet of love, rules both these signs so one might think this is a match made in heaven. The Taurus–Libra couple have a lot in common: an appreciation of the arts and beauty, comfort and material delights. However, Taurus is a more practical and grounded sign, preoccupied with wealth and acquisition, while Librans are more interested in accumulating people rather than objects in their life's journey. Ms Taurus doesn't possess the same gracious, light energy of the charming Mr Libra.

This relationship is more workable as a friendship rather than as a loving union. Both can learn much from the other: Ms Taurus can learn to loosen up and sharpen her communication skills, and Mr Libra can become more decisive and practical.

Mr Libra is more open to social interaction and has a willingness to please. He often won't express his needs in the relationship, whereas his Taurean mate will call a spade a spade and not waste precious time weighing up the pros and cons.

In the bedroom: These two signs are both ruled by Venus, so their union has the potential to be hot and heavy. She desires a strong physical bond and he'll want a creative kitten in the sack, so if they meet somewhere in the middle, then there'll be no turning back!

♎ Mr Libra + Ms Gemini ♊

Sign	Libra	Gemini
Symbol	Scales	Twins
Ruler	Venus	Mercury
Type	Cardinal	Mutable
Element	Air	Air

Astrologically, the combination of Ms Gemini and Mr Libra is what is referred to as a trine aspect, which means the flow of energy between these two signs is one of harmony and unity. They are both fairly impulsive in love, more so Ms Gemini, and both being air signs means they have a natural affinity to enjoy the same things – particularly communication. Ms Gemini is attracted to the charming, dedicated and romantic Mr Libra who is equally smitten by her ability to keep him on his toes and entertain him with her wit.

Air signs seem to lack the depth and intensity of the water and earth signs, meaning their relationships work on a more superficial level as both don't like to ponder the shortcomings of their relationship. Ms Gemini may at times become impatient with Mr Libra's indecisiveness because she is very quick to make up her mind, but his Venusian charm will always manage to win her over.

Both these signs are characterised by a narcissistic streak, often causing the Gemini and Libran to be preoccupied with their own thoughts and limiting their ability to truly understand what they need from a relationship. Mr Libra will need a relationship far more than Ms Gemini, who is more inconsistent about what she wants and doesn't always convey her true feelings or desires to a partner. Instead, she will often tell him what she thinks he wants to hear rather than being truthful and straightforward.

Mr Libra is idealistic in love, putting his beloved on a pedestal and seeing her as something more than mortal. He needs to be more realistic in his relationships and Ms Gemini needs to be less fickle and more honest in what she wants if this is to be a lasting union.

In the bedroom: Although these two air signs will become one in bed, it is unlikely they will experience the same wild abandonment and consuming passion of two earth or fire combinations. But sex between Ms Gemini and Mr Libra will be changeable and delightful.

♎ Mr Libra + Ms Cancer ♋

Sign	Libra	Cancer
Symbol	Scales	Crab
Ruler	Venus	Moon
Type	Cardinal	Cardinal
Element	Air	Water

Ms Cancer and Mr Libra will have an interesting relationship. She is the deeper and more sensitive of the two, and he appears to hide his true feelings and rely more on his superficial nature. If the Cancerian woman can dig below the surface of this charming Libran, she will tap into the deeper side of his nature. Although attractive to all star signs, the Libran man will bring out the crab's more sensitive and emotional nature, as he will be insistent on understanding her moods, feelings and vulnerabilities since he is a born psychologist.

This couple has an artistic flair and will make their domestic life a feature of this union. Both are cardinal signs, suggesting they are initiators; however, Librans are renowned for their procrastination, a trait Ms Cancer will find frustrating at times. They both need partners but search for different things. Ms Cancer is more likely to look for deeper qualities in her mate; conversely, he will be happy with a pretty face and to judge the book by its cover, rather than opening pages and finding the mystique that lie waiting within.

If this Libran man is willing to expose his vulnerabilities and share his true emotions with his Cancerian mate, this might work; however, it is more likely she will only ever see the shallow quality of her mate. Sadly for Mr Libra, he will lose a deep passionate and nurturing partner, which is exactly what he really needs.

In the bedroom: Sex between Mr Libra and Ms Cancer is like riding a seesaw – sometimes it's breathtaking, but at other times her mistrusting nature and his lack of depth can cause them to come crashing down to earth. But because they're both sentimental souls they'll be able to put their differences aside for a good dose of loving!

♎ Mr Libra + Ms Leo ♌

Sign	Libra	Leo
Symbol	Scales	Lion
Ruler	Venus	Sun
Type	Cardinal	Fixed
Element	Air	Fire

Mr Libra and Ms Leo have a strong social connection because they both enjoy involving other people in their lives. Her attractiveness and colourful personality will be admired by her Libran mate, and she will find that he will put her up on a pedestal where she feels most comfortable.

Mr Libra, by nature, likes balance and harmony, so when his lioness roars too loudly on occasions – she is prone to temper tantrums – he will turn a blind eye. They share a love of beauty and both have a strong creative ability, which includes an eye for design and colour. Given their many similarities in this sphere, Ms Leo and Mr Libra will come to appreciate and admire each other's talents.

The Libran man will be happy to provide his lioness with the respect and loyalty she insists upon in a relationship; as well, he will allow her to strut her stuff rather than cramping her style. Since they both stand out in a crowd, it will be hard for them not to be drawn to each other's magnetic and alluring personalities. They are traditionalists, so when they decide the union is working they'll be more inclined to agree to marry rather than simply coasting along. It is a great combination if Mr Libra doesn't get too miffed at Ms Leo's constant need to be the centre of attention.

In the bedroom: Fire and air is usually a good match since both are the romantics of the zodiac and enjoy the fuss they make of each other. Ms Leo will be turned on by the charming and complimentary Libra, who loves a lot of foreplay.

♎ Mr Libra + Ms Virgo ♍

Sign	Libra	Virgo
Symbol	Scales	Virgin
Ruler	Venus	Mercury
Type	Cardinal	Mutable
Element	Air	Earth

In their own way, Mr Libra and Ms Virgo have a desire for perfection. The virgin thrives in an environment where there is order and harmony. She likes her life to be neat and tidy and will make improvements if she feels they are necessary. Mr Libra also relishes an orderly domain and both will work together to create balance. But where these two differ is that Ms Virgo is much more of a hands-on worker, whereas Mr Libra is more likely to want to give orders rather than pitching in and getting his hands dirty.

He is much more of a charming, sweet-talker who never likes to get to the point, preferring instead to keep everyone happy, but Ms Virgo – who always gives 100 per cent in her relationships – will have no qualms about speaking the truth, so she may be too blunt and critical for this passive fence-sitter. Mr Libra will never want to rock the boat and is likely to suffer in silence if something is bothering him. Because commitment is a top priority for these two, if they do end up in a long-term union, it will take a lot for either one to end the relationship if things aren't working out.

In the bedroom: Virgoans are fairly practical, even when it comes to sex, but the right encouragement and nurturing from her Venusian man might be just enough to awaken a strong sensual side to her nature. She may even throw caution to the wind and surprise her man with her sexual spontaneity.

♎ Mr Libra + Ms Libra ♎

Sign	Libra	Libra
Symbol	Scales	Scales
Ruler	Venus	Venus
Type	Cardinal	Cardinal
Element	Air	Air

Too much of a good thing can often become boring. Mr and Ms Libra have much in common, but they may be too focused on the superficial rather than on deeper and more meaningful aspects of a fulfilling union. As two air signs, they will spend plenty of time talking and analysing their partnership to achieve the right balance. Both will want the perfect union and will always be trying to strive for that ideal. Because this pair values romance, they will enjoy setting the mood and creating the right atmosphere to indulge in their fantasies. They are natural diplomats with a desire to please, yet might need to be more honest with each other. Neither wants to been seen as the 'bad guy' in this relationship.

The most frustrating aspect for this pairing seems to be their indecisiveness. Librans are noted procrastinators and fence-sitters, so how will they ever reach a decision? Because they are cardinal signs, this might not be too much of a problem. Both are initiators as long as they are not given too many alternatives.

This couple blends beautifully when it comes to playing house together, as both have an artistic streak as well as an affinity for the finer things in life. Venus, the planet of love and beauty, rules and so they will both have a preoccupation with the aesthetics and pleasures of life. As a couple they will always strive for perfection and harmony in their union, and their mutual desire for companionship will see them sharing most aspects of their life together.

In the bedroom: As long as they are prepared to get their feathers ruffled, there will be no stopping this pair, who will spend many hours communicating and perfecting their lovemaking techniques. Remember, practice makes perfect!

♎ Mr Libra + Ms Scorpio ♏

Sign	Libra	Scorpio
Symbol	Scales	Scorpion
Ruler	Venus	Pluto
Type	Cardinal	Fixed
Element	Air	Water

Mr Libra will find Ms Scorpio initially alluring and erotic and will want to get to know this mysterious woman; however, she is a dark horse and will not want to give too much away. Mr Libra loves to discuss all things, particularly his one-on-one relationships, which is something Ms Scorpio is reluctant to do.

Air is all about communication and water runs still and deep, so these two signs will have a problem relating. Ms Scorpio has a way of entrapping her man and because Mr Libra is so charming and personable, she will be initially attracted to him; however, her intense and dominating manner may frighten him away. The difficulty with this connection is that Mr Libra is sociable, communicative and very attractive to the opposite sex as well as his own, so Ms Scorpio may see her sting come out in a jealous tirade on occasions. Mr Libra abhors such outbursts because he needs peace and tranquillity in his relationships. He will view this behaviour as unjustified and, above all, unfair.

These two have very different personalities. Mr Libra lacks the depth that this passionate woman needs and he will not understand her demands and frustrations. Ms Scorpio, on the other hand, is too emotional and intense for the peace-loving, non-confronting Libran. She is decisive and knows her own mind only too well. His inability to make up his mind will see her cast her spell elsewhere.

In the bedroom: The boudoir is the best room in the house for these two. And if they can spend their entire life behind closed doors, the relationship might just stand a chance.

♎ Mr Libra + Ms Sagittarius ♐

Sign	Libra	Sagittarius
Symbol	Scales	Archer
Ruler	Venus	Jupiter
Type	Cardinal	Mutable
Element	Air	Fire

This is a great match because fire and air excites and entices each other. Both Mr Libra and Ms Sagittarius have a natural zest for life and are open individuals who share the same passion for learning and exchanging ideas and thoughts. These two are also very sociable and will be happy to share their life with others. Their natural optimism and their ability to relate well to people give them many opportunities to experience a rich and textured lifestyle. Both are romantic idealists, so they will be happy to work on improving their relationship. Mr Libra will be drawn to the fun-loving adventurous archer who will be constantly dragging him to participate in whatever her passion desires – be it a seat in the saddle or seat in the fast lane. The archer is a fun-loving girl who likes to play hard.

The one thing that might set these two apart is the foot-in-mouth disease that can afflict Ms Sagittarius. She lets it all hang out, much to the embarrassment of Mr Libra, who is far too diplomatic to really say how it is. Ms Sagittarius is known be a bit of an embarrassment on occasions, but if Mr Libra can relax and see the humour of such situations and her genuine intent (she does not have a mean bone in her body), then all will be well.

Mr Libra likes to do everything with his mate, but the archer needs some space at times. Such differences will need to be discussed in advance so that each knows where they stand; however, if difficulties do crop up they will be quickly solved, because this pair has a great sense of empathy and compassion for each other.

In the bedroom: Mr Libra dedicates himself to pleasing and his skill lies not only in his physical manoeuvres, but also in his ability to be a selfless lover, getting the most satisfaction when he sees his lover squirm for more.

♎ Mr Libra + Ms Capricorn ♑

Sign	Libra	Capricorn
Symbol	Scales	Goat
Ruler	Venus	Saturn
Type	Cardinal	Cardinal
Element	Air	Earth

These two will respect each other's attributes but this will not be enough to bind them. Mr Libra's wishy-washy and indecisive ways will be frustrating for the definitive goat, who wants to know where she is heading in the relationship. Mr Libra's romancing will not be enough for this hard-nosed girl, who is more turned on by practical considerations than by zealous passion. She takes her relationships seriously and will feel her Libran man is in love with love rather than with her. He, in turn, will feel unappreciated, as he needs his ego stroked many times a day.

The Capricornian woman is not the type to allow her heart to rule her head so will not succumb to the whims of her Venusian man. She has a tendency to isolate herself emotionally and Mr Libra will be unsure how to penetrate what seems to him a cold, cold heart.

These two signs seem to come from different perspectives: he is a born romantic and places his lady on a pedestal, but Ms Capricorn won't be comfortable on a throne that could be overturned at any moment. She would rather be on the ground where she can make her own way to the top in her own time and in her own way.

These signs make a challenging aspect astrologically. On a fundamental level, they are too different to make adjustments and compromises.

In the bedroom: The qualities of earth and air are very different. Mr Libra will want to discuss and analyse his relationship at length while Ms Capricorn will want to get down to business.

♎ Mr Libra + Ms Aquarius ♒

Sign	Libra	Aquarius
Symbol	Scales	Water bearer
Ruler	Venus	Uranus
Type	Cardinal	Fixed
Element	Air	Air

These two signs are an excellent combination. Both are interested in social justice and equality, and will always be supportive of each other's needs and projects. Both are skilful communicators and will spend many hours engaged in verbal discussions. These two are not comfortable with emotional intensity, but would rather enjoy an intellectual approach to their relationship, preferring logic and evaluation over emotions.

The main theme that seems to run through this combination is this pair's ability to be open minded and fair. Mr Libra is perhaps more needy because he is a romantic and wants everything to be perfect when he sails into the sunset with his beloved by his side. Ms Aquarius, however, will want to seek adventure independently rather than needing to have her mate constantly under her feet.

She is the more impersonal of the two and is interested in freedom and not becoming trapped, so Mr Libra will need to make some adjustments if he wants a relationship with the water bearer, who is a strange paradox of conservatism and unconventionality. Because Mr Libra has a strong desire to conform to please his mate, he just might find he is the one making more compromises in this relationship.

In the bedroom: Mr Libra will display his usual talent to bring Ms Aquarius to nirvana, yet he'd better not dilly-dally too long, as her interest will wane and she will be planning her next move outside the confines of the bedroom.

♎ Mr Libra + Ms Pisces ♓

Sign	Libra	Pisces
Symbol	Scales	Fish
Ruler	Venus	Neptune
Type	Cardinal	Mutable
Element	Air	Water

These two are romantics at heart. They will have an interesting exchange because both are interested in love and relationships and will be totally committed to each other. Ms Pisces takes the award for being the most sensitive and intuitive of the water signs. She comes from a feeling perspective and her passion can be a little overwhelming for the Libran guy, who is very much in his head and will rarely understand the depth of this woman. They each seek perfection from their relationships and will project their ideals on to each other, only to feel disappointed in the light of day.

This pair shares a flair for the artistic and the creative and will stimulate each other by expressing their mutual talents. The fish has escapist tendencies and will be somewhat self-deluded, always making adjustments and compromises for her mate. Mr Libra will also make compromises for his lady because he will see her as a gifted, sensitive and gentle person.

Water and air don't usually mix well, but these two are an exception; both will be interested in plain sailing on calm waters rather than bobbing about in turbulent seas. This combination has a magical quality based on the ruling planets. He is ruled by the planet Venus, so love and harmony are his focus, while the little mermaid has Neptune ruling over her, which gives her a sensitive and highly-idealistic flavour, making their relationship harmonious.

In the bedroom: She needs little encouragement – one touch and she is away in her own space, taking her Prince Charming to a place he has never been, let alone even dreamt of.

Celebrity Mr Libra: Sting

Singer, born 2 October 1951 in Newcastle-on-Tyne, England

```
Personal planets: Sun in Libra
                  Moon in Libra
                  Mercury in Virgo
                  Venus in Virgo
                  Mars in Leo
```

I think I mentioned to Bob (Geldolf) I could make love for eight hours. What I didn't say was this included four hours of begging and then dinner and a movie.

– Sting

Singer and political activist Gordon Sumner, better known as Sting, is a man who typifies the Libran spirit with his artistic brilliance and his interest in human causes. His romantic nature would make him want to woo and romance his lady, making her feel very special. Venus in the sign of Virgo gives him a faithful and disciplined approach to his relationship. He would naturally be attracted to a woman who displays the Virgo tendency to make him comfortable and supported.

His obvious attractiveness, both physically and mentally, makes him a man most women would desire. Libran men have a considerable charm and he is no exception to the rule. Sting's marriage to Trudie Styler is an interesting one. She is a Capricorn and, as a rule, this combination is not particularly compatible. His own chart has a strong Virgo theme, giving him some weighty earth elements; these fit harmoniously with her Sun sign. His Libran Sun is connected to the planet Saturn, giving him a grounded and more disciplined approach to life, which is in contrast to the more superficial and 'flighty' side of his Libran nature.

Sting and Styler are keen environmentalists – they share a mutual drive to conserve the planet – and together make a formidable business partnership. They established the Rainforest Foundation in 1989 to protect a great tract of the South American Amazon wildness, which they considered to be a part of the planet worth saving.

As a Capricorn, Styler is likely be the more dominant of the two. And even Sting acknowledges that: 'She is the stronger in the relationship; I'm the dizzy blond'. The relationship indicates an awareness of their mutual strengths and differences. Sting is attracted to the decisiveness and practical nature of his Capricornian partner, while his diplomacy and sense of justice holds great appeal for her. These two individuals can bring their unique qualities to the table and respect each other's differences.

Styler is steadfast and committed to her relationship – a requirement Sting needs to be emotionally satisfied. Her Mars in Pisces suggests she would be attracted to a Neptunian type of man, who is creative and into music and culture. She would be hard pressed to find a man who surpasses Sting's creative talents and imaginative mind.

SCORPIO (24 October–22 November)

♏

Ruled by the planet Pluto
Water sign
Fixed
Feminine energy

In general ...

Scorpio is an intensely passionate water sign and is often regarded as the most sexually oriented and erotic sign of the zodiac.

Both sexes always maintain an exterior facade self-control and disciplined energy, giving nothing away about how they really feel on an emotional level. This secretive energy can be frustrating because they have an incredible ability to extract information from their partners but will reveal nothing themselves. Beneath this facade of strength lies a well of emotions that will rarely surface until they feel they are in a safe and trusted union. Their sensitivities and insecurities are manifested in issues of control and obsessive behaviour, which are a direct result of feeling a lack of parental love and support in their childhood. This makes them crave love and affection.

Scorpios are needy and possessive when it comes to their relationships and will stop at nothing to possess their loved one. The difficulty that most Scorpios face is their determination to control people close to them, which can lead to alienation and relationship difficulties.

Sex is used as a vehicle to transport the Scorpio to a higher place, where love and bonding become the strongest features of a relationship. Scorpios of both sexes use their sexuality and magnetism as a way of controlling their partners, and can do so very effectively. They can sting their partner into submission and then back off after having claimed victory. Their wounded target is often left confused, bewildered as to the underlying motive and wondering if there is a future for the relationship.

As a fixed sign, Scorpios demonstrate endurance and loyalty, and if they bond with a partner, they will stay faithful and committed. But there will always be a strings-attached policy in their partnerships. Scorpios like to control most situations and, often as a result of their own shortcomings and insecurities, will become exceedingly jealous and possessive. Most Scorpios have an alluring quality with a penetrating view that can see right though the object of their desire. This is the very quality that captivates the opposite sex.

As a typical water sign, Scorpios have a need to experience depth and intensity in their connections; lukewarm relationships will not be enough for them. They want to feel an emotional, mental and physical connection with their partners, who can often feel overwhelmed by their partner's constant need for love and attention. This deep intensity can lead to rejection, ironically the very thing Scorpios fear the most from their relationships. Scorpios might be too intense for some but a relationship with a Scorpio can be a transformative experience – not recommended, however, for the faint-hearted.

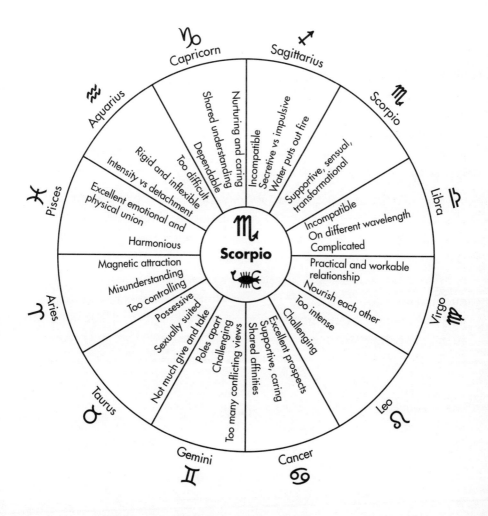

How a Scorpio personality might match up with other star signs

Ms Scorpio — an overview

The Scorpio woman is a creature who will sting when she feels under threat, quickly immobilising her victim with her sharp and sarcastic tongue. This woman is a force not to be reckoned with. Her alluring, composed and sensual manner will catch the attention of many prospective partners who will be fascinated as to what lies beneath those penetrating and mysterious eyes.

Ms Scorpio is a woman who seeks emotional intensity from her relationships. She needs to feel in control and is often labelled a sexual predator, which is unfair since she uses sex only as an initial connection for a deeply emotional and transcending union. So desirous is she to obtain the love and affection she feels she lacked in her early life that she will use her sexuality to cement long-term relationships. A Scorpio woman is highly tuned into what her man needs and will have the knack of drawing him out without giving too much of herself away. She will skilfully penetrate his soul, exposing his vulnerability in the process, which will make her appear stronger and more in control of the relationship.

Her magnetism is a drawcard for many and, once she feels safe and trusting in a relationship, she will be a committed, loving and, above all, loyal mate. This woman is on a lifelong search for love and security and will endure many crises in her life. She is on a mission of personal transformation and has a tremendous reserve of energy and tenacity to find her ideal. As a fixed mode of expression, she knows her own mind well and will find it difficult to make compromises in her relationships. The attention-seeking Ms Scorpio has a strong possessive streak and, because she is fundamentally insecure, it can lead to moments of intense jealousy.

This femme fatale craves a partnership to quash her fear of loneliness and abandonment, yet will never compromise herself in a relationship that is shallow and superficial. She needs her mate to have the same understanding and emotional dependency as her if all is to be well in the realms of love.

Famous Scorpio women

* Marie-Antoinette
  (French queen)
* Grace Kelly
  (actor/princess)
* Sylvia Plath
  (poet/writer)

* Hillary Clinton
  (former US first lady/senator)
* Marie Curie (scientist)
* Whoopi Goldberg
  (actor/comedian)

Combinations

♏ Ms Scorpio + Mr Aries ♈

Sign	Scorpio	Aries
Symbol	Scorpion	Ram
Ruler	Pluto	Mars
Type	Fixed	Cardinal
Element	Water	Fire

Mr Aries will be attracted to the deep, sensual nature of Ms Scorpio, giving this union all the trimmings of a passionate love affair, but the security-craving scorpion is likely to be too intense for the easy-going ram, who might find himself drowning in a sea of emotions.

Ms Scorpio is secretive and non-trusting by nature – the very opposite of the open, down-to-earth Arian man. This water-sign woman is needy, controlling and possessive, all of which will eventually drive him to seek solace elsewhere. Although she will be intensely loyal and committed in their relationship, he will be overwhelmed by it all. He has an open and forthright nature and will be dragged down by Ms Scorpio's secretive habits. Basically, she is passionate about her relationships, whereas he can take them or leave them.

This pair will have trouble communicating because Ms Scorpio has a tendency to keep her feelings hidden and, consequently, Mr Aries is often left in the dark. Eventually this tension will erupt, causing anger and frustration on both sides. The scorpion's brooding, jealous and controlling nature will suffocate her Arian mate.

Scorpios have a tendency to control their relationship through sex, which initially attracts Mr Aries; however, it is commitment and emotional consistency she seeks and he doesn't match up. Because Scorpio is a fixed sign, change doesn't come easily, whereas Mr Aries is constantly attracted to change. What started out as such a promising relationship has nowhere to go. Slowly the flames will die and Mr Aries will pack his bags in search of a far less complex liaison.

In the bedroom: These two sexually charged signs will share plenty of erotic pleasures. Ms Scorpio will let her man take the lead but by no means will she be a passive lover.

♏ Ms Scorpio + Mr Taurus ♉

Sign	Scorpio	Taurus
Symbol	Scorpion	Bull
Ruler	Pluto	Venus
Type	Fixed	Fixed
Element	Water	Earth

Sex will be the driving force in this union as lust and more lust is primarily what these two signs have in common. Both Scorpios and Taureans desire a close, possessive relationship where they feel number one. Because these two signs are both in a fixed mode of expression, they are not adaptable to change and can become totally committed once they feel they have trust in their relationships.

Ms Scorpio is often afraid of rejection and will engage in certain controlling behaviour patterns to feel in charge of the relationship. Her Taurean mate will lap up the attention. These signs share a similar intensity in their relationship: both are very devoted and will become extremely protective of each other. If either feels there is an injustice done to their lover, they will be quick to spring to their defence. Loyalty is what seems to keep these two on an even keel; it is the common thread that binds them. Mr Taurus will ensure the vulnerable Ms Scorpio is always in a safe haven. In turn, she will use her mysterious charm to magnetise her man.

Taureans and Librans do not communicate their emotions easily. Ms Scorpio is secretive and untrusting and Mr Taurus has a tendency to bury his head in the sand. Hence it is important for this couple to recognise that this trait might cause some difficulties in their relationship. All in all, however, this is a good and powerful combination because the watery Scorpio will always shower her bull with love and affection.

In the bedroom: Erotic and devouring are the best two words to describe the lovemaking between Mr Taurus and his Scorpio lover. They both expect to be loved completely and not simply because they're great in the sack.

♏ Ms Scorpio + Mr Gemini ♊

Sign	Scorpio	Gemini
Symbol	Scorpion	Twins
Ruler	Pluto	Mercury
Type	Fixed	Mutable
Element	Water	Air

The union of Mr Gemini and Ms Scorpio is not a match made in heaven. The energy these two exude is very different. She expects commitment from her man, which is one quality he struggles with. She tends to scare the boyish Gemini with her brooding and secretive disposition and he will never be able to handle her possessive and controlling ways.

This man abhors any female who wants to pin him down and her jealous streak will send him running into the arms of someone more easy-going and fun-loving. Nothing scares a Gemini guy more than commitment and, because Ms Scorpio needs guarantees, issues of trust will creep into the pairing process, forcing an impasse that will rarely see the two of them head down the road of love. This man is far too interested in himself to provide the deep and intuitive Ms Scorpio with a caring and sensitive partner. She, in turn, is security-conscious and manipulative and rarely will she fall for the wishy-washy, smooth-talking Gemini charm.

He needs a woman who will share his thirst for knowledge and information, and his desire to communicate with people from all walks of life. Ms Scorpio, however, is a far more self-contained and secretive soul who will become insanely jealous when she has to share her gregarious Gemini with the plethora of other woman he claims are 'just friends'. These two are polarised in their needs and desires. Mr Gemini will soon tire of Ms Scorpio's efforts to contain his free-spirited soul.

In the bedroom: Mr Gemini is more likely to sink than swim when confronted by Ms Scorpio's passionate yearnings. She will be fascinated by the twin, desperate to penetrate the deep secrets locked within. But his wandering and detached spirit will eventually force this woman into the bed of a more sensual and dedicated lover.

♏ Ms Scorpio + Mr Cancer ♋

Sign	Scorpio	Cancer
Symbol	Scorpion	Crab
Ruler	Pluto	Moon
Type	Fixed	Cardinal
Element	Water	Water

When Ms Scorpio and Mr Cancer come together in love, there is an amazing transformative energy force that will transport them into a deep and intense union. They both have a tremendous ability to survive the most arduous and tough encounters in their lives. Not for nothing are they known as the survivors of the zodiac. In fact, on most occasions, they will grow stronger from these testing and traumatic experiences.

Although both are initially reticent when it comes to love and protective of their secrets and souls, when the crab initiates and the scorpion responds it will be a fulfilling and enduring relationship. Since both are water signs, they need partners who are deeply responsive. Neither treats their relationship lightly, which can lead to petty jealousies. However, the mutual understanding between them eliminates fear and anxiety generated by jealously.

Mr Cancer has strong ties with his mother, endowing him with an understanding of women and their vulnerabilities, so he is happy to indulge Ms Scorpio in her constant desire for attention. They hide their aggressive tendencies well but if either is under threat, they will stop at nothing to protect each other. And because they are both complex characters who suffer mood swings, they will be tolerant of each other's occasional outbursts.

Mr Cancer and Ms Scorpio are people who need time out and crave a certain amount of privacy and solitude to re-energise themselves.

In the bedroom: A very powerful sexual force exists between the crab and scorpion. It will be a blending of their bodies and minds when these two water signs join in the bedroom.

♏ Ms Scorpio + Mr Leo ♌

Sign	Scorpio	Leo
Symbol	Scorpion	Lion
Ruler	Pluto	Sun
Type	Fixed	Fixed
Element	Water	Fire

These two are passionate and intense in their desire to have a relationship but compromise is always an important part of it. In many ways, they share similar personalities: both are control freaks and have a tendency to want to take the dominant role in the relationship.

However, their tactics are different: Mr Leo is open, vocal and demonstrative and says it how it is, which can cut Ms Scorpio to the quick. Although she might know where she stands with him, more often than not he won't with her, because of her secretive nature and her suspicion of his bravado and his need for public adoration.

Her sting will ultimately be more lethal than his roar and Mr Leo will wind up being the one to make more sacrifices in the relationship. As a fire sign, he likes a woman who is direct and honest in her feelings but Ms Scorpio is distrusting of most men until they prove their self-worth. Mr Leo is too proud to play games he has no chance of winning. The scorpion is likely to be too demanding and jealous for the lion, who usually has a string of admirers waiting in the wings.

In the bedroom: Both being fixed signs, these two are equally self-contained and need to feel emotionally secure before they reveal themselves sexually to a partner. Both will be keen to initiate proceedings and want to have sexual dominance over the other. It can be all-out passion if one plays a more submissive role at times. Bring on the game of cat and mouse!

♏ Ms Scorpio + Mr Virgo ♍

Sign	Scorpio	Virgo
Symbol	Scorpion	Virgin
Ruler	Pluto	Mercury
Type	Fixed	Mutable
Element	Water	Earth

Mr Virgo is not compatible with the suspicious Ms Scorpio, whom he finds too closed and secretive. He is an open book and will always communicate his feelings, often at times too bluntly and honestly, but Ms Scorpio is not a trusting soul and will keep her man in the dark. For some males this can be a turn on, as Ms Scorpio has an air of mystique and an alluring quality that is often interpreted as a strong sexual energy.

Mr Virgo is a man who thrives on challenges and he needs his sense of self-confidence boosted rather than being undermined. Both he and Ms Scorpio have issues regarding tolerance: they don't like weakness, and tend to be judgemental of each other. This couple has a strong sense of commitment and will be supportive of each other if a connection is made, but Mr Virgo is too 'straight' to buy into the complexities of the watery Scorpio who needs constant reassurance about her position in the relationship.

He will find Ms Scorpio's tendency to be jealous frustrating because he considers himself to be a trusting and loyal mate, and doesn't take to her undermining approach easily. If these two can get past first base, Ms Scorpio can provide enough water to make Mr Virgo's earthy qualities flourish.

In the bedroom: Sexually, there won't be an easy connection between these two because neither gives themselves completely in this union. Their key to sexual compatibility is for both to let go of their fears and throw themselves into it when the lights go out.

♏ Ms Scorpio + Mr Libra ♎

Sign	Scorpio	Libra
Symbol	Scorpion	Scales
Ruler	Pluto	Venus
Type	Fixed	Cardinal
Element	Water	Air

Mr Libra will find Ms Scorpio initially alluring and erotic and will want to get to know this mysterious woman; however, she is a dark horse and will not want to give too much away. Mr Libra loves to talk and discuss all things, particularly his one-on-one relationship, something this girl is reluctant to do.

Air is all about communication and the water around Ms Scorpio runs still and deep, so this pair will have a problem relating. Ms Scorpio has a way of cornering her man and she will find the charming and personable Mr Libra initially attractive. He, on the other hand, is likely to find her intense and dominating manner quite intimidating and he might run for cover. The difficulties for this relationship lie in the fact that Mr Libra is a sociable and communicative beast and is also very attractive to the opposite sex, as well as his own. This will cause Ms Scorpio to erupt in the occasional jealous tirade. Mr Libra abhors such outbursts; he is after peace and tranquillity in his relationships and will view this behaviour as unjustified and unfair.

These two have very different personalities. The Libran man lacks the depth this passionate woman needs and he will not understand her demands and frustrations; and Ms Scorpio is too emotional and intense for this peace-loving, non-confrontational man. She is decisive and knows her own mind only too well. His inability to make up his mind will see her cast her spell elsewhere.

In the bedroom: The boudoir is the best room in the house for these two. And if they can spend their entire life behind closed doors, their relationship might just stand a chance.

♏ Ms Scorpio + Mr Scorpio ♏

Sign	Scorpio	Scorpio
Symbol	Scorpion	Scorpion
Ruler	Pluto	Pluto
Type	Fixed	Fixed
Element	Water	Water

This relationship is driven by an abundance of passion and volatility. Both desire physical and emotional intimacy, which is fine; however, the intensity with which these two operate can be explosive and, with both coming from a place of possessiveness, issues of trust and commitment might pose a problem. Jealousies can often undermine this union.

Mr and Ms Scorpio don't give too much away and because both are the brooding silent types, neither will be prepared to be the first to communicate their feelings and dissatisfaction. As fixed signs, they are stubborn and single-minded in their approach to each other, never bowing under pressure and remaining absolute in their resolve to be the stronger in the relationship.

On the plus side, they find each other irresistibly attractive and can read each other's mind. Both find superficiality uncomfortable but will gravitate towards forming a deep and meaningful shared bond. They will share the same passion for a relationship and their obsessive quality will be respected rather than misunderstood.

The common denominator for this Scorpio pairing is their need for love, approval and respect. They know exactly want they want from each other and can identify with their partner's insecurities and hang-ups. They often share the same childhood wounds, giving them a clearer insight into each other's motives and needs. Mr and Ms Scorpio can help each other move closer towards their true aspirations and will attain a more fulfilling life and partnership into the bargain.

In the bedroom: Sex, sex and more sex! This couple are gifted in the art of lovemaking and with matching libidos they will soar to great heights of passion. Sex is merely a tool for them to transcend to a higher plane of unity.

♏ Ms Scorpio + Mr Sagittarius ♐

Sign	Scorpio	Sagittarius
Symbol	Scorpion	Archer
Ruler	Pluto	Jupiter
Type	Fixed	Mutable
Element	Water	Fire

Initially Ms Scorpio will find this man a challenge. He is everything she's not – outgoing, open and communicative. She is closed, secretive and guarded, while he has the proverbial foot-in-mouth disease. She is a careful deliberator of words and actions and needs a mate she can control and obsess over, whereas he is the optimistic, gregarious guy who cannot stand emotional confinement. What do these two have in common? The one thing that connects them is a fascination for their differences. Both come from vastly different perspectives yet they secretly admire each other's qualities.

A relationship might prove too difficult in the long run but they could have a lot of fun for a while, given that they both have a strong sex drive and find each other physically attractive. Although Mr Sagittarius doesn't have the same physical intensity as his Scorpio mate, he enjoys the conquest. She would be an alluring partner who would keep her man guessing. She is likely to be too controlling, jealous and obsessive for the independent archer, since he is a free-wheeler who needs his space.

Ultimately, this woman will be too much trouble for the simple Sag male who wants to have a beer with his mates or fly his hang-glider over a canyon. She finds his lack of commitment and his philandering ways too burdensome. The archer is a free spirit who fears being trapped by a controlling and suffocating woman. She wants only to be loved, yet she is often misunderstood by the fire types, who lack the patience to let her true colours shine through. Her water would dampen the fire spirit of this man and eventually put out the flame of passion. He would simply cause her too much grief.

In the bedroom: Both seek intensity beyond the pure physical pleasure, so this will be an uplifting experience for them both. Fire and water blend well in the bedroom. Mr Sagittarius craves this sensation-oriented woman with whom he will fall in love. Lust equates to love in his eyes, and that gets him every time.

♏ Ms Scorpio + Mr Capricorn ♑

Sign	Scorpio	Capricorn
Symbol	Scorpion	Goat
Ruler	Pluto	Saturn
Type	Fixed	Cardinal
Element	Water	Earth

This partnership has an affinity and is considered one of the best combinations of the earth and water signs. Ms Scorpio and Mr Capricorn seem to bring out the positive qualities in each other. Both take their relationship seriously and won't waste time making their intentions known. They won't play games with each other because both are into truth and integrity and will respect the other's values and viewpoints. The only catch here is that the Capricornian man is a pragmatist and, because Ms Scorpio needs a certain amount of intensity in her relationships, the goat might appear too aloof or detached for this sensitive creature. Her emotional senses are strong and his err on the side of insensitivity.

Power preoccupies them both. It gives her some validation as a woman and he likes the power that comes with prestige. Both view success as a powerful tool.

Ms Scorpio can be of great assistance to her man with her loyal and committed demeanour and will be only too happy to stand by him in all situations. Never fire up a Scorpio woman or question her motives, especially when it comes to those she loves. She has a rather nasty sting that may take hours to heal. Mr Capricorn will value her single-minded drive and support. These two can fly high together in more ways than one; they are passionate and intense in different ways, yet still have a desire to merge and enjoy a long and satisfying union.

In the bedroom: Any problems these two have will get ironed out in the bedroom. Mr Capricorn is only too happy to be stung by the venom of this passionate lady and, with both sharing a similar intensity in their lovemaking, Ms Scorpio will always be waiting for her Billy Goat Gruff!

♏ Ms Scorpio + Mr Aquarius ♒

Sign	Scorpio	Aquarius
Symbol	Scorpion	Water bearer
Ruler	Pluto	Uranus
Type	Fixed	Fixed
Element	Water	Air

Ms Scorpio will find this elusive man too detached and indifferent for her. Air signs appear cold and impersonal in their intimate relationships and Ms Scorpio is a woman who thrives on emotional and physical intimacy. She needs to feel appreciated and very much acknowledged, and her Aquarian man will not have the awareness and intensity she requires to feel secure in the relationship.

The water bearer is often unpredictable and unconventional; he needs a partner who lets him do his own thing rather than confining him. And it is unlikely to be Ms Scorpio. She is a control freak and won't be at all comfortable to see her man pursuing universal love instead of concentrating all his love and attention on her. Her need for a relationship is far greater than his and she may feel his detachment hurtful and unsympathetic.

Both these signs are fixed elements, so a certain degree of stubbornness and wilfulness will creep into this relationship. Who will be the one to compromise? Ms Scorpio and Mr Aquarius are strongly opinionated people and will rarely concede that they are in the wrong. Because they have firmly entrenched personalities, they rarely make allowances for the differences of others.

Ms Scorpio is too sensual and passionate for Mr Aquarius, who is intimidated by her sexual prowess and would rather have a playful companion with whom he can carry on a conversation than a partner who stretches him emotionally. He comes from an intellectual perspective and she comes from an emotional standpoint.

In the bedroom: Although their libidos are quite different, Ms Scorpio's innate ability to turn him on will excite Mr Aquarius, who is open to all things new, especially when it comes to sex! He loves to experiment and learn new tricks and couldn't ask for a better teacher than Ms Scorpio. The bedroom is where this pair will leave their differences at the door and get to have the most fun together.

♏ Ms Scorpio + Mr Pisces ♓

Sign	Scorpio	Pisces
Symbol	Scorpion	Fish
Ruler	Pluto	Neptune
Type	Fixed	Mutable
Element	Water	Water

This woman and man come together harmoniously, especially as both share water elements that contain the same deep, sensitive and intuitive qualities. Water has no boundaries, so this couple will be constantly overflowing with passion and feeling.

Mr Pisces is perhaps the nurturer in this union and will temper his Scorpio woman when she gets up to her stinging and controlling ways; she, in turn, will be a willing ear to his emotional hang-ups and escapist tendencies. The water signs tend to be emotionally sensitive and vulnerable people and are reluctant to express their intimate feelings. At the outset, the crab and the fish might dance around each other for a while to build up a protective wall. When at last they feel secure, it will be a union of substance.

They are both interested in some form of spiritual development and growth, which is where the fish can teach his woman a thing or two about the aesthetic side of life. Ms Scorpio, on the other hand, can encourage him to develop his creative and intuitive side. These two have well-developed instincts, allowing them to tap into each other's minds. And although Mr Pisces may lose his way on occasions – he is well known for his escapist tendencies – Ms Scorpio will always save him from a sea of confusion. She is a master analyst who can bring this man to his senses. The fixed and rigid partner in this relationship, she will always be one step ahead of this vulnerable man. He, in turn, will win her over with his sensitive and compassionate manner. The fish needs to feel a powerful connection with his woman, and who better to fit the role than the intense, magnetic Scorpio.

In the bedroom: Sex between the Piscean man and Scorpio woman will be more then just a physical expression of their love for each other. She will be moved to find that she's found a mate who understands her needs on a deeper and spiritual level.

Celebrity Ms Scorpio: Julia Roberts

Actor, born 12.16 am 28 October 1967 in Atlanta, Georgia, USA

Personal planets: Sun in Scorpio
                   Moon in Leo
                   Mercury in Scorpio
                   Venus in Virgo
                   Mars in Capricorn

I believe that two people are connected at the heart and it doesn't matter what you do, or who you are or where you live; there are no boundaries or barriers if two people are destined to be together.

– Julia Roberts

In *Pretty Woman*, the film that really made her a household name, Julia Roberts portrayed a prostitute who falls in love with her handsome and eligible client, and they live happily ever after. Roberts's character, Vivian Ward, resembles the actor's own personality, yet it has taken the star some time to find her Prince Charming. The 'happily ever after' ending might be true now, but she has kissed plenty of frogs along the way.

Roberts is a true Scorpio, with the passion and intensity that is synonymous with this deeply emotional and sensitive sign. She stands no nonsense from her man and demands his respect. She needs to be in control and does not allow her mate to see her insecurities and vulnerabilities. Her chart points to a strong earth element, which indicates she is a self-sufficient woman who doesn't need a mate to provide her with financial and emotional security. Her love needs are strong; however, she will never compromise herself if her relationship proves to be unsatisfying and will seek new frontiers where she can express her rich imagination and feel valued. Sometimes this realisation comes at the speed of light, which will see her end unions that are unsuitable. Her Venus in the sign of Virgo would make her quite discriminating in her choice of a partner.

Roberts's relationships have been with men who are earth, fire and air signs but rarely the water element, indicating her predisposition for thinking and aspiring personas. She likes earthy, sensation-oriented men and is not attracted to the type of man who is sensitive, intense and emotionally vulnerable, and usually representative of water signs like herself. Perhaps her own Scorpio energy compensates for this. She might have enough of these qualities so she doesn't need to take on the challenges that come with these emotions.

Her former fiancée, Kiefer Sutherland, is a Sagittarius, which is compatible with Roberts's Moon sign in Leo. Both are fire elements, which would have given the relationship a spark and a strong physical attraction. Each would have felt inspired by the other's creative streak and abilities. Sutherland would always have felt protective and sympathetic towards her, yet would have acknowledged her self-assurance and her ability to have fun. This is always an important ingredient for keeping the fire energy alive and happy.

Another of Roberts's beaus, Gemini Jason Patric, would have made her feel very comfortable. And although he would have satisfied her communicative needs and stimulated her mind, their Sun signs ultimately came from different perspectives. Roberts would have found his Gemini ways too impersonal and non-committal, while he would have found her Scorpio energy fascinating, yet too controlling.

Her current marriage to Aquarian Danny Moder, an air sign with a strong water composition in his chart, shows how Roberts can now face up to the more powerful aspects of her mate, which refect her own intensities. She will relish in the passion and depth that this union holds, rather than wanting to control the relationship in true Scorpio mode. She has met her match with a man who shares her passion to regenerate and transform their union into a lasting bond.

Mr Scorpio – an overview

Mr Scorpio is man of contrasts. As a water sign, he has a sensitive and vulnerable side to his nature, yet his personality also contains an angry and aggressive quality. This man can be charming and passionate one minute, yet, if he's under threat, can turn around completely to expose a ruthless, unforgiving and hostile persona. This duplicity results in the Scorpio man having relationship problems because he will never admit guilt. He is often considered the most complex sign of the zodiac, the dark, silent and brooding type who gives nothing away, yet will want to extract every pound of flesh from his mate. It is so important for him to maintain control in his relationships that his behaviour can be completely unreasonable at times.

This man craves emotional and physical intimacy and will use his skills in the bedroom with great tactile ability. Each manoeuvre is carefully planned and orchestrated to combat his own insecurities and vulnerabilities, leading him to take charge for proceedings. When he feels he has won, he will pull back, leaving his partner craving more of his sensual delights. His art of seduction leaves the other signs for dead. It is no wonder he has the reputation for being the most sexual of all signs. Sex for Mr Scorpio needs to be a transformative experience rather than just a physically gratifying act and it is viewed as a prelude to a more intense and emotional bonding that transcends the physical plane.

This man enjoys a woman who appreciates a deep and intense connection and, when he finds a mate that shares his passion, he is a devoted and consistent lover. There can be no middle of the road with this man; he wants all or nothing. His partner must be committed emotionally, spiritually and sexually.

The Scorpio man has exceptional intuitive skills and can tap into his partner's mind with ease, sensing what she needs from him. He is attracted to the elusive type who provides him with a challenge, but he will not stand for a flirtatious woman. He has a jealous streak that can turn his sharp tongue into a dangerous sting, inflicting severe emotional pain on his victim. However, beneath this smokescreen of dominating and manipulative behaviours lies a vulnerable man who really wants just to love and be loved in return.

Famous Scorpio men

* Bill Gates
  (founder of Microsoft)
* Art Garfunkel and
  Paul Simon (musicians)
* Ethan Hawke (actor)

* Auguste Rodin (sculptor)
* Pablo Picasso (artist)
* Theodore Roosevelt
  (US president)

Combinations

♏ Mr Scorpio + Ms Aries ♈

Sign	Scorpio	Aries
Symbol	Scorpion	Ram
Ruler	Pluto	Mars
Type	Fixed	Cardinal
Element	Water	Fire

Ms Aries will be attracted to the deep, sensual nature of Mr Scorpio, making this union overflow with all the trimmings of a passionate love affair. But the security-craving Scorpio may become too intense for the easy-going Arian woman, who will find herself drowning in a sea of emotions – his that is!

Mr Scorpio is secretive and non-trusting by nature, which is the opposite of the trusting, direct and open Arian woman. She will have no qualms about telling him what she thinks but will find it frustrating that he doesn't share the same frankness with her. He will have a lot of time for her spunk and get-up-and-go attitude, but his need for emotional closeness will make her jumpy.

Ms Aries is fairly down-to-earth, simple and spontaneous, while her Scorpio lover is a far more complex character. His brooding, jealous and controlling nature will suffocate Ms Aries, who doesn't have the energy or inclination to fight a losing battle. She is an impulsive and independent woman and he's much more secretive and anti-social.

In the bedroom: Slowly the sparks will fly but not for long in the bedroom. Ms Aries will pack her bags and head to greener pastures where she will feel free from the ever-present constraints of the sexually charged Mr Scorpio.

♏ Mr Scorpio + Ms Taurus ♉

Sign	Scorpio	Taurus
Symbol	Scorpion	Bull
Ruler	Pluto	Venus
Type	Fixed	Fixed
Element	Water	Earth

Passion will ignite this pair because they both share a deep level of commitment, loyalty and security, and both are also extremely possessive. Fundamentally they are compatible; however, Ms Taurus is less complicated and less intense than Mr Scorpio, who will at times try to manipulate her good nature. He is too demanding and has a tendency to play power games in his relationships, whereas the single-minded bull, who is fiercely loyal, has a less-controlling nature.

Although both will show a strong sense of commitment in the relationship, Ms Taurus will at times become overwhelmed by Mr Scorpio's nasty sting and his power games. Sexually they can complement each other because they are both strong, sensual beings.

Ms Taurus will have no qualms about standing up for herself, which is where the union may fall apart, because the scorpion's temperament is unrelenting – rarely will he make the first move to back down in a dispute. If they can temper their combative streaks and enjoy the sensuality the relationship has to offer, the compatible bull and the scorpion can be very happy together. Both have a faithful nature and, when committed, will be staunch companions. Ms Taurus will make her mate feel secure and nurtured, which is comforting for the secretive and suspicious Scorpio, who might have suffered rejection in his childhood and is looking for guarantees in life. This is something his Taurean mate can provide.

In the bedroom: There'll be a strong physical chemistry between these two. The Scorpio man will enjoy his Taurean girl's possessive nature and she'll understand the deep-seated passion that burns deep within him.

♏ Mr Scorpio + Ms Gemini ♊

Sign	Scorpio	Gemini
Symbol	Scorpion	Twins
Ruler	Pluto	Mercury
Type	Fixed	Mutable
Element	Water	Air

Mr Scorpio is too deep and intense for the light-hearted Ms Gemini, who loves to spread her wings like a butterfly, flitting from one place to another, spreading her light and captivating audiences along the way. He will start to brood and become insanely jealous, because he doesn't understand the flighty ways of the ever-changing Gemini lass. He needs her in his corner, under his thumb, where he can control her movements and keep a watchful eye over his possession. But Ms Gemini will never allow any man to control her impulsive ways; she can't be tamed and the more her Scorpio mate tries to hold on to her, the more elusive she will become, until she has vanished completely.

Mr Scorpio is a fixed water sign, so his inflexible attitude will create tension in this union. He will find that Ms Gemini is too interested in her own world and will not give him the attention he so desperately craves to feel wanted and desired. This man is a passionate being and needs depth and intensity in all his undertakings, especially in his relationships. He is guided by a keen sense of intuition and will be put off by Ms Gemini's flirtatious yet harmless ways. Because Mr Scorpio is so untrusting, he will never really believe what she has to say, and he could well be right, as she can be very fickle and a true chameleon.

Mr Scorpio needs a lady that he can smother with love but Ms Gemini will find this claustrophobic and uncomfortable – this girl needs loads of space as well as variety.

In the bedroom: Sex to a Scorpio is the meaning of life itself, but to a Gemini woman it's simply one of life's little pleasures. She is likely to find her Scorpio lover far too absorbed and serious about sex. She might find her mind wandering off into the ether during their lovemaking.

♏ Mr Scorpio + Ms Cancer ♋

Sign	Scorpio	Cancer
Symbol	Scorpion	Crab
Ruler	Pluto	Moon
Type	Fixed	Cardinal
Element	Water	Water

These water signs have a natural affinity with each other. Mr Scorpio and Ms Cancer are both passionate creatures, which will result in them forming an intense relationship. They share a particularly sensual energy that tends to highlight their union. However, because Cancerians and Scorpios can overwhelm each other emotionally, they need to recognise that if they don't pull back on occasions, they will be drowned in a sea of emotions.

Because this pair has experienced some emotional discontent in their early years, they can be guarded and self-protective in their relationships. The cardinal Cancerian, however, can initiate well and will be the instigator in trying to bring the secretive Scorpio out of his shell. Mr Scorpio is controlling because he is mistrusting of those close to him, but it will be Ms Cancer's gentle and non-aggressive approach that will coax him into being more open and honest with her.

Mr Scorpio's planetary ruler is Pluto; hence he needs to feel in control of his relationship. His behaviour and attitude will match the equally intense persona of his Cancerian partner. Although they have different ways of dealing with their emotions, she views his intensity as a reassurance of how he feels. Given their similarities, this union has all the hallmarks of success.

In the bedroom: If these two understand what each other needs, there'll be no limit to the sexual heights they can reach. As long as there are no ripples in the water, they will meld as one and drown in a sea of passion.

♏ Mr Scorpio + Ms Leo ♌

Sign	Scorpio	Leo
Symbol	Scorpion	Lion
Ruler	Pluto	Sun
Type	Fixed	Fixed
Element	Water	Fire

Challenging aspects in this union will doom this pair to constant power struggles. Ms Leo is a fire sign, which surfaces in her strong, freedom-loving and idealistic streak. This girl doesn't like to be controlled and Mr Scorpio will try to manipulate her into following his desired course of action – usually to no avail. Leo and Scorpio are both fixed signs; they are stubborn and neither is likely to compromise or readily give in to the other.

The planetary ruler of Ms Leo is the Sun, giving her an open, generous and brightly shining demeanour. This is in opposition to Mr Scorpio's Plutonic energy, which makes him more secretive, jealous and manipulative, and is exhibited in his intense and controlling manner. The lioness wants to be free and independent, and her constant string of admirers will cause her Scorpio mate much grief. His energy will be too dark and draining for the lioness, who much prefers to be out and about, lapping up attention from her adoring fans rather than being stuck in a relationship with a brooding, control-freak.

Ms Leo can be egotistical at times and needs constant admiration and respect from people around her. Mr Scorpio will fight a losing battle against his lover's incessant need for the limelight.

In the bedroom: Initially an intense, physical attraction can ignite these two, but Mr Scorpio's overwhelming need to possess her will stifle Ms Leo's self-expression. None of the trickery Mr Scorpio uses so successfully on some of the other women of the zodiac will work on the lioness, who is rarely tempted out of the den, since she can see through his slippery and sneaky facade.

♏ Mr Scorpio + Ms Virgo ♍

Sign	Scorpio	Virgo
Symbol	Scorpion	Virgin
Ruler	Pluto	Mercury
Type	Fixed	Mutable
Element	Water	Earth

Both Mr Scorpio and Ms Virgo have sharp tongues and will not hold back on finding fault or criticising each other. This attitude works in the negative: Mr Scorpio seems to undermine Ms Virgo's sense of self-confidence and he is too insecure to be able to handle her nit-picking and criticisms.

These two signs are too uptight for each other and the fixed energy of Mr Scorpio will rarely give in to the demands of Ms Virgo. There's a judgmental quality in this union that tends to put pressure on the relationship from time to time. Although they are both fiercely loyal and committed individuals, Ms Virgo will feel that the over-protective, possessive and controlling attitude of Mr Scorpio is too demeaning, and she will sense his mistrust.

She is an open book and will always be upfront in her dealings with people. On the other hand, Mr Scorpio is hidden and secretive and, although he might claim he is not dishonest, that is open to interpretation. As far as Ms Virgo is concerned, holding back information is a form of dishonesty. This couple doesn't tend to rush into love. They usually prefer a slower road to romance.

In the bedroom: Their sexual connection will rarely get off the ground. Mr Scorpio's persistent approach will be rebuffed and Ms Virgo will find this man too intense. But if these two can just learn to be themselves, their lovemaking will have no boundaries.

♏ Mr Scorpio + Ms Libra ♎

Sign	Scorpio	Libra
Symbol	Scorpion	Scales
Ruler	Pluto	Venus
Type	Fixed	Cardinal
Element	Water	Air

This combination will have all the typical conflicts that seem to dominate a union between an air girl and her water man. Ms Libra wants things to be light and uncomplicated and, above all, is after a strong line of communication with her partner. This deeply intense, complicated and secretive man, however, will be too moody for her. The Libran lady's physical beauty and alluring personality will dazzle Mr Scorpio, but will also intensify his insecurities and bring out his jealous streak.

She thrives on verbal exchanges and needs an open and honest man. Mr Scorpio seems to have a problem opening up to her. By doing so, he feels he is relinquishing control, so he will leave Ms Libra in the dark, which will seem totally unfair to her.

Water runs deep and the Scorpio man needs constant reassurance. This air lady seems too detached and emotionally cool for this passionate man. They come from different emotional planes and will not fit well together. Ms Libra will always want to keep the peace and will pretend all is well and happy, yet Mr Scorpio's penetrating mind will be able to deduce that this is not the case, which will lead to further complications.

In the bedroom: This man is known for his sexuality and has the capacity to turn most women on. Ms Libra is no exception. However, sex for the Scorpio man needs to combine the physical act with emotional intimacy – a problem for his Libran lover. She is too detached for this intense man, who will always be able to satisfy his mate, but will have the feeling that the scales are tipped more in her favour.

♏ Mr Scorpio + Ms Scorpio ♏

Sign	Scorpio	Scorpio
Symbol	Scorpion	Scorpion
Ruler	Pluto	Pluto
Type	Fixed	Fixed
Element	Water	Water

If this pair finds some middle ground, all will be fine and dandy. However, because both are Scorpios, they have the same qualities of intensity, jealously and need for control. There seems to be a thread of insecurity between these two that is disturbing. As fixed modes of expression, they will not grant each other enough slack to feel comfortable.

Much lies beneath the surface of this pairing and with neither opening up to the other, a web of mistrust and insecurity is created. Although they have the same physical, emotional and spiritual needs in a relationship, and are capable of transcending the limitations of their personalities, they will never give way – always needing to be the dominant one in this union. This can turn quickly into a stalemate where their underlying vindictiveness and sarcasm can emerge.

On the plus side, as always with a pairing of the same signs, there are familiar feelings that can be quite comforting and supportive, because the couple can empathise with each other. A union such as this can be very powerful, as well as challenging, and it can accelerate or degenerate quickly. The answer lies in how evolved these two are and what things life experience has taught them. Scorpios have the ability to overcome the most difficult of adversities and regenerate themselves – if they want to! Mr Scorpio and Ms Scorpio can generate the power and resolve to harness their energy to merge in a union that transcends all their difficulties – yet only they will know when the time is right.

In the bedroom: Sex, sex and more sex! This couple are gifted in the art of lovemaking and with matching libidos, they will soar to great heights of passion. Sex is merely a tool for them to transcend to a higher plane of unity.

♏ Mr Scorpio + Ms Sagittarius ♐

Sign	Scorpio	Sagittarius
Symbol	Scorpion	Archer
Ruler	Pluto	Jupiter
Type	Fixed	Mutable
Element	Water	Fire

Mr Scorpio will be immensely attracted to this 'simpatico' girl, who seems to breeze through life without a care in the world. He is the secretive type and finds it bewildering that she can be so open and communicative. She will be disarmed by Mr Scorpio's strong physical presence and his fixed gaze, which seems to penetrate her very core. Before long, however, this magnetic attraction will lose its pull and each will find the difference of their personalities a turn-off.

Mr Scorpio will feel threatened by the archer's elusive and flighty ways and if he starts to exert some control over her, she will want to flee. His brooding and moody stance will be foreign to the archer woman, who has an optimistic approach to life. She will always view life as being a cup that is half-full rather than half-empty. He will not tolerate her independent streak and lack of commitment. This girl needs to explore life free of restrictions and will be happy to go it alone if she has to. Mr Scorpio has to have a mate who feels as intensely as he does. He needs a total merging of mind, body and soul, which this woman cannot provide.

Water energy is intense and feelings run deep. As much as fire wants to share in the magic of love, Ms Sagittarius will always be too idealistic for this man who would love to tie a lead to her pretty little wrist and keep her close at all times. But, alas, this will only dull her flame even further.

In the bedroom: Mr Scorpio will admire and appreciate the enthusiasm with which the archer launches into sex. But this girl may be too forthright and outspoken for the sensitive Scorpio man. Her notorious foot-in-mouth blunders might spill over into the bedroom, fatally wounding the ego of her brooding lover.

♏ Mr Scorpio + Ms Capricorn ♑

Sign	Scorpio	Capricorn
Symbol	Scorpion	Goat
Ruler	Pluto	Saturn
Type	Fixed	Cardinal
Element	Water	Earth

These two will rarely take their relationship lightly. Initially there will be a bit of a stand-off while they sum each other up. Despite their initial fascination, they will need to test the waters before committing. Mr Scorpio and Ms Capricorn are not the gushy types. They will be slow to expose their inner feelings and express their emotions until they feel on safe ground. Mr Scorpio will be attracted to this female, who is on a mission to achieve emotional and economic security, and he will respect her strength and ambitious quality. Ms Capricorn is attracted to the strong and controlled disposition of this man, who will help her to achieve her goals. This is a dynamic duo and they will accomplish much in their relationship, largely because they are interested in the serious aspects of life rather than its frivolous and social side.

Mr Scorpio may brood and become moody on occasions when he feels his goat is too distant and not focused enough on him. He is emotionally challenged and needs to feel loved and acknowledged, and it will alarm him if he thinks his Capricornian love is too preoccupied with her own goals to express her need for him. It is easy for her to lose patience with the Scorpio's controlling and intense ways, and his reluctance to share his inner thoughts.

Ms Capricorn is the more emotionally detached of the two and it will take all the skills of the passionate Scorpio man to bring this woman to her knees. These two signs are the right mix to bring out the best in each other. With a bit of consideration and thought, it can be a highly successful union in all ways.

In the bedroom: Both have a strong sexual drive and Mr Scorpio has to live up to his reputation by never leaving his goat thinking it might be better down the track. He likes her to beg for more at every turn.

♏ Mr Scorpio + Ms Aquarius ♒

Sign	Scorpio	Aquarius
Symbol	Scorpion	Water bearer
Ruler	Pluto	Uranus
Type	Fixed	Fixed
Element	Water	Air

This man and woman are too different in their emotional makeup to become permanent lovers. Mr Scorpio is a man who craves emotional intensity and thrives on the highs and lows of a relationship where he is in control. The more complex it is, the more responsive he is. By comparison, Ms Aquarius is an idealistic, freedom-loving girl, who is more inclined to love her mates than become entangled in a complex tirade of emotions with this intense man.

Her detached and indifferent demeanour will create some discord between them and, because they are both fixed signs, neither will give in and nor will they be receptive to some compromise. Both Mr Scorpio and Ms Aquarius are stubborn and headstrong and will lock horns often. She will not stay in this relationship too long; her scream 'don't fence me in' will be heard far and wide. In turn, he will find that this woman doesn't understand his need for intimacy, commitment and stability. She wants to explore life free from restrictions, in her own time and in her own way. This will not suit Mr Scorpio who needs a woman by his side – or at least on a short leash that he can reel in when he so desires.

These two are on different wavelengths. He is possessive and controlling and is inclined to jealous outbursts, whereas she has a tendency to provoke him with her insensitive, detached demeanour. He is a private man and wants to be with her; she is a social creature, who wants to the save the world and will only fit him in when she wants to.

Air is detached and non-feeling; water is intense and emotional. She will find it hard to swim in this sea of emotion and will have to keep her head above water to survive this union.

In the bedroom: Ms Aquarius is more interested in discovering life on Mars than flying to the Moon and back with her Scorpio lover. He might take some time to float back down to reality after a romantic interlude, while she'll already be thinking about her next adventure.

♏ Mr Scorpio + Ms Pisces ♓

Sign	Scorpio	Pisces
Symbol	Scorpion	Fish
Ruler	Pluto	Neptune
Type	Fixed	Mutable
Element	Water	Water

These two will share a strong bond based on intuition and compassion. The water elements that bind them are a powerful force that gives a deep and intense quality to this relationship. Mr Scorpio and Ms Pisces are aware of each other's shortcomings, yet will be tolerant and supportive of them.

The fish will often make the sacrifices in this relationship because she is the softer and more submissive of the two. She can be seduced by this man because she has a tendency to view her relationships through rose-coloured glasses. She needs a strong man who can anchor her emotionally, and no man could do it as efficiently as Mr Scorpio, who is the master of control.

Ms Pisces will value this man's attention and interest in her. She needs validation and Mr Scorpio will cherish her devotion and selfless love. Both are inclined, at times, to repress their emotions and will need to keep their channels of communication open if they want to feel secure with each other.

Water signs are complex creatures who doubt their self-worth yet, in time, they can learn to trust each other with their love. This can be a mystical union because both can conjure the intrigue that is characteristic of their signs. They share a desire to turn their union into a purposeful relationship that transcends all boundaries. If Mr Scorpio can hang on to his fish and not let her swim downstream to escape to the underworld – where she may indulge in sex, drugs and rock'n'roll – these two are looking at a long and successful union.

In the bedroom: Sex will be an all-consuming experience when the fish and scorpion unite. It will be a melding of the mind, body and spirit in a sea of emotions.

Celebrity Mr Scorpio: Prince Charles

British royal, born 9.14 pm 14 November 1948 in London, England

```
Personal planets:  Sun in Scorpio
                   Moon in Taurus
                   Mercury in Scorpio
                   Venus in Libra
                   Mars in Sagittarius
```

Do you seriously expect me to be the first Prince of Wales not to have a mistress?

– Prince Charles

Prince Charles's ruling planet is Pluto, which rules rebirth and transformation. As such, his life, like a phoenix, has seen him rise like from the ashes to be reborn and survive the many adversities he has had to face.

His Scorpio Sun represents his strong-willed and fixed nature, coupled with intensity and a passion-fuelled persona. He is a man who needs intimacy and love, and his desire for emotional intensity is characteristic of a childhood lacking in physical and emotional bonding. Prince Charles is fearful of emotional rejection and so has a tendency to withhold his true feelings to avoid feeling exposed and vulnerable. This quality is often misunderstood, seen instead as a form of secrecy and control. Many Scorpios need to learn to trust and share their true feelings with the people they love so they can move forward and flourish in a relationship.

His chart indicates he has a balanced outlook on life and values justice and equality in his partnerships. His Venus in the sign of Libra makes him someone who needs to share his life with another who is also interested in peace and harmony. His Mars in the sign of Sagittarius gives him a love of adventure and strong moral beliefs. He needs a mate who shares his passion and interest, yet someone who will allow him room to move.

His first marriage to Diana Spencer, a Cancerian, was a complex affair, although they both shared some very strong affinities in their charts. Her water Sun sign was in harmony with his Scorpio Sun yet, as water signs, they both tended to bottle up their feelings, too afraid to share and be open and trusting with each other. She felt vulnerable and rejected because of Charles's inability to express his intimate thoughts and feelings; he, in turn, felt misunderstood, resulting in hostility on both sides.

His relationship and subsequent marriage to Camilla Parker-Bowles, who is also a Cancerian, is supported by their mutual interests and their compatible Moon signs. These are important ingredients for endurance and emotional compatibility. He has a Taurus Moon, which makes him hanker after a secure, comfortable relationship with plenty of nurturing, and Camilla's Moon in Cancer means she can supply her prince with the loving and support he desires. Her strong loyal streak contributes to Charles's sense of confidence, allowing him to be open with his emotions and willing to share his feelings and needs with her. Their relationship has stood the test of time and shows how the crab and the scorpion are able to build a happy long-term future together.

SAGITTARIUS (23 November–21 December)

Ruled by the planet Jupiter
Fire sign
Mutable
Masculine energy

In general ...

The Sagittarian is represented in the zodiac as a centaur – a half-man, half-horse, an archer who aims his arrow towards the sky in search of new frontiers and conquests. His mission is to keep moving, to look for his next adventure, in order to broaden his mind and find greener pastures. The archer's journey is always more fun than arriving at his destination.

Sagittarians, who are honest gypsies at heart, greatly value their independence and freedom. They are always in search of the ideal philosophical pursuit and have a preoccupation with travel, especially for the knowledge gained through the journey. Above all else is their need to feel passionate about something which, more often than, involves a project that gives their life a purpose rather than a relationship.

However, Sagittarians are infectious and easy-going personalities, and have their fair share of fun and excitement with their lovers. They have a positive and opened-minded attitude towards most things, yet live by a strong moral code and value fairness and justice. Considered the 'lucky' sign of the zodiac, things just seem to fall in place for them. It is as if they have their own guardian angel watching over them as they breeze through life and relationships, seemingly without a care.

Sagittarians are extremely attractive to the opposite sex, mainly because of their open and honest approach. But what you see is what you get. They are definitely not the mysterious and silent types. Although well received for the most part, the one thing that seems to get them into trouble is their candour. They share their own secrets so openly and are so frank that they can't understand why everyone is not like them. They expect the same traits in their mates and are disappointed when they are let down. Not everyone is as trusting and willing to expose themselves as they are.

Sagittarians are known for their honesty and are noted for their foot-in-mouth blunders. When accused of being hurtful and lacking tact, they will be quite offended. Sagittarians are not malicious but rather naive.

A relationship with a Sagittarian is usually based on friendship and camaraderie and, as long as there is plenty of fun and variety along the way, it will be an enjoyable experience on the merry-go-round of life.

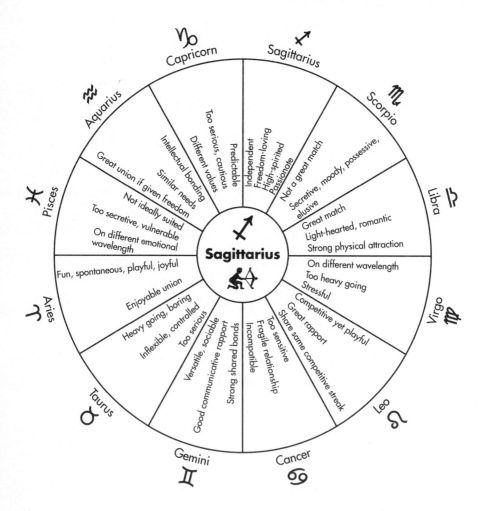

How a Sagittarian personality might match up with other star signs

Ms Sagittarius - an overview

Ms Sagittarius is often seen as one of the boys. She has a streak of tomboy in her, which makes her a wonderful playmate for many in the zodiac. Her love of fun and adventure will give her a reputation of being a passionate lover of life. Like Mr Sagittarius, she dislikes any sort of confinement and will feel uncomfortable if her man doesn't grant her the space and independence she needs.

The Sagittarian girl is idealistic when it comes to relationships, always believing at the start that she has met the man of her dreams. Then the relationship becomes too predictable and mundane, at which point she will feel hemmed in and panic. This woman is a straight shooter who doesn't think before she speaks, and her blunt approach is often a wounding experience for those on the receiving end. Her arrow can often pierce the heart of a faint-hearted male, who is desperate to have this charismatic lady by his side. If he can stand the truth and be reminded of his failings, he stands a chance in this relationship.

Ms Sagittarius is also a woman who is open to learning. She is the eternal student, so she needs a mate to share her love of travel and philosophy and to help her broaden her horizons. She is happiest pounding the pavement, in her joggers or bareback on a horse, but she is not the domestic goddess that some men require. This girl is not into pretence and glamour and will always be more receptive to the simple pleasures in life. She is the eternal optimist who views life from a broad perspective.

Sagittarius is a mutable sign, so this girl is especially adaptable and can fit well into most social scenarios. However, if you want to win her heart, the less complex approach the better. Sit her under the stars, break open the bottle and whisper words of wisdom in her ears, and she will tumble into your arms.

Famous Sagittarian women

* Jane Austen (writer)
* Dionne Warwicke (singer)
* Margaret Mead (anthropologist)
* Tina Turner (singer)
* Bette Midler (singer/actor)
* Jane Fonda (actor/activist)

Combinations

♐ Ms Sagittarius + Mr Aries ♈

Sign	Sagittarius	Aries
Symbol	Archer	Ram
Ruler	Jupiter	Mars
Type	Mutable	Cardinal
Element	Fire	Fire

Both these signs enjoy freedom, independence and sporting pursuits. Because the ram and the archer are enthusiastic about life's pleasures, they will relish a relationship that gives them the freedom and space they need. These fire signs are open and honest with each other – what you see is often what you get, which can be a carefree combination of frivolity, playfulness and spontaneity. Both are very open-minded and will be honest about what they need from a relationship.

The archer's thirst for knowledge and her itchy feet for greener pastures keep her Arian lover on his toes. She loves adventure and will never let the grass grow under her feet, a vitality particularly attractive to Mr Aries. He likes that his partner has an open-mind and a non-judgmental view of the world, which he can share.

Mutual understanding between these signs is strong; they don't like boundaries in their relationships. Mr Aries and Ms Sagittarius live in the moment, sometimes with little regard for tomorrow. Both have a tendency to rush headlong into any situation, so there is little room for peace and quiet in this union. But, as fire signs, they love the idea of being in love and might quite easily end up walking down the aisle.

In the bedroom: As lovers, the sparks can fly because the archer and ram are both highly sexed and adventurous in the bedroom. There will be no stopping the bedroom antics of these two fire signs!

♐ Ms Sagittarius + Mr Taurus ♉

Sign	Sagittarius	Taurus
Symbol	Archer	Bull
Ruler	Jupiter	Venus
Type	Mutable	Fixed
Element	Fire	Earth

The key words for Ms Sagittarius are growth and idealism. She is the optimist of the zodiac and the adventurer who craves knowledge – always looking to spread her wings and travel to greener pastures. Mr Taurus will not find this conducive to the type of relationship he desires, which is steadfast, predictable and conservative. She will find him too limiting and boring and, although she will be appreciative of his grounding influence on occasions, in the long run she will see it as a form of control and restriction. Because Ms Sagittarius values her freedom above all else, she will feel like a caged animal while her Taurean mate, resentful of her ability to soar, will try to clip her wings.

This is not a good mix, as the fiery Sagittarian does not want to be grounded; she needs excitement and is not interested in the same material trappings as her Taurean man, who loves material security and comfort. Ultimately these two are likely to head in different directions, but if Mr Taurus is willing to give Ms Sagittarius some space, she will come home from her adventures to recuperate and enjoy the home fires and cosy environment he has created. If things don't fall into place for the security-loving Mr Taurus, he will eventually stamp his hoof and demand an end to this lopsided union.

In the bedroom: The initial sexual chemistry will be strong between the earth man and fire woman. He'll love her raw sex appeal and animal instinct and he'll make her feel complete.

♐ Ms Sagittarius + Mr Gemini ♊

Sign	Sagittarius	Gemini
Symbol	Archer	Twins
Ruler	Jupiter	Mercury
Type	Mutable	Mutable
Element	Fire	Air

Sparks are likely to fly when Mr Gemini and Ms Sagittarius lay eyes on each other. Both mutable signs, their air and fire elements blend well together and both are freedom- and adventure-loving souls. Neither likes to keep the home fires burning and both prefer relationships free from boundaries and constraints.

These independent souls will enjoy a spontaneous and exciting relationship with excellent communication. Mr Gemini can often be insincere, plying a potential love partner with falsehoods in order to win her heart. But the confident and feisty Ms Sagittarius will rarely buy into this barrage of bulldust. Instead, if she can rely on what is revealed in his eyes, she will find the truth.

Jealousy will not be an issue for either sign, particularly Ms Sagittarius, who has a huge collection of friends and acquaintances she likes to spend time with. Mr Gemini has much to gain from his archer mate, who has a strong thirst for knowledge and an equally strong desire to share it with those willing to learn.

Astrologically, these signs are in opposition to one another, but this can ignite a magical pull between them. If Mr Gemini can evolve into a more caring and sympathetic soul, then his Sagittarian love might just be able to commit long term to this perennial player.

In the bedroom: These two have a tendency to use ploys to evoke jealousy in each other that often leads them to engage in plenty of makeup sex. Neither makes a particularly loyal partner, often attracted to new and exciting adventures.

⚹ Ms Sagittarius + Mr Cancer ♋

Sign	Sagittarius	Cancer
Symbol	Archer	Crab
Ruler	Jupiter	Moon
Type	Mutable	Cardinal
Element	Fire	Water

Mr Cancer will be far too introverted for the outgoing and adventurous Ms Sagittarius, who prefers a relationship that allows her plenty of freedom and space. Most of the astrological signs respect and admire the Sagittarian energy and Mr Cancer is no exception. He will find this girl uplifting and positive; she will rarely display the same intensity and moodiness that afflicts him.

These signs have very different needs from a relationship. The sensitive crab will seek a mate who can give him security, loyalty and an inner sense of peace, whereas the zany Sagittarian 'foot-in-mouth' miss will be too loud, brash and tactless for him. He relishes in home delights and would much rather snuggle up than take up her offer of any boisterous or daring escapades. Although of a gentle nature, he is not that timid that he can't rise to the challenge when he wants to.

But it is her inability to commit that frustrates this man more than anything else. He likes certainties and guarantees and, because he is ruled by the Moon, he is an exceptionally nurturing partner. On the other hand, Ms Sagittarius is ruled by the planet Jupiter, which makes her crave many experiences and things in abundances. Even though Mr Cancer might find a relationship with this happy-go-lucky, fun girl rather exciting at the outset, ultimately he will be too possessive to make a permanent go of this union.

In the bedroom: If blended correctly water and fire can create a simmering sexual union. The crab will be enchanted by his fiery, physical lover and Ms Sagittarius will be equally captivated by her deep and mysterious man.

♐ Ms Sagittarius + Mr Leo ♌

Sign	Sagittarius	Leo
Symbol	Archer	Lion
Ruler	Jupiter	Sun
Type	Mutable	Fixed
Element	Fire	Fire

The planetary rulers of Leo and Sagittarius – the Sun and Jupiter, respectively – are all about living life to the fullest. The two fire signs crave excitement and will stop at nothing to expand their horizons and fulfil their need to express their fiery, dynamic energies. Fire signs need an outlet for their overflowing creative energy, and this can come in the form of an inspiring relationship where two people can express their mutual desires without compromising their individuality.

Both Mr Leo and Ms Sagittarius are exceptionally physical beings; he's especially masculine, and she will always find a strong, well-built and confident man appealing. The lion, in turn, will find an athletic physique and shapely thighs a huge turn-on. But if the archer is too independent, her lion will become disheartened with her perceived lack of attention and commitment to him.

Ms Sagittarius is a woman who needs to respect her partner and feel protected, and the proud and regal Mr Leo will be an ideal mate for her. But his sometimes controlling and demanding demeanour can irritate the freedom-loving Ms Sagittarius, who values her independence and will fight fiercely to hang on to it. Even though these fire signs have a natural affinity, they also have a competitive streak that can dampen the Sagittarian's enthusiasm for her Leo lover.

In the bedroom: These two will enjoy a good romp under the covers! Both possess a strong physical energy and can horse around for hours.

♐ Ms Sagittarius + Mr Virgo ♍

Sign	Sagittarius	Virgo
Symbol	Archer	Virgin
Ruler	Jupiter	Mercury
Type	Mutable	Mutable
Element	Fire	Earth

To begin with, this union can seem quite compatible because both the Virgoan male and Sagittarian female share mutual interests – especially a desire for sport and outdoor pursuits. However, Mr Virgo is a perfectionist, so it won't be good enough for him to throw the tent in the backseat and head off to unknown adventures. He would rather spend time on making sure the pegs and other attachments are neatly packed into their box. That seems to sum up the fundamental difference between these two. Mr Virgo is a man who uses his discriminatory powers to the letter and near enough is not good enough for him. Ms Sagittarius, however, has already moved on to the next adventure, not bothering to count the number of pegs in the box.

She is an idealist and he a realist who defines his world in neat compartments. Conversely, Ms Sagittarius will always have a Utopian view of her universe and will be disappointed by this man's analytical and, at times, critical nature. For her, the journey is often more exciting than arriving at her destination and the more opportunities she has to fill her mind with the wonders of the world, the happier she will be. Mr Virgo will find this energy too frenetic and unsettling, despite the fact that he is an active participant in life. Everything he does needs to be checked out beforehand, so rarely will they be at the same place at the same time.

In the bedroom: Ms Sagittarius may be too spontaneous and boisterous for this methodical and practical earthy man. Sadly, there might not be much room for any 'hanky panky'.

♐ Ms Sagittarius + Mr Libra ♎

Sign	Sagittarius	Libra
Symbol	Archer	Scales
Ruler	Jupiter	Venus
Type	Mutable	Cardinal
Element	Fire	Air

This is a great match because fire and air excite and entice each other. Both Mr Libra and Ms Sagittarius have a natural zest for life and are open individuals who share the same passion for learning and exchanging ideas and thoughts. These two are also very sociable and will be happy to share their life with a partner. Their natural optimism and their ability to relate well to people give them many opportunities to experience a rich and textured lifestyle. Both are romantic idealists, so they will be happy to work on improving their relationship. Mr Libra will be drawn to the fun-loving adventurous archer who will be constantly dragging him to participate in whatever her passion desires – be it a seat in the saddle or seat in the fast lane. The archer is a fun-loving girl who likes to play hard.

The one thing that might set these two apart is the foot-in-mouth disease that can afflict Ms Sagittarius. She lets it all hang out, much to the embarrassment of Mr Libra, who is far too diplomatic to really say it how it is, openly. Ms Sagittarius is known be a bit of an embarrassment on occasions, but if Mr Libra can relax and see the humour of such situations and appreciate her genuine intent (she does not have a mean bone in her body), then all will be well.

The Libran man likes to do everything with his mate but the archer needs some space at times. This will need to be discussed in advance so both know where they stand; however, if difficulties do crop up, they will be quickly solved because these two have a great sense of empathy and compassion for one another.

In the bedroom: Mr Libra dedicates himself to pleasing, and his skill lies not only in his physical manoeuvres, but also in his ability to be a selfless lover, getting the most satisfaction when he makes his lover squirm for more.

↗ Ms Sagittarius + Mr Scorpio ♏

Sign	Sagittarius	Scorpio
Symbol	Archer	Scorpion
Ruler	Jupiter	Pluto
Type	Mutable	Fixed
Element	Fire	Water

Mr Scorpio will be immensely attracted to this 'simpatico' girl, who seems to breeze through life without a care in the world. He is the secretive type and finds it bewildering that she can be so open and communicative. She will be disarmed by Mr Scorpio's strong physical presence and his fixed gaze that seems to penetrate her very core. Before long, however, this magnetic attraction will lose its pull and each will find the difference of their personalities a turn-off.

Mr Scorpio will feel threatened by the archer's elusive and flighty ways and if he starts to exert some control over her, she will want to flee. His brooding and moody stance will be foreign to the archer woman, who has an optimistic approach to life. She will always view life as being a cup that is half-full rather than half-empty. He will not tolerate her independent streak and lack of commitment. This girl needs to explore life free of restrictions and will be happy to go it alone if she has to. Mr Scorpio has to have a mate who feels as intensely as he does. He needs a total merging of mind, body and soul, which this woman cannot provide.

Water energy is intense and feelings run deep. As much as fire wants to share in the magic of love, Ms Sagittarius will always be too idealistic for this man who would love to tie a lead to her pretty little wrist and keep her close at all times. But, alas, this will only dull her flame even further.

In the bedroom: Mr Scorpio will admire and appreciate the enthusiasm with which the archer launches into sex. But this girl may be too forthright and outspoken for the sensitive Scorpio man. Her notorious foot-in-mouth blunders might spill over into the bedroom, fatally wounding the ego of her brooding lover.

↗ Ms Sagittarius + Mr Sagittarius ↗

Sign	Sagittarius	Sagittarius
Symbol	Archer	Archer
Ruler	Jupiter	Jupiter
Type	Mutable	Mutable
Element	Fire	Fire

This dynamic duo will enjoy each other because they share a passion for the same things. They have much in common, both loving to develop their minds and being eager participants in life. They value their independence and freedom, so they will respect each other's need for space. And they come from the same perspective: each desires a relationship built on truth and honesty.

Equally energetic and passionate, this Sagittarian duo will encourage each other to throw themselves into whatever adventure might arise. Sagittarians are by nature impulsive, and a double dose in a relationship might create havoc, yet these two seem to always have luck on their side. When they get into a mess they can always see the humour of the situation, rather than the downside.

Fire signs are open and enthusiastic, often jumping in where angels fear to tread. And the archer is no exception – noted for candour and honesty, Ms Sagittarius is not so keen to have a dose of her own medicine and, even though she does have a happy-go-lucky disposition, she often feels somewhat misunderstood.

Ms Sagittarius expects her male counterpart to be intuitive and know what she needs from the relationship, as he does from her. Both are reluctant to ask for what they want and may become disillusioned when their ideals are not met. This fiery Sagittarian duo has much in common, however, the usual difficulties crop up when they want similar things. Two fire signs can share the same flame for passion, but one might want to shine more brightly.

In the bedroom: What turns these two on is a meeting of the minds. When this happens, there is plenty of physical action to satisfy this lusty pair.

♐ Ms Sagittarius + Mr Capricorn ♑

Sign	Sagittarius	Capricorn
Symbol	Archer	Goat
Ruler	Jupiter	Saturn
Type	Mutable	Cardinal
Element	Fire	Earth

Mr Capricorn is just what this girl needs. He is a practical and grounded man who can temper her volatile and impulsive nature, and persuade her to keep her feet on the ground. In turn, Ms Sagittarius is what he needs: a strong-spirited, optimistic girl who can encourage him to see the positive and fun-loving side of life. Sadly, however, what they need is not necessarily what they want. She is more interested in developing her mind. Her security is not based on material accomplishments but rather on recognising that she can be free to do what she wants, unlike her conservative Capricornian mate who loves structure and order in his life.

The archer is happiest living a nomadic lifestyle, which will allow her to explore a different side of life. He, however, will not cope with her desire to chase rainbows. She wants to see the fruits of his labours, yet is only interested in eating the fruit. And although she admires the goat's virtues – caution, discretion and conservatism – she is too bohemian to lock herself into the practicalities and the mundane, and will see him as being far too pragmatic.

The goat is a traditionalist and takes himself far too seriously, according to the adventurous archer. Her fiery spirit is too out of control for this man, who needs to feel a sense of purpose and direction in his life. Ms Sagittarius's only direction is out of the goat's clutches and into a more colourful and zany space, where she can indulge herself with the fun-loving pursuits that turn her on.

In the bedroom: This is always a fun place for these two. The goat can relax and allow the archer to give him much-needed pampering. In turn, he will treat her to a serious dose of lovemaking, since he prides himself on being the best in all areas of his life.

↗ Ms Sagittarius + Mr Aquarius ≈

Sign	Sagittarius	Aquarius
Symbol	Archer	Water bearer
Ruler	Jupiter	Uranus
Type	Mutable	Fixed
Element	Fire	Air

These are two cool customers, although Mr Aquarius is the cooler and more detached of the two. Despite their need for independence, fire signs also need lots of admiration and attention. These are not qualities Mr Aquarius easily bestows on his woman, who will feel neglected as a result. He is not as responsive and as personal as she would like, yet she cannot be too critical of this man, as she doesn't like to be possessed herself.

However, they have much in common. Each values their freedom and independence and has a desire to grow intellectually. They share a passion for communication and will stimulate each other with their insights and wisdom. Ms Sagittarius will value this man's loyal and honest approach. Both are interested in serving mankind and will be able to support each other's vision for global peace and harmony. But this is where the similarities end. The Aquarian man is unconventional and open to all things and, although his archer maiden is far from straight-laced, she has a strong moral code and will not indulge in this man's off-beat ways.

He can always justify his behaviour intellectually, which won't suit the romantic and idealistic Ms Sagittarius, who needs her man to show some emotion rather than repress his feelings. And because of his fixed nature, she will be the one making the compromises. Her mutable mode of expression makes her more adaptable and tolerant.

This duo will make far better friends than lovers because they will enjoy each other's attributes without the strings attached, which is ideal – especially because neither is very good at tying the other's laces.

In the bedroom: Mr Aquarius's love of experimentation is at its best in this room, where he can try out his new tricks. Ms Sagittarius – the perpetual and eager student – will be only too willing to learn something new.

♐ Ms Sagittarius + Mr Pisces ♓

Sign	Sagittarius	Pisces
Symbol	Archer	Fish
Ruler	Jupiter	Neptune
Type	Mutable	Mutable
Element	Fire	Water

The water and fire in the hearts of these two will attract each other initially but may not be sustaining in the long run. She will be drawn to the mystical and sensitive fish and he will be attracted to her outgoing and adventurous spirit. They both have a love of transcending boundaries: Ms Sagittarius with her quest to search for spiritual truth, and Mr Pisces with his desire to escape the confines of his mundane existence to find his soulmate.

With both being mutable signs, there will be much give and take in their relationship. However, it will be more take than give if Ms Sagittarius has her way. Mr Pisces is into making sacrifices for this optimistic woman and she will not allow him to wallow in his world of escapism. She will encourage her man to follow the high road of life and lead him to a place where he can pursue his talents.

These two share the same romantic ideals and have a harsh time facing the realities of a relationship when it carries too much baggage. It is best that they keep the target of domestic bliss out of their lives and concentrate more on the creative aspect of their romance. The archer may have to temper her critical side because Mr Pisces' sensitive nature will cause him to lose faith in her if she is too blunt.

He is a man who needs encouragement and support, and he might find Ms Sagittarius too dogmatic and impatient for him. The dreamy fish likes to swim to the bottom of the ocean occasionally to indulge in his own private fantasies. Ms Sagittarius will be left up in the air, wondering where her lover has escaped to this time.

In the bedroom: The fish is a creature who loves to escape and where better than into the arms of Ms Sagittarius, whose lusty appetite will devour this man in one swoop. She will be licking her lips for more of that tasty morsel.

Celebrity Ms Sagittarius: Jane Fonda

Actor/activist, born 9.14 am 21 December 1937, New York, USA

```
Personal planets:  Sun in Sagittarius
                   Moon in Leo
                   Mercury in Capricorn
                   Venus in Sagittarius
                   Mars in Aquarius
```

It's never too late – never too late to start over, never too late to be happy.

—Jane Fonda

Jane Fonda has worn many Sagittarian caps during her life – all with the true archer's flair and panache. From an actor to a political activist to a highly successful fitness guru to a philanthropic environmentalist – all her endeavours have fitted her Sagittarian persona. She has expressed the archer's enthusiasm and passion in all her undertakings.

True to Sagittarian form, Fonda has been outspoken and courageous in her beliefs, treading where angels have feared to along the way. She continues to live her life to the fullest, making every moment of every day count for something. This archer girl's list of accomplishments is tied into her passions.

As a true Sagittarian, Fonda's restless spirit is one that hungers for adventure and dynamic experiences. Along the way, she has grasped any new opportunities that presented themselves and has dedicated herself courageously to the causes she feels so passionate about. Both her Sun and Moon are in fire signs, so she has idealistic views and is prone to disappointment when outcomes are not what she anticipates. This perception also flows into her relationships. Her Venus in Sagittarius indicates that she needs her lover to be her best friend. He has to be honest and a straight-shooter, as well as someone she can have fun with.

Fonda's Mars in Aquarius gives her a need to communicate with her man, yet she can seem impersonal. The air quality is uncomfortable with intimacy and her first marriage to film director Roger Vadim, an Aquarian, would have given her some awareness as to how detached this Uranian energy can be. Fonda would have needed his attention, but he didn't, or couldn't, show her the compassion and warmth she required. In turn, she was reluctant to ask for what she needed, instead sacrificing her hidden desires.

Her second marriage to political activist Tom Hayden, also a Sagittarian, would have seen them fulfilling their philosophical needs and exposing the dynamism in each other. In true Sagittarian spirit, they would have bonded through a shared cause. Her third marriage to US entrepreneur Ted Turner, a Scorpio, would have been coloured by some interesting affinities and challenges. As a true Scorpio, he found the courage and focus to rebuild his life after a period of adversity, when he managed to steer his father's ailing business into an empire. As Fonda has risen on many occasions to reinvent herself successfully, Turner has too. The union was often referred to as an 'electrically charged relationship' that knew no boundaries, except of course within the confines of their marriage.

Fonda has now parted ways with Turner after their 10-year marriage and is busy writing her memoirs, saying: 'One of the things I want to make clear (in my book) is that separation or divorce doesn't necessarily represent failure.'

Mr Sagittarius – an overview

The male archer will stand out in a crowd and is an attractive partner for a woman who wants a life of fun, variety and adventure. His openness and uncomplicated personality are very appealing and his elusive air has women in hot pursuit. He is a hunter, however, and will rarely be drawn to a girl who does the chasing. Mr Sagittarius loves the early stages of a relationship, when things are hot and steamy. He will fall instantly in love, only to find that as things progress, the whole affair becomes too mundane for him and far from what he imagined.

He needs a girl who will allow him plenty of independence and freedom to pursue his other passions and will always grant her the same favours. This man thrives on mental exploration and will always be interested in diversity. He requires a constant stream of new information to satisfy his active mind and will be kept interested if his mate can provide him with some mental stimuli. He is more suited to friendships than a deep relationship because he is adverse to commitment. Happy as long as he doesn't feel locked in, the archer will become a caged beast if he thinks he is tied down – desperate to escape his perceived confinement.

He is a man who can roar like a lion one minute and then purr like a kitty-cat five minutes later. Not one to bear grudges and resentments, he will be an easy mate to live with, as long as he doesn't feel bogged down by domesticity. This man wants to be in the outdoors, away from the constrictions of everyday life. He loves to feel the wind blowing in his hair as he sails into unchartered waters, and if he hears the faint tinkle of wedding bells, he'll run even further away to find another damsel who will share his love of adventure and independence.

Famous Sagittarian men

* Mark Twain (writer)
* Winston Churchill
  (British prime minister)
* Walt Disney
  (animator/producer)
* Pope John XXIII (Pope)
* Kirk Douglas (actor)
* Beethoven (composer)

Combinations

♐ Mr Sagittarius + Ms Aries ♈

Sign	Sagittarius	Aries
Symbol	Archer	Ram
Ruler	Jupiter	Mars
Type	Mutable	Cardinal
Element	Fire	Fire

This couple's love of sport and the great outdoors makes for a compatible union. They both embrace life with equal enthusiasm and will derive pleasure from experiences they can share together. Mr Sagittarius will be a breath of fresh air for Ms Aries, who will flourish in a relationship free from the controlling and manipulative clutches of some of the other signs of the zodiac.

Both fire signs, these two are open and honest with each other – what you see is often what you get. Although Mr Sagittarius is known for his 'foot-in-mouth disease', he is more charming and refined than Ms Aries, a trait she finds appealing. The archer's thirst for knowledge and his need to try new experiences is what keeps Ms Aries on her toes. She loves adventure, so these two would have a great time globetrotting.

Mutual understanding between these signs is strong; neither likes boundaries in their relationships. Since both have a tendency to rush headlong into any situation, there is little room for peace and quiet in this union. Ms Aries and Mr Sagittarius live in the moment, sometimes with little regard for tomorrow. But as fire signs, both love the idea of being in love and might quite easily end up walking down the aisle together.

In the bedroom: Both the ram and the archer are extremely passionate lovers who will make responsive and affectionate bedfellows. Ms Aries may become jealous or miffed when he breaks his promises, but the sensual and energetic archer will make up for that in more ways than one!

♐ Mr Sagittarius + Ms Taurus ♉

Sign	Sagittarius	Taurus
Symbol	Archer	Bull
Ruler	Jupiter	Venus
Type	Mutable	Fixed
Element	Fire	Earth

Mr Sagittarius and Ms Taurus don't seem to have much in common. Her practical no-nonsense attitude to life is in complete contrast to the adventuresome, freedom-loving archer. Ms Taurus will find her Sagittarian man attractive and, in some respects, be in a bit in awe of his ability to move so freely through life with such an optimistic and philosophical outlook. She is more materialistic and comfort-oriented and gets too bogged down with the nitty-gritty of daily life. The archer appreciates some of the grounding qualities that his lady bull provides, but her complacency and smothering tends to stifle his outward expression.

Ms Taurus is ruled by Venus making her needy with a partner and the comforts and security of life, whereas Mr Sagittarius prefers a less-structured and more dynamic lifestyle where he can come and go as he pleases and satisfy his lustful nature. Ms Taurus will seem like a mother figure to the impish archer. He likes to fire his arrow in many directions and finds her too stifling as a love interest. She in turn will find the archer too fickle and will not share his passion for energetic, daredevil pursuits, instead preferring a mate who will be happier to work alongside her pulling out weeds in the garden.

The bull is a domesticated creature and her archer companion will not provide her with the luxuries and comforts she desires. She would much prefer a weekend in a five-star resort than in a tent in the Himalayas.

In the bedroom: A Taurean woman shows her love best through touch and a Sagittarian man needs to express himself both physically and verbally. They will have different sexual needs, but a little give and take will go a long way towards helping these two reach nirvana in the bedroom!

♐ Mr Sagittarius + Ms Gemini ♊

Sign	Sagittarius	Gemini
Symbol	Archer	Twins
Ruler	Jupiter	Mercury
Type	Mutable	Mutable
Element	Fire	Air

These two have some common traits and understand each other on some levels but Ms Gemini is a communicator in a superficial sense, whereas Mr Sagittarius is the eternal student, the philosopher and the adventurer, and cannot be bogged down by the inconsequential issues of life.

Ms Gemini has a lot to learn from her archer, who is constantly aiming his arrow higher at the horizon and, if she is patient enough to listen to his wisdom, this could be an exciting partnership. Both have a strong sense of adventure and love to horse around, although she lives more in her head and is not as physically active. And with neither of them being domesticated, they are happiest following their passions rather than playing house.

If Ms Gemini is willing to let her archer guide her through the journey of life, this bond could last an eternity; however, the ever-changing faces of the twin will, at times, frustrate the deeper, more philosophical Sagittarian guy. On the bright side, both Geminis and Sagittarians look for greener pastures and are motivated by new frontiers, so life together will never be dull. The combination of air and fire signs means they will have a certain idealism in their relationship, despite a tendency towards a wandering eye. This, however, gives them common ground for greater understanding of each other.

The qualities that define this relationship are freedom and independence, which are extremely important to both parties. Mr Sagittarius has an ability to relate well to people and will understand his Gemini mate's need to socialise, which he will not interpret as flirtatious but rather as an expression of her personality.

In the bedroom: He might be more physical than he is mental, but that doesn't mean the twin and archer won't blend in bed to become one. The archer will definitely be the more demonstrative and fiery mate in this sexual pairing.

♐ Mr Sagittarius + Ms Cancer ♋

Sign	Sagittarius	Cancer
Symbol	Archer	Crab
Ruler	Jupiter	Moon
Type	Mutable	Cardinal
Element	Fire	Water

These two have fundamentally different natures. Mr Sagittarius is interested primarily in freedom, variety and greener pastures, and for him the journey is often the more meaningful part of his experiences. Ms Cancer, on the other hand, needs guarantees and assurances, so she will not feel protected and nurtured by her archer man, whom she sees as too elusive and selfish. She tends to cling to her past and will always run back to the fold when she feels vulnerable, which will be very often if she finds herself with a Sagittarian man.

Her water elements, intensity and mood swings will not be readily understood or tolerated by the optimistic and expansive mind of the Sagittarian guy. He is a lover of the outdoors, nature and challenges, while she is more the domesticated creature with a flare for creating harmonious and nurturing environments. Ms Cancer will be too single-minded to allow her archer mate to have the space and freedom he requires in his relationships. He will only exacerbate her insecurities and sense of instability by the very essence of his hedonistic and insensitive nature.

This crab will be too rigid, staid and possessive for her Sagittarian guy, who will find her energy and disposition stifling and boring. The archer likes to shoot his arrow in many directions and this will ultimately be the undoing of this duo.

In the bedroom: 'Shoot that bow and arrow through my hear-ah-ah-art,' croons the crab. But the archer man might miss the mark with this woman; she wants deep and fulfilling passion from their sexual union and he's more after physical gratification.

✒ **Mr Sagittarius + Ms Leo** ♌

Sign	Sagittarius	Leo
Symbol	Archer	Lion
Ruler	Jupiter	Sun
Type	Mutable	Fixed
Element	Fire	Fire

Mr Sagittarius and Ms Leo make a dynamic duo. The element of fire fuels this union with intensity, passion, idealism and a sense of adventure. This couple plays well together, each encouraging the other to pursue their own interests, yet will always show a unified front.

Mr Sagittarius will encourage Ms Leo to broaden her outlook and help whet her appetite for adventure; in turn, Ms Leo will ground the impulsive archer. They are both free-thinking, independent, energetic individuals who share a passion for life. Both have tremendous self-confidence and rather dominating egos and never buy into the negative aspects of each other's personalities. The lioness and the archer have a healthy perspective on life and rarely harbour hidden agendas – what you see is what you get.

Each has an optimistic attitude towards life and together can merge their creative and insightful attitudes into a partnership that is destined for success. Rarely will they make their partner feel jealous; they allow each other the other space to enjoy friendships outside their relationship. These fire signs are larger than life and participate in a variety of pursuits, so they can bring a lot of this external stimulus into the union and will learn much from each other.

In the bedroom: Sexually these two are highly compatible: they don't have to prove themselves and can relax and have fun. Their playful expression is the key to keeping these two on their sexual toes. But sometimes the honesty and frankness of the archer may wound the high and mighty lioness, who likes to hear only praise of her positive traits. Overall this duo's physical passion is intense but there's plenty of fun along the way.

♐ Mr Sagittarius + Ms Virgo ♍

Sign	Sagittarius	Virgo
Symbol	Archer	Virgin
Ruler	Jupiter	Mercury
Type	Mutable	Mutable
Element	Fire	Earth

These two have a mutual interest in the outdoors. They love adventure and, being on the same wavelength, can engage in a lively exchange of ideas. Truth and honesty is paramount to their relationship. Ms Virgo will be attracted to her honest and, at times, too-blunt Sagittarian man because she also calls a spade a spade.

In this relationship, Ms Virgo will learn a lot about tolerance and patience and how to develop a sense of humour. Mr Sagittarius does everything in a big way because his ruling planet, Jupiter, is the planet of expansion, enthusiasm and abundance. Ms Virgo, on the other hand, is more cautious and conservative, preferring to analyse a situation before throwing herself in at the deep end like her archer mate.

Being a fire sign, Mr Sagittarius is idealistic in life and love, and since he is the eternal optimist, his energy and drive for new frontiers will be a little bit overwhelming for the discriminating Ms Virgo. Mr Sagittarius will find the virgin's nagging nature a drain on his free-spirited outlook. But she's only complaining because she likes to keep things orderly, especially at home, and can become annoyed with her Sagittarian man's messy and scattered energies.

In the bedroom: Ms Virgo is a loyal and committed lover, unlike her philandering Sagittarian mate who can be quite promiscuous. These two can learn from each other and have a lustful connection, but a long-term romantic relationship is unlikely.

↗ Mr Sagittarius + Ms Libra ♎

Sign	Sagittarius	Libra
Symbol	Archer	Scales
Ruler	Jupiter	Venus
Type	Mutable	Cardinal
Element	Fire	Air

The magic of air and fire will always send sparks flying and this pair will have an immense attraction for one another. Mr Sagittarius and Ms Libra seem to have an easy time in life and will be attracted to each other's uncomplicated style. She is drawn to his optimistic and fun-loving nature and he is lured by her physical beauty. But, more importantly, and more appealing for this archer, is his Libran love's ability to communicate and freely express herself. Ms Libra is interested in mental exploration and has a highly developed mind. Like her archer mate, she values learning and education, leading this pair to spend plenty of time in pursuit of excitement and social interaction.

Ms Libra and her archer share the same values and will be keen to encourage each other's talents and interests. Her refined manner and social appeal may at first be a little overwhelming for this basic, laid-back guy, who would rather hang out in his sports gear than don a tuxedo. Yet they seem to have a good flow of communication and a willingness to please each other, so there will be compromises along the way. She might get her man to wear a tie on the odd occasion and he might convince her that she looks just as stunning in her tracksuit as in her 'glammed-up' gear.

Ms Libra will be happy to give this man room to move, which will be much appreciated by Mr Sagittarius, whose 'don't fence me in' attitude is typical of this star sign.

In the bedroom: Physical intimacy for Ms Libra and her archer is one of sheer joy. These two have plenty of fun together, combining humour and passion when the lights go out.

♐ Mr Sagittarius + Ms Scorpio ♏

Sign	Sagittarius	Scorpio
Symbol	Archer	Scorpion
Ruler	Jupiter	Pluto
Type	Mutable	Fixed
Element	Fire	Water

Initially Ms Scorpio will find this man a challenge. Mr Sagittarius is everything she's not – outgoing, open and communicative. She is closed, secretive and guarded, while he has the proverbial foot-in-mouth disease. She is a careful deliberator of words and actions and needs a mate she can control and obsess over, whereas he is the optimistic, gregarious guy who cannot stand emotional confinement. What do these two have in common? The one thing that connects them is a fascination for their differences. Both come from vastly different perspectives yet they secretly admire each other's qualities.

A relationship might prove too difficult in the long run but they could have a lot of fun for a while, given that they both have a strong sex drive and find each other physically attractive. Although Mr Sagittarius doesn't have the same physical intensity as his Scorpio mate, he enjoys the conquest. She would be an alluring partner who would keep her man guessing. She is likely to be too controlling, jealous and obsessive for the independent archer, since he is a free-wheeler who needs his space.

Ultimately, this woman will be too much trouble for the simple Sag male who wants to have a beer with his mates or fly his hang-glider over a canyon. She finds his lack of commitment and his philandering ways too burdensome. The archer is a free spirit who fears being trapped by a controlling and suffocating woman. She wants only to be loved, yet she is often misunderstood by the fire types, who lack the patience to let her true colours shine through. Her water would dampen the fire spirit of this man and eventually put out the flame of passion. He would simply cause her too much grief.

In the bedroom: Both seek intensity beyond the pure physical pleasure, so this will be an uplifting experience for them both. Fire and water blend well in the bedroom. Mr Sagittarius craves this sensation-oriented woman with whom he will fall in love. Lust equates to love in his eyes, and that gets him every time.

⚹ Mr Sagittarius + Ms Sagittarius ⚹

Sign	Sagittarius	Sagittarius
Symbol	Archer	Archer
Ruler	Jupiter	Jupiter
Type	Mutable	Mutable
Element	Fire	Fire

This dynamic duo will enjoy each other because they share a passion for the same things. They have much in common, both loving to develop their minds and being eager participants in life. They value their independence and freedom, so they will respect each other's need for space. And they come from the same perspective: each desires a relationship built on truth and honesty.

Equally energetic and passionate, this Sagittarian duo will encourage each other to throw themselves into whatever adventure might arise. Sagittarians are by nature impulsive, and a double dose in a relationship might create havoc, yet these two seem to always have luck on their side. When they get into a mess they can always see the humour of the situation, rather than the downside.

Fire signs are open and enthusiastic, often jumping in where angels fear to tread. And the archer is no exception – noted for candour and honesty, Ms Sagittarius is not so keen to have a dose of her own medicine and, even though she does have a happy-go-lucky disposition, she often feels somewhat misunderstood.

Mr Sagittarius expects his female counterpart to be intuitive and know what he needs from the relationship, as she does from him. Both are reluctant to ask for what they want and may become disillusioned when their ideals are not met. This fiery Sagittarian duo has much in common, however, the usual difficulties crop up when they want similar things. Two fire signs can share the same flame for passion, but one might want to shine more brightly.

In the bedroom: What turns these two on is a meeting of the minds. When this happens, there is plenty of physical action to satisfy this lusty pair.

♐ Mr Sagittarius + Ms Capricorn ♑

Sign	Sagittarius	Capricorn
Symbol	Archer	Goat
Ruler	Jupiter	Saturn
Type	Mutable	Cardinal
Element	Fire	Earth

Mr Sagittarius and Ms Capricorn are more suited to being business partners than lovers. They value each other's attributes and can mutually benefit from shared skills. The goat admires the archer's ability to relate to a cross-section of people and is attracted to his sunny and optimistic approach to life. Secretly she wishes she could feel as optimistic and comfortable with herself as he does. Mr Sagittarius sees the goat as a woman of substance, who is on a mission to climb the ladder of success; however, his journey arises from different motivations. She is hard-nosed and has to have a purpose in life, whereas he is happy to go where the mood takes him.

Although he is impressed by her ability to stay focused on her goals, he will be discouraged by her lack of playfulness and her 'duty before pleasure' attitude. He is an adventurer and, with a well-developed inner child, will find her scolding ways too stifling. Ms Capricorn also likes to feel in control of her life, which includes her relationships. Mr Sagittarius will prove too elusive for her. She will never be able to trap this man into submission.

Mr Sagittarius will admire the loyalty and devotion this woman shows; however, he needs a mate who can allow him the freedom he so desperately craves, and it is unlikely to be Ms Capricorn. She hankers for the emotional security of a partnership and, being the most conservative sign of the zodiac, will start to tinkle wedding bells in his ear. But these will sound like alarm bells to the free-spirited Mr Sagittarius, who is likely to duck for cover.

In the bedroom: The goat might well be struck by Cupid's arrow, but this practical no-nonsense woman will want to schedule her romantic interludes into her organiser. The foot-in-mouth archer must be careful not to offend his sensitive Capricornian lover, who is unlikely to submit until he can prove to her that his philandering days are well and truly over.

♐ Mr Sagittarius + Ms Aquarius ♒

Sign	Sagittarius	Aquarius
Symbol	Archer	Water bearer
Ruler	Jupiter	Uranus
Type	Mutable	Fixed
Element	Fire	Air

Mr Sagittarius will be attracted to this highly intelligent and off-beat girl, who will drive him wild with her indifference. She will prove a real challenge: he will chase her up hill and down dale until she finally succumbs and his arrow finds her heart. 'Once you have found her, let her go' should be the advice offered to an archer faced with this scenario, because the water bearer will prove too headstrong for this easygoing man. She is a woman who values independence even more than he does and she will be more involved with humanitarian causes.

Mr Sagittarius will feel somewhat neglected because he is used to being the centre of attention and is, himself, often pursued by a string of admirers. He will view her indifference as somewhat of a slight. But rather than making his needs known, Ms Aquarius will be left guessing as to why her man is brooding in the corner, so unlike his usual sunny disposition.

Ms Aquarius has difficulty in expressing her emotions, which results in her being considered too cold or too impersonal for the hot-blooded archer, whose passionate streak will turn to ice if kept out in the cold too long.

This couple's love of adventure and desire to seek new frontiers will kick-start the relationship, but Ms Aquarius will never get out of the driver's seat and help push this union along. She is a fixed sign and is much too stubborn to be the one to concede when something needs fixing. It will be up to the optimistic Mr Sagittarius to wake up and smell the roses and recognise that this was a wonderful journey, albeit at times frustrating, while it lasted.

In the bedroom: These two will enjoy a good romp under the covers. Rarely will there be strings attached and pressure to perform. Both are freedom-loving but they can be possessive about their property, so it wouldn't be wise for Mr Sag to think his Aquarian lover's unconventional attitude means he can slip between the sheets with another woman.

♐ Mr Sagittarius + Ms Pisces ♓

Sign	Sagittarius	Pisces
Symbol	Archer	Fish
Ruler	Jupiter	Neptune
Type	Mutable	Mutable
Element	Fire	Water

This risque man will attract Ms Pisces, who will see him as a dashing knight who will pluck her from the depths of the ocean and transport her to nirvana. Ms Pisces will, of course, have her rose-coloured glasses on and will see only what she wants. She is a true romantic and will ignore the more negative sides of her mate, namely his lack of subtlety and his hedonistic demeanour. Instead she will focus on his optimistic, outgoing and honest attributes. In turn, he will be attracted to her creativity and her subtle disposition. Ms Pisces will bring out the gentle side of the archer's nature and he will feel a sense of protectiveness towards this seemingly demure and compassionate woman.

Both need to be spiritually bonded and enjoy the romantic aspects of the partnership, rather than the daily grind. Mr Sagittarius and Ms Pisces could be together forever if they could indulge in the excesses of life without having to come down to earth. But they both have an aversion to commitment and don't like to be pinned down. All will run smoothly until Mr Sagittarius wants to stretch his legs and wanderlust sets in.

Essentially, the archer will be too energetic and restless for the fish, who is much more laid back and contented to just sail along. And although Ms Pisces will be happy for her mate do his own thing, she will start to feel disillusioned when she realises she is the one always making the sacrifices, and she is likely to end up the martyr in the relationship. In restless times, she will keep the peace by retreating to her cave and burying herself into her own private world, not letting the wayward Mr Sagittarius in until he has redeemed himself and carried her off to conquer new horizons.

In the bedroom: The archer will find the fish extremely alluring, but she needs deep, sensitive loving rather than just the physical closeness he seeks. But, if they can tune into each other's psyches, their bodies will follow suit in spectacular fashion.

Celebrity Mr Sagittarius:
Frank Sinatra

Singer/actor, born 3 am 12 December 1915 in Hoboken, New Jersey, USA

```
Personal planets: Sun in Sagittarius
                  Moon in Pisces
                  Mercury in Sagittarius
                  Venus in Capricorn
                  Mars in Leo
```

I am supposed to have a PhD on the subject of women. But the truth is I flunked more often than not. I am very fond of women. I admire them and, like all men, I don't understand them.

– Frank Sinatra

He may not have understood women but that didn't stop ol' blue eyes from testing the waters time and time again. He even made it to the altar four times, which is a rarity for a Sagittarian man, who loves women but steers away from commitment.

Frank Sinatra was a man of passion who embraced his goals with a sense of purpose. His strong and fiery temperament hid a surprisingly shy persona. He felt more comfortable around people he knew well and was not a man to open up emotionally to others.

Sinatra's Moon in Pisces endowed him with a highly imaginative and creative talent, which he used to forge a successful career in the entertainment industry. But his Moon was less positive in other ways: the famed singer was prone to excesses and mood swings. His one earth component meant he needed to be both emotionally and financially secure, so he was steadfast on his mission to become successful. Sinatra was open to learning anything new, which is reflected in the way he developed his own distinctive style of crooning in the early 1950s.

His Venus in Capricorn saw Sinatra drawn to women who had a certain style and sophistication but who were also elusive and played hard to get.

One of his former wives, beautiful Capricornian Ava Gardner, typified the female goat's approach to relationships. She played it cool with Frank and left all the chasing up to him. When she finally succumbed, she insisted on the traditional trappings of marriage – earth signs like to do things the right way. Ultimately, their differences proved too great, although she has been quoted as saying he was 'the love of her life'.

Sinatra's chart shows an abundance of water elements, which made him especially sensitive. Throughout his many relationships he developed a protective wall to enable him to avoid pain and suffering if the union broke down, which it did on many occasions – like his marriage to actor Mia Farrow. An Aquarian, Farrow was emotionally detached and independent. Although he would have been attractive to this free-spirited and creative woman, she was too cool for him and did not stroke his ego nearly enough.

His last marriage to Libran Barbara Marks appeared to hold more gentle and harmonious aspects. Sinatra's Moon in Pisces would have attracted him to this gentle and empathetic woman. She would have bought peace and harmony into his life, which would have soothed his fiery and, at times, temperamental personality, which became more pronounced in his old age.

CAPRICORN (22 December–20 January)

ℏ Ruled by the planet Saturn
Earth sign
Cardinal
Feminine energy

In general ...

Capricornians are the zodiac's most serious, hardworking personalities. All work and no play is their motto; their focus in life is to keep climbing the mountain until they reach the pinnacle of success, regardless of how many times they slip up. They will be steadfast in their purpose. Social acceptance and status measure high on Capricornians' list of priorities and they are attracted to partners who can help elevate them to the position they desire. Marrying above their station gives them the status they need to feel secure. Success means power and power is an attractive commodity to most Capricornians.

They have the same motivation to succeed in their personal life as much as in the business arena, so they take their relationships very seriously. Cautious and reserved in the early stages of a union, they need time to express their feelings. Although they might be physically motivated, they can put their lustful needs on the back burner until they feel in control of the situation. Then they will allow their defences down ever so cautiously. Spontaneity is not their strongest asset but, once committed, they will make dedicated and loyal partners.

Because Capricornians have an adversity to divorce, it will take a very unhappy goat to take the initiative to severe a union. Family is number one with them, and their concern with their public persona and with what is acceptable behaviour means they will always honour their commitments and marital vows. Capricorn is not a sign associated with the archetype of love and passion; rather they have a more pragmatic approach to love. They are very sensual beings, yet keep this under wraps until they feel safe within a relationship.

Capricornians value respect and loyalty above the more mystical qualities of love and need a mate who shares these characteristics. Their ruling planet Saturn seems to be permanently on their shoulder, whispering 'you can do better', because they are very aware of their responsibilities and are constantly striving for perfection. Such dedication to hard work means they often place duty before pleasure; however, work is fun to a Capricornian. A relationship with this goat will be not be a frivolous experience but one that encompasses fidelity and physical security.

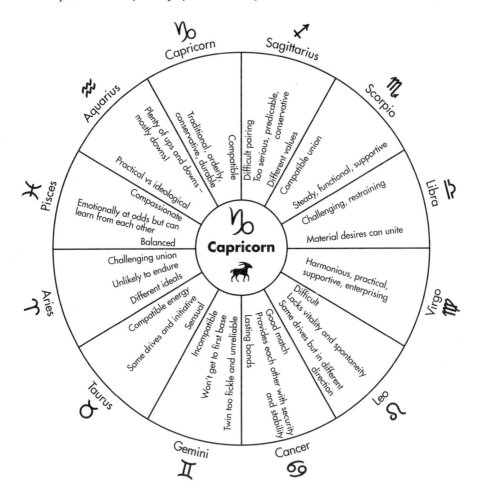

How a Capricornian personality might match up with other star signs

Ms Capricorn – an overview

Regardless of which persona Ms Capricorn adopts – be it the archetype Mother Earth or the staunch professional woman – her capabilities and skills will be hard to match. She is a woman who has learnt from childhood to put business and responsibilities ahead of pleasure, so she is not a frivolous character but a woman who takes her life and relationships seriously. Ms Capricorn has strong ambitions in all her undertakings. She keeps her emotions under wraps because she wants to feel in control. Emotional outbursts are not this woman's style. Her hard exterior, which makes her appear distant and unapproachable at times, is just a front for this discerning woman. When she finally connects with that certain someone, she will be ready to give her all and can turn from a mountain goat to sex kitten in a flash.

Her understanding of the world revolves around the practical and tangible. What you see is real. Ms Capricorn doesn't indulge herself with fantasies and romance. She is more a hands-on type of woman who will always be happy to support her man. She will be happier still, however, if she can have her own goal to aspire to rather than living her life just through her partner. Her relationships are a little slow to get off the ground because she takes time to process all the data before she indulges herself, but once she has stepped over the line, she will be a steadfast and willing participant.

Ms Capricorn is a cardinal sign so she has the aggression to fulfil her drive to succeed professionally. She also carries this energy through to her relationships, which she takes very seriously, as she does her whole life. Her ruling planet Saturn is not always looked upon in the fondest of terms. It represents limitations, hard work and structure, and this is how this woman views her life. She will be happy to partake in her man's successes yet will be just as willing to get her hands dirty and toil in the soil if needs be. Like her male counterpart, she will be more fun to be with as time goes by, and she will learn to relax and indulge in some of life's frivolities, taking the time to smell the roses.

Famous Capricornian women

* Shirley Bassey (singer)
* Ava Gardner (actor)
* Helena Rubinstein
  (cosmetics queen)
* Janis Joplin (singer)
* Joan of Arc (French saint)
* Heidi Fleiss
  (Hollywood madam)

Combinations

♑ Ms Capricorn + Mr Aries ♈

Sign	Capricorn	Aries
Symbol	Goat	Ram
Ruler	Saturn	Mars
Type	Cardinal	Cardinal
Element	Earth	Fire

Astrologically these two signs are in a difficult aspect, which indicates that there will be differences in their natures. Ms Capricorn is ambitious, pragmatic and practical, and her ruling planet Saturn requires her to work hard at her relationships – and that's what she expects from her mate. Although she can teach her Arian lover about the practicalities of life, she is too conservative and serious for this Casanova. Her lack of spontaneity and her serious disposition do not fit well with the playful frivolity of the Arian male.

Ms Capricorn is very serious about her relationships and not as spontaneous as Mr Aries. Before she allows herself to become too passionate, she needs some form of commitment. If he persists in his efforts to crack through her tough exterior, he will find a committed and successful woman, but rarely does he have the patience or tenacity to persist with such a seemingly arduous task.

The fiery warmth of the Arian persona will melt the cold heart of Ms Capricorn, but ultimately her seriousness, lack of frivolity and managerial qualities will be too heavy going for adventurous Mr Aries. He will crave a more carefree union and eventually break free from this structured and rigid relationship which stifles his creativity.

In the bedroom: These two rarely make it to the bedroom because Mr Aries finds Ms Capricorn too straight-laced and conservative to make an exciting lover. She'll lack spontaneity, preferring sex in the bedroom, while the impulsive and excitable ram can hardly make it beyond the backseat of the car!

♑ Ms Capricorn + Mr Taurus ♉

Sign	Capricorn	Taurus
Symbol	Goat	Bull
Ruler	Saturn	Venus
Type	Cardinal	Fixed
Element	Earth	Earth

This combination has a strong connection and seems to get on well, with both thriving on building a structured lifestyle with all the trappings of wealth. These two will work hard to achieve this and will support and appreciate one another's desire for material accumulation.

Ms Capricorn can appear a little detached and aloof – in fact, rather cold and pragmatic – however, she is also very defensive of her mate and will protect him with all her might. In turn, Mr Taurus will thrive on Ms Capricorn's practical application to life and will value her support to attain success.

Earth signs need to learn how to express these needs verbally so that partners can gain an insight into each other's frustrations and, if these two can break down the communication barriers, they will build a close-knit and secure future together and enjoy the fruits of their labours.

Because this pair shares a conservative attitude towards life, they will proceed with caution until they feel a genuine trust. Then things will start to speed up. Both are also interested in long-term commitments and will always prefer marriage to merely living together. Mr Taurus will be attracted to the ambitious quality Ms Capricorn displays and she, in turn, will support and encourage her man at every turn.

Mr Taurus desires a partner who will give him the security he craves and who is also genuine in her affection. These earth signs have a mutual affinity and are often considered to be the builders of the zodiac – the ones who create a comfortable and secure lifestyle for themselves.

In the bedroom: Although suited on many levels, physical passion is unlikely to be the driving force behind this union. But that's not to say they won't find a comfortable physical relationship together. Romance and long-lasting sexual compatibility is on the cards for these two earth stars.

♑ Ms Capricorn + Mr Gemini ♊

Sign	Capricron	Gemini
Symbol	Goat	Twins
Ruler	Saturn	Mercury
Type	Cardinal	Mutable
Element	Earth	Air

The hard-working, practical and tenacious Capricornian will rarely fuel the fires of passion within the freedom-loving, adventure-seeking Gemini. Mr Gemini hardly lets the dust settle beneath his feet before he leaps to his next conquest, while Ms Capricorn rarely moves before she feels the security of solid earth beneath her.

Geminis and Capricornians have different needs and desires from a relationship: she'll want an emotionally secure and mature man while he'll be after a more flexible and freedom-loving woman. The Capricornian lass likes guarantees – certainly in everything she undertakes – so she will need to believe her relationship is genuine and has a good chance of permanency before she commits entirely to the union with her Gemini beau. She seeks the truth while he struggles to reveal it. Mr Gemini usually shuns emotional stability but, ironically, while he may resent this very quality in his Capricornian love, it will be the very thing that lures him back to the union because some part of his psyche secretly harbours a need for security.

Ms Capricorn is hardworking and committed to every task she undertakes and a relationship is no exception so, despite the emotional highs and lows this relationship brings, she will try to make it work because to admit defeat is something she struggles with.

In the bedroom: Sexually this couple may not set the house on fire but, because both can be fairly independent, their lovemaking creates a strong but not all-consuming bond between them.

♑ Ms Capricorn + Mr Cancer ♋

Sign	Capricorn	Cancer
Symbol	Goat	Crab
Ruler	Saturn	Moon
Type	Cardinal	Cardinal
Element	Earth	Water

These two are very similar in their desire for security and financial independence. Mr Crab will admire the Capricornian girl's managerial abilities and commitment to achieving her goals. She is a pragmatic soul and gets on with her life with minimal fuss and few hang-ups. This woman is on a mission to succeed that will embrace all areas of her life. Failure is not a word she relates to and she will aim to give her all in a relationship.

Although their life goals seem to be the same, by nature Cancerians and Capricornians get to where they want via different approaches. Mr Cancer displays a more emotional and needy vulnerability in relationships, which is not always understood by the more stoical Capricornian. In turn, her lack of warmth and affection will at times cause some dissension in the union. He's a tactile creature who needs physical responsiveness from his mate so he may have to teach his Capricornian girl to be a bit more touchy-feely.

Mr Cancer's worrying nature can be tempered by Ms Capricorn's no-fuss, solution-oriented personality, which can help keep the intense emotions of her man on a more grounded and balanced level. If the Capricornian can modify her desire for professional success and spend more time with her Cancerian mate, this union will be very workable and can be a prosperous one for both parties.

In the bedroom: The crab and the goat take lovemaking just as seriously as they do other aspects of their lives. He will draw out the sensuality of this woman and will take her to heights of intimacy that will surprise and thrill her.

♑ Ms Capricorn + Mr Leo ♌

Sign	Capricorn	Leo
Symbol	Goat	Lion
Ruler	Saturn	Sun
Type	Cardinal	Fixed
Element	Earth	Fire

Both Ms Capricorn and Mr Leo have a desire to make it in a worldly sense. Respect and commitment tie these two together; however, more in a commercial than romantic sense. A less passionate Leo male might be aroused by the managerial and organisational skills of this woman, but the true lionhearted spirit of fun, frivolity and adventure isn't compatible with this distant and aloof Capricornian. She projects a serious and responsible disposition which does not attract Mr Leo, who needs a woman who can enhance his sense of status.

Mr Leo's fire is infectious and volatile, and Ms Capricorn will see him as superficial and lacking in commitment. He needs an open-minded and fun-loving woman with whom he can laugh but, alas, the goat is more focused on climbing her mountain and reaching the pinnacle than letting her hair down. Ms Capricorn is often attracted to partners who can speed her rise to prominence and will often marry someone who is above her station. The motto 'I use' is about the Capricornian's ability to utilise the talents and abilities of others to move forward. Mr Leo is too opinionated and caught up with his own rise to fame to have the inclination to help her along that path.

In the bedroom: Sexually these signs don't really gel. Ms Capricorn's drive is not so much in the bedroom as in the boardroom. And the lion will be far too concerned with pleasing himself to worry about pleasing his goat as well.

♑ Ms Capricorn + Mr Virgo ♍

Sign	Capricorn	Virgo
Symbol	Goat	Virgin
Ruler	Saturn	Mercury
Type	Cardinal	Mutable
Element	Earth	Earth

The Virgoan man will enjoy this woman because he sees in her a steady and practical mate who can participate and work systematically towards their mutual goals. Two earth signs might seem a little lacklustre because their focus is often work-orientated and each seems to bring out a strong work ethos in the other.

Capricornians and Virgoans are two signs in the zodiac that can be compared with a good wine. They mature and ripen well with age. Because they are committed to pleasing each other, the virgin and the goat will always have a lively sexual rapport. Although slow movers initially, once Mr Virgo has trapped his mountain goat they both will ascend to higher ground in this union. Both are very grounded and have high expectations of themselves so neither will find this disconcerting.

The element of earth that runs through this pair's veins is about reality and practicality, so each will give 100 per cent commitment to this relationship. There will be no hidden agendas to contend with. What you see is what you get. These earthy guys will create a solid base where they can play house and service one another's needs. Both are slow to connect but it will be Ms Capricorn's cardinal energy that will initiate a connection and Mr Virgo will keep the ball rolling.

In the bedroom: Earth signs usually make very compatible sexual partners. Sex will solidify their already strong connection. Both are much better expressing themselves on a physical level.

♑ Ms Capricorn + Mr Libra ♎

Sign	Capricorn	Libra
Symbol	Goat	Scales
Ruler	Saturn	Venus
Type	Cardinal	Cardinal
Element	Earth	Air

These two will respect each other's attributes but this will not be enough to bind them. Mr Libra's wishy-washy and indecisive ways will be frustrating for the definitive goat, who wants to know where she is heading in the relationship. Mr Libra's romancing will not be enough for this hard-nosed girl who is more turned on by practical considerations than by zealous passion. She takes her relationships seriously and will feel her Libran man is in love with love rather than with her. He, in turn, will feel unappreciated as he needs his ego stroked many times a day. The Capricornian woman is not the type to allow her heart to rule her head so she will not succumb to the whims of her Venusian man. She has a tendency to isolate herself emotionally and Mr Libra will be unsure how to penetrate what seems to him a cold, cold heart.

These two signs seem to come from different perspectives: he is a born romantic and places his lady on a pedestal but Ms Capricorn won't be comfortable on a throne that could be overturned at any moment. She would rather be on the ground where she can make her own way to the top in her own time and in her own way. These signs make a challenging aspect astrologically. On a fundamental level they are too different to make adjustments and compromises.

In the bedroom: The qualities of earth and air are very different. Mr Libra will want to discuss and analyse his relationship at length while Ms Capricorn will want to get down to business.

♑ Ms Capricorn + Mr Scorpio ♏

Sign	Capricorn	Scorpio
Symbol	Goat	Scorpion
Ruler	Saturn	Pluto
Type	Cardinal	Fixed
Element	Earth	Water

These two will rarely take their relationship lightly. Initially there will be a bit of a stand-off while they sum each other up. Despite their initial fascination, they will need to test the waters before committing. Mr Scorpio and Ms Capricorn are not the gushy types. They will be slow to expose their inner feelings and express their emotions until they feel on safe ground. Mr Scorpio will be attracted to this female, who is on a mission to achieve emotional and economic security, and he will respect her strength and ambitious quality. Ms Capricorn is attracted to the strong and controlled disposition of this man who will help her to achieve her goals. This is a dynamic duo and they will accomplish much in their relationship, largely because they are interested in the serious aspects of life rather than its frivolous and social side.

Mr Scorpio may brood and become moody on occasions when he feels his goat is too distant and not focused enough on him. He is emotionally challenged and needs to feel loved and acknowledged, and it will alarm him if he thinks his Capricornian love is too preoccupied with her own goals to express her need for him. It is easy for her to lose patience with the Scorpio's controlling and intense ways, and his reluctance to share his inner thoughts.

Ms Capricorn is the more emotionally detached of the two and it will take all the skills of the passionate Scorpio man to bring this woman to her knees. These two signs are the right mix to bring out the best in each other. With a bit of consideration and thought, it can be a highly successful union in all ways.

In the bedroom: Both have a strong sexual drive and Mr Scorpio has to live up to his reputation by never leaving his goat thinking it might be better down the track. He likes her to beg for more at every turn.

♑ Ms Capricorn + Mr Sagittarius ♐

Sign	Capricorn	Sagittarius
Symbol	Goat	Archer
Ruler	Saturn	Jupiter
Type	Cardinal	Mutable
Element	Earth	Fire

Ms Capricorn and Mr Sagittarius are more suited to being business partners than lovers. They value each other's attributes and can mutually benefit from shared skills. The goat admires the archer's ability to relate to a cross-section of people and is attracted to his sunny and optimistic approach to life. Secretly she wishes she could feel as optimistic and comfortable with herself as he does. Mr Sagittarius sees the goat as a woman of substance, who is on a mission to climb the ladder of success; however, his journey arises from different motivations. She is hard-nosed and has to have a purpose in life, whereas he is happy to go where the mood takes him.

Although he is impressed by her ability to stay focused on her goals, he will be discouraged by her lack of playfulness and her 'duty before pleasure' attitude. He is an adventurer and, with a well-developed inner child, will find her scolding ways too stifling. Ms Capricorn also likes to feel in control of her life, which includes her relationships. Mr Sagittarius will prove too elusive for her. She will never be able to trap this man into submission.

Mr Sagittarius will admire the loyalty and devotion this woman shows; however, he needs a mate who can allow him the freedom he so desperately craves, and it is unlikely to be Ms Capricorn. She hankers for the emotional security of a partnership and, being the most conservative sign of the zodiac, will start to tinkle wedding bells in his ear. But these will sound like alarm bells to the free-spirited Mr Sagittarius, who is likely to duck for cover.

In the bedroom: The goat might well be struck by Cupid's arrow, but this practical no-nonsense woman will want to schedule her romantic interludes into her organiser. The foot-in-mouth archer must be careful not to offend his sensitive Capricornian lover, who is unlikely to submit until he can prove to her that his philandering days are well and truly over.

♑ Ms Capricorn + Mr Capricorn ♑

Sign	Capricorn	Capricorn
Symbol	Goat	Goat
Ruler	Saturn	Saturn
Type	Cardinal	Cardinal
Element	Earth	Earth

This is a relationship built on respect and mutual affinities. Capricornians of both sexes are hard working and practical by nature. They don't feel comfortable with emotional displays, so they will feel comfortable sharing their own kind of intimacy. Together they make a formidable couple, who share the same aspirations. Although they will tread cautiously with each other in the early stages of a relationship, they will quickly come to realise how much they have in common, which is work, work and more work. This pair finds work exciting and they will always have a project on the backburner to keep them interested.

Because they lean towards the traditional in more ways than one, they will opt for the more socially acceptable union of marriage, rather than 'living in sin'. They need to be seen as pillars of society, so they will be in sync when it comes to 'proper' behaviour. Capricorns are 'the builders' of the zodiac and represent the mountain goat climbing to higher ground, which is exactly what these two will do: climb to their kingdom and live in their castle. Never ones for self-indulgent behaviour, they will support each other along the way and, even if one trips up, there will always be a kind and strong shoulder to lean on.

The downside of this match occurs when two Capricornians are too focused on reaching the summit to have fun on the journey. These two can be too resolute in achieving their goals and forget about the playful and simple things in life. If they can drop their guard at times, they may be in for a pleasant surprise.

In the bedroom: 'It won't happen over night but it *will* happen' could well be the motto for Capricornian lovers. Because these two usually keep their emotions in check, eventually they will relish the chance to share a deep and intimate love with someone they trust and with whom they share a mutual understanding.

♑ Ms Capricorn + Mr Aquarius ♒

Sign	Capricorn	Aquarius
Symbol	Goat	Water bearer
Ruler	Saturn	Uranus
Type	Cardinal	Fixed
Element	Earth	Air

The goat and the water bearer have much in common: each has a certain mission in life. Both have excellent minds and will respect each other's skills and talents, but they do have their differences. Ms Capricorn is focused on personal success and achievement, whereas Mr Aquarius has humanitarian aspirations and is focused on helping the world.

Even though they are individuals who don't need to bask in each other's glory, Ms Capricorn might feel her man is too detached and indifferent at times and is not as attentive as she would like him to be. But both lack the ability to be responsive on an emotional level and, when things get tough, will find it hard to get through to each other. Her good deeds will never go unnoticed or be taken for granted but the Aquarian man is not good at knowing how to be responsive. His manner is unpredictable: he will be all lovey-dovey one minute and impersonal the next. Yet he is completely in the dark about this pattern of behaviour. His ruling planet Uranus, which is rebellious and unpredictable, can be blamed when he is off doing his own thing. But Saturn, who co-rules Aquarius, is responsible when he is attentive and supporting his mate.

Ms Capricorn has a traditional side to her personality and, with her, everything has an order and fits into a plan. Her off-beat man will never be that conventional and, in fact, will be much more unorthodox in his approach to life. She may see glimmers of hope at times; however, Ms Capricorn loves consistency and Mr Aquarius will be consistent only in his inconsistency! Both are visionaries yet how they accomplish their dreams will differ. If she is willing to sit back and take a magic carpet ride with Mr Aquarius, she might find she enjoys being swept off her feet.

In the bedroom: Sex is not an obsession for either Capricornians or Aquarians. But she will relish the unpredictable bedroom antics of her zany lover and together they will dedicate themselves to the task at hand.

♑ Ms Capricorn + Mr Pisces ♓

Sign	Capricorn	Pisces
Symbol	Goat	Fish
Ruler	Saturn	Neptune
Type	Cardinal	Mutable
Element	Earth	Water

Ms Capricorn loves to have a hobby to pursue but fishing is not high on her list. But it might be just what she needs to relax and enjoy herself instead of playing the busy wife and homemaker or the determined, driven entrepreneur. To catch the elusive Piscean is challenging, yet Ms Capricorn will have all the skills she needs to snare this man. But will she be happy with her catch? This is the million-dollar question.

Both can benefit from this association. Ms Capricorn can learn to express the more feeling side of her nature, while she can teach the fish a thing or two about order and management. If they have the patience to learn to adjust to their differences, this can be a wonderful meeting of the minds as well as a strong physical connection. Ms Capricorn is not one to readily show her sensual and lusty appetite, yet beneath her reserved demeanour is a girl who needs to be appreciated and loved. Mr Pisces will be that man. He can sense what this lady needs and will be able to draw out her more charismatic side. She, in turn, will ground her fish and help him consolidate his talents with her practical approach and flair for achievement.

Ms Capricorn will be the one in charge of this relationship, which will suit her fish. He will be only too happy for her to take the lead and show the way because he recognises he can't stay submerged forever. Ms Capricorn is well able to take control if she sees her fish dive too deeply into his own private world and indulge in his one or two addictions. She will be the discriminating one and will endeavour to bring this romantic man back to earth where he will soak up the earthly pleasures his Capricornian lover can provide.

In the bedroom: Ms Capricorn will be direct and assertive when it comes to sex, like she is about most things in her life. Water and earth signs share a depth of passion that will set the room on fire. She will want to get down to business, while the imaginative and creative fish will be only too happy to lead her on a sexual journey of self-discovery.

Celebrity Ms Capricorn:

Helena Rubenstein

Cosmetics queen, born 25 December 1870, in Kracow, Poland

```
Personal planets:  Sun in Capricorn
                   Moon in Aquarius
                   Mercury in Capricorn
                   Venus in Capricorn
                   Mars in Virgo
```

Personally, I think if a woman hasn't met the right man by the time she is 24, she may be lucky.

– Helena Rubinstein

Capricornian Helena Rubinstein was one of the world's most successful beauty and cosmetics entrepreneurs of the twentieth century. Her great rival in the trade was Elizabeth Arden, coincidentally also a Capricorn, which might suggest that the voraciousness of this industry was handled best by strong and committed people. Rubinstein's vision created an opportunity for woman to address their vanity, and the cliché 'beauty is only skin deep' became a reality as skin-conscious women adopted her products as part of their beauty routines. Her initial magical potion was just the beginning of a long career in the industry as her product line continued to grow and dominate the market for many decades.

True to form, Rubinstein's Capricornian spirit saw her dedicate herself to this passion her entire life, actively contributing to her growing empire until she died at the age of 94. Her parents encouraged her potential and she migrated from Poland to Australia at the age of 18 to start a life that would become the success she dreamed of, never letting up on her drive to reach her goal. Rubinstein's chart shows she had most of her planets in earth signs, which gave her a grounded and enduring personality. She was a dedicated and driven woman who consolidated her past successes and continued to build her future. Her relationships were not her primary drive, although she remained a faithful wife. Her first marriage to

Polish-American writer Edward Titus was a relationship that gave her an insight to the artistic and literary world, yet she didn't have the time to devote to her marriage, or the arts, and the marriage was over within 10 years. Her husband's philandering ways and his own insecurities brought the marriage undone. However, she would have been faithful and committed in her marriage; both her Venus and Mars were in earth elements, which gave her a strong loyal and committed focus.

Her second marriage to Russian Prince Artchil Gourielli-Tchkonia, an Aquarian 20 years her junior, showed her interest in marrying someone that had a station in life – not that she really needed someone to elevate her at this stage. But the strong Capricornian theme running through her chart suggests that the status may have given her emotional security and fulfilled the cliché that Capricorns are like a wine – they get better with age – and start to feel younger as they become older. His Aquarian energy would have given her a free rein to continue along her career path without restriction and he would have been sympathetic to her vision.

Mr Capricorn – an overview

The goat is a man of few words but when he falls in love, he will let you know. Mr Capricorn is not the romantic type to gush and fawn over his beloved, but views romance as a more serious business. Self-control and caution are important for the goat and, as the typical earth sign, the slow and steady approach is the safest. He also needs to feel emotionally protected and will therefore take plenty of time to assess if a woman is the one for him before he makes a move. Mr Capricorn has difficulty relating. He is the silent type, never expressing how he truly feels. However, what he lacks in the charm stakes he makes up for in his attributes of loyalty and commitment.

His need for security – both professional and personal – will see Mr Capricorn stay true to a relationship. Rarely will he rock the boat and make waves that might end a union because he values family and marriage, and will always remain a dutiful and faithful husband who takes his commitments seriously.

Mr Capricorn has a burning ambition to achieve success and prosperity and is tenacious in his will to focus, so he is not averse to forming a union that can help him on his journey. Many Capricornian men are attracted to women who come from higher social standing, which gives them the status and respectability they long for. He is a man who will always provide and be protective of his loved one. However, he is not a pushover and his mate will have to provide him with some sensual pleasures in return.

He is a workaholic so he needs a mate who can understand his passion and be only too happy to enjoy the fruits of his success, rather than be critical of the time he spends at work. This man is great at compartmentalising, so his relationship fits neatly into one of his boxes. His romances are just one part of a life he toils hard at, so he will need a partner who is just as pragmatic and has doesn't demand his all.

Mr Capricorn starts to enjoy his life more as he becomes older – when he feels more relaxed and comfortable with himself. So girls, you might have to wait for the old goat before you can have some real fun.

Famous Capricornian men

* Muhammad Ali (boxer)
* Federico Fellini (film director)
* Cary Grant (actor)
* Elvis Presley (singer)
* Rudyard Kipling (writer)
* Martin Luther King (civil rights leader)

Combinations

♑ Mr Capricorn + Ms Aries ♈

Sign	Capricorn	Aries
Symbol	Goat	Ram
Ruler	Saturn	Mars
Type	Cardinal	Cardinal
Element	Earth	Fire

Mr Capricorn is interested in guarantees and long-term security, which Ms Aries will struggle to provide. Astrologically, these two signs square each other, which suggests that there will be difficulties in finding a happy medium.

Mr Capricorn is ambitious, pragmatic, conservative and single-minded and ruled by the planet Saturn, which represents hard work, tenacity and direction. He will make an excellent provider for Ms Aries, who may admire his success and the trappings of wealth. Ms Aries will be initially attracted to the strength and commitment Mr Capricorn gives her and he'll equally enjoy her free-spirited approach to life and her bubbly personality.

The fiery warmth of the Arian persona will melt the cold heart of the Capricornian. But because the goat can sometimes keep his true feelings under wraps, he may end up losing the woman he loves because he simply can't tell her how he really feels – unlike Ms Aries who calls a spade a spade and has no problem doing so. But ultimately his seriousness and lack of frivolity will not be enough to keep the home fires burning. Ms Aries will crave a more carefree union and will break free from this structured and rigid relationship that may stifle her creativity.

In the bedroom: Mr Capricorn is self-disciplined and cautious, even in the bedroom, which can be extremely frustrating for a voracious woman likes Ms Aries, who jumps headlong into most situations.

♑ Mr Capricorn + Ms Taurus ♉

Sign	Capricorn	Taurus
Symbol	Goat	Bull
Ruler	Saturn	Venus
Type	Cardinal	Fixed
Element	Earth	Earth

These two earth sign possess a favourable combination of similar qualities. They share the same ideals and values and are both driven to accumulate resources to help them lead a comfortable and secure lifestyle. Taureans will provide the perfect home setting for the Capricornian man, who will appreciate his partner's ability to be the perfect wife, hostess and homemaker

Mr Capricorn and Ms Taurus will stay committed to one another and see divorce as a last resort. Both have supportive natures and a mutual understanding of the practicalities of life and it is the interest of materialistic security that helps keep this pair together. Mr Capricorn is interested in social status and respect, so Ms Taurus is the ideal partner to help him in his rise to fame and fortune. Loyalty, integrity and commitment feature very strongly in this match. They will provide each other with tenderness and love in and out of the bedroom, and be appreciative of the other's enduring love and devotion.

Money is important to both the Taurean and Capricornian, but only as a means to provide comfort and security to the former, and power and prestige to the latter. Behind every great man there's an equally strong, determined woman and Ms Taurus is no exception. She and her earth sign mate will make a formidable couple – he as a great leader and she alongside him as his loyal supporter.

In the bedroom: The goat never finds it easy to express his desires but, with the right encouragement, Ms Taurus and her man will be swinging from the chandeliers in no time!

♑ Mr Capricorn + Ms Gemini ♊

Sign	Capricron	Gemini
Symbol	Goat	Twins
Ruler	Saturn	Mercury
Type	Cardinal	Mutable
Element	Earth	Air

The energy is so different between these two that rarely would they attract each other as a prospective partner. Ms Gemini values her freedom and will find the goat too conservative and boring to keep her interested. He is a pragmatic and steady creature who values integrity, loyalty and commitment from his mate – traits that Ms Gemini definitely lacks. She is not the sort of woman who can help this ambitious goat further his status in life. He needs someone who will walk methodically and slowly beside him, sharing in his quest to achieve fortune and success.

Ms Gemini doesn't share Mr Capricorn's persistence and interest in commitment and success and his desire for social status and security. His ambitious streak is fuelled by his ruling planet Saturn, often referred to as the 'cosmic cop'. He values tenacity and hard work and is far too disciplined in his approach to life for Ms Gemini. He will harshly judge her sense of frivolity and fun and lack of commitment. She will be too much of a featherweight to compete in his corner of the ring.

The Capricornian guy requires solidity and dependability from his partner and, although they both seek independence, he still will want to be the boss in this match. In turn, Ms Gemini will not give up her independence for the promise of security and financial gains.

In the bedroom: Both the Gemini and Capricornian approach sex from the same perspective. Neither is necessarily after a mind-altering experience but rather a comfortable and pleasurable one. He'll skip with joy if his Gemini lover is receptive to his playful, physical advances; in turn, she'll appreciate words to arouse her desires.

♑ Mr Capricorn + Ms Cancer ♋

Sign	Capricorn	Cancer
Symbol	Goat	Crab
Ruler	Saturn	Moon
Type	Cardinal	Cardinal
Element	Earth	Water

These signs are steeped in tradition and family values. Mr Capricorn is ruled by Saturn, which represents hard work, responsibility and discipline, all of which he can bring into his relationship with Ms Crab. She respects his tenacity, admires his responsible attitude and enjoys the material benefits he can provide her with. Mr Capricorn is very much commitment oriented and will value his family life with the same degree of intensity as Ms Cancer, but he can project a cold, hard exterior at times.

He is a pragmatic soul and does not understand the emotional needs of his Cancerian partner, who is prone to mood swings that baffle the stoic and seemingly emotionless goat. His aloof attitude will at times create disharmony in their union because, by nature, Ms Cancer needs a tactile, demonstrative man – something the Capricornian is most definitely not.

All is not lost, however. Despite his lack of compassion and understanding, Mr Capricorn will be able to provide his Cancerian lover with the financial security and stability she seeks. In turn, she is well able to melt the icy bravado of her mountain goat.

In the bedroom: The Cancerian woman will take the Capricorn man to undiscovered heights of sexual pleasure. She does appreciate the commitment and loyalty he gives her which will allow her to open up and really be herself.

♑ Mr Capricorn + Ms Leo ♌

Sign	Capricorn	Leo
Symbol	Goat	Lion
Ruler	Saturn	Sun
Type	Cardinal	Fixed
Element	Earth	Fire

Ms Leo has much to gain from the steady, reliable and stable Mr Capricorn; however, these qualities don't always excite the lioness. She gains her security by participating in life, whereas he gains his from financial success. And she likes to live in a world of colour, vitality and excitement – needing to express her creativity through whatever turns her on; Mr Capricorn is far too reserved and earthed for that.

Although both need recognition, it comes from different sources. For her, it's a platform where she can strut her stuff, which is an area where he will not want to compete. He is more interested in receiving accolades for his ability to accumulate money.

On a relationship level, the Capricornian guy prefers a one-to-one intimate connection and is inclined to become quite possessive and jealous of his Leo girl, who has no shortage of adoring males waiting to make their move. She is much more gregarious and outgoing than her Capricornian mate, who will turn his back on anything he considers shallow and frivolous.

In the bedroom: Capricornian men crave success in all their undertakings and their performance in the bedroom is no exception. He will be an attentive and persistent lover because he wants to please his partner and teach her a thing or two, but he might very well become frustrated that Ms Leo's hedonistic attitude dominates all areas of her life.

♑ Mr Capricorn + Ms Virgo ♍

Sign	Capricorn	Virgo
Symbol	Goat	Virgin
Ruler	Saturn	Mercury
Type	Cardinal	Mutable
Element	Earth	Earth

These two earth signs have a mutual respect for each other; they share the same virtues, which seem to be an important ingredient for stability and longevity. Mr Capricorn and Ms Virgo have a practical and pragmatic approach to life – a no-fuss, get-on-with-it attitude. Their hardworking energies lead to success in business and combine to build a happy relationship together. Ms Virgo will appreciate Mr Capricorn's commitment, his stable persona and his logical mind.

Trust is a strong link between this pair. It brings Ms Virgo and Mr Capricorn closer together and allows them to open up and share their expectations and intimacies. Ms Virgo will take comfort in her loyal, Capricornian mate, who not only can provide a consistent and stable environment, but be her devoted protector as well. This couple's driving force is that they share the same vision for the future: they are builders and yet can encourage one another to learn to relax a little and take time out to smell the roses.

In the bedroom: The sexual attraction between Mr Capricorn and Ms Virgo will grow from strength to strength as they learn to respect and appreciate each other's values. Both can harbour feelings of sexual inadequacy, but this is a relationship based on mutual trust so it won't be long before both are enjoying a romp in the hay.

♑ Mr Capricorn + Ms Libra ♎

Sign	Capricorn	Libra
Symbol	Goat	Scales
Ruler	Saturn	Venus
Type	Cardinal	Cardinal
Element	Earth	Air

The Libran energy is particularly attractive to Mr Capricorn, who will admire the social skills and controlled personality of this woman. He is preoccupied with status and is often attracted to a partner who can elevate him socially. And Ms Libra is adaptable to most social situations and relates well to people, qualities the mountain goat aspires to. She will admire his business acumen, and his focus on achieving and knowing his own mind so well.

These signs can learn much from each other yet, sadly, the negatives seem to outweigh the positives, which leaves Ms Libra feeling uncomfortable because the scales are not perfectly balanced. The goat will be too critical of her need to surround herself with life's little luxuries and comforts, which can lead to some friction in the camp. She is a communicator and needs to talk about everything – especially feelings and relationships. He is a private person and too reserved, and will often appear too detached for the romantic Ms Libra.

Both signs are emotionally cool: fundamentally both will feel in the dark as to where they stand with each other. The air sign girl might appear too superficial for the stoic, pragmatic goat, and he will be far too grounded for her.

Mr Capricorn and Ms Libra have conventional leanings and can be caught up with what they see as an appropriate form of behaviour. They will always favour a socially accepted marriage over living together, and so might end up married for convention's sake rather than for lust and romance.

In the bedroom: The intimate side of this relationship can make or break it. If it works, it will be sustaining and will heat up an otherwise lukewarm bond.

♑ Mr Capricorn + Ms Scorpio ♏

Sign	Capricorn	Scorpio
Symbol	Goat	Scorpion
Ruler	Saturn	Pluto
Type	Cardinal	Fixed
Element	Earth	Water

This partnership has an affinity and is considered one of the best combinations of the earth and water signs. Mr Capricorn and Ms Scorpio seem to bring out the positive qualities in each other. Both take their relationship seriously and won't waste time making their intentions known. They won't play games with each other because both are into truth and integrity and will respect the other's values and viewpoints. The only catch here is that the Capricornian man is a pragmatist and, because Ms Scorpio needs a certain amount of intensity in her relationships, the goat might appear too aloof or detached for this sensitive creature. Her emotional senses are strong and his err on the side of insensitivity.

Power preoccupies them both. It gives her some validation as a woman and he likes the power that comes with prestige. Both view success as a powerful tool.

Ms Scorpio can be of great assistance to her man with her loyal and committed demeanour and will be only too happy to stand by him in all situations. Never fire up a Scorpio woman or question her motives, especially when it comes to those she loves. She has a rather nasty sting that may take hours to heal. Mr Capricorn will value her single-minded drive and support. These two can fly high together in more ways than one; they are passionate and intense in different ways, yet still have a desire to merge and enjoy a long and satisfying union.

In the bedroom: Any problems these two have will get ironed out in the bedroom. Mr Capricorn is only too happy to be stung by the venom of this passionate lady and, with both sharing a similar intensity in their lovemaking, Ms Scorpio will always be waiting for her Billy Goat Gruff!

♑ Mr Capricorn + Ms Sagittarius ♐

Sign	Capricorn	Sagittarius
Symbol	Goat	Archer
Ruler	Saturn	Jupiter
Type	Cardinal	Mutable
Element	Earth	Fire

Mr Capricorn is just what this girl needs. He is a practical and grounded man who can temper her volatile and impulsive nature, and persuade her to keep her feet on the ground. In turn, Ms Sagittarius is what he needs: a strong-spirited, optimistic girl who can encourage him to see the positive and fun-loving side of life. Sadly, however, what they need is not necessarily what they want. She is more interested in developing her mind. Her security is not based on material accomplishments but rather on recognising that she can be free to do what she wants, unlike her conservative Capricornian mate who loves structure and order in his life.

The archer is happiest living a nomadic lifestyle, which will allow her to explore a different side of life. He, however, will not cope with her desire to chase rainbows. She wants to see the fruits of his labours, yet is only interested in eating the fruit. And although she admires the goat's virtues – caution, discretion and conservatism – she is too bohemian to lock herself into the practicalities and the mundane, and will see him as being far too pragmatic.

The goat is a traditionalist and takes himself far too seriously, according to the adventurous archer. Her fiery spirit is too out of control for this man, who needs to feel a sense of purpose and direction in his life. Ms Sagittarius's only direction is out of the goat's clutches and into a more colourful and zany space, where she can indulge herself with the fun-loving pursuits that turn her on.

In the bedroom: This is always a fun place for these two. The goat can relax and allow the archer to give him much-needed pampering. In turn, he will treat her to a serious dose of lovemaking, since he prides himself on being the best in all areas of his life.

♑ Mr Capricorn + Ms Capricorn ♑

Sign	Capricorn	Capricorn
Symbol	Goat	Goat
Ruler	Saturn	Saturn
Type	Cardinal	Cardinal
Element	Earth	Earth

This is a relationship built on respect and mutual affinities. Capricornians of both sexes are hard working and practical by nature. They don't feel comfortable with emotional displays, so they will feel comfortable sharing their own kind of intimacy. Together they make a formidable couple, who share the same aspirations. Although they will tread cautiously with each other in the early stages of a relationship, they will quickly come to realise how much they have in common, which is work, work and more work. This pair finds work exciting and they will always have a project on the backburner to keep them interested.

Because they lean towards the traditional in more ways than one, they will opt for the more socially acceptable union of marriage, rather than 'living in sin'. They need to be seen as pillars of society, so they will be in sync when it comes to 'proper' behaviour. Capricorns are 'the builders' of the zodiac and represent the mountain goat climbing to higher ground, which is exactly what these two will do: climb to their kingdom and live in their castle. Never ones for self-indulgent behaviour, they will support each other along the way and, even if one trips up, there will always be a kind and strong shoulder to lean on.

The downside of this match occurs when two Capricornians are too focused on reaching the summit to have fun on the journey. These two can be too resolute in achieving their goals and forget about the playful and simple things in life. If they can drop their guard at times, they may be in for a pleasant surprise.

In the bedroom: 'It won't happen over night but it *will* happen' could well be the motto for Capricornian lovers. Because these two usually keep their emotions in check, eventually they will relish the chance to share a deep and intimate love with someone they trust and with whom they share a mutual understanding.

♑ Mr Capricorn + Ms Aquarius ♒

Sign	Capricorn	Aquarius
Symbol	Goat	Water bearer
Ruler	Saturn	Uranus
Type	Cardinal	Fixed
Element	Earth	Air

Earth and air seem to be at odds with one another. Mr Capricorn likes to have his feet firmly planted on terra firma and needs to know where he is going. So resolved is the mountain goat in his ambition that he plans his path down to the finest detail; Ms Aquarius, however, is a woman who enjoys wandering wherever her mood takes her. She is freedom-loving, rebellious and impulsive – all traits the goat won't allow himself to indulge in. She is a lover of humankind and is on a mission to save the world.

Both share the same energy and passion to achieve, yet Mr Capricorn needs appreciation and validation along the way. He is not as strong and secure as he leads people to believe and will feel left out in the cold by his Aquarian ice-maiden. Even with all his managerial talents, this woman is one he won't be able to control. She is a girl who can create relationship problems because she doesn't know how to give herself emotionally. She can seem impersonal and is often misunderstood as being disinterested and detached.

Air signs are regarded more as thinkers than feeling types. Her emotions run deep, but her Capricornian man will not understand them easily. He will see her as single-minded and fixed in her ideas – never the one to compromise. They do, however, share a common bond because Ms Aquarius is co-ruled by the planets Saturn and Uranus, and the Saturnine energy shared by Mr Capricorn will attract her to the trappings of success. She will delight in the finery this man has to offer.

In the bedroom: Mr Capricorn is likely to be too practical and down-to-earth for this ethereal and imaginative Ms – especially when it comes to his bedroom antics. Her changeability will be unsettling, making it hard to know exactly where she's at and what she wants from him.

♑ Mr Capricorn + Ms Pisces ♓

Sign	Capricorn	Pisces
Symbol	Goat	Fish
Ruler	Saturn	Neptune
Type	Cardinal	Mutable
Element	Earth	Water

He is pragmatic and she is a romantic. He is discriminating and she lacks discernment. He is ambitious and she is an escapist. He is a saviour and she is a victim. Will these two really make it as a couple? Yes, but only if they are willing to learn and develop, and incorporate a little portion of each other's virtues into their psyches.

The fish and the goat seem worlds apart. He stands firmly on the mountain top for all to see and revels in his accomplishments, while the fish hides deep in the ocean with King Neptune by her side, swimming free of restraints.

This is a relationship in which each can see what they are lacking and will appreciate the other's efforts to make things work. Mr Capricorn will love the artistic and gentle qualities this soft lady can provide, while she will be grateful for his physical support and his encouragement of her talents. As different as these two seem, it is a partnership that has much potential. Earth needs water to sustain it, so Mr Capricorn will be grateful to his Piscean mate for keeping him from perishing and allowing him the opportunity to grow spiritually.

Their challenges provide a landscape of opportunity for learning and developing. Ms Pisces will make the adjustments and sacrifices for this man because she can see he is honourable and, above all, virtuous in his pursuits. This thoughtful woman will suit Mr Capricorn because beneath his veneer of strength and composure lies a vulnerable man who needs a gentle soul to coax out his well-hidden soft side. She can guide him on his quest for power for the good of all rather than for his own selfish desires.

In the bedroom: There's no stopping the unbridled passion between a sensitive and seductive fish and her eager goat. He will feel relaxed and comfortable in the arms of a woman who is happiest when giving pleasure to others.

Celebrity Mr Capricorn: Elvis Presley

Singer, born 4.35 am 8 January 1935 in Tupelo, Mississippi, USA

```
Personal planets:  Sun in Capricorn
                   Moon in Pisces
                   Mercury in Capricorn
                   Venus in Capricorn
                   Mars in Libra
```

Do what's right for you, as long as it don't hurt no one.

– Elvis Presley

Elvis, the 'king of rock 'n' roll', was a man who had many faces. Throughout his life, his talent touched a great many people around the world. But, in true Capricornian style, he was not content to be just a guitar-playing singer; he was also driven to carve a name for himself in the film industry, which he felt would be a true measure of his success.

As far as relationships are concerned, Capricornian men seem to have a closer bond with their mothers than their fathers, and Elvis was no exception. His love and respect for his mother was widely known and her influence played a major role throughout his life and coloured his future relationships, making him desirous of a relationship that was traditional and respectful.

His relationship with his Gemini wife Priscilla was indicative of Elvis's innate drive to be associated with someone from a respectable background. Even though she was very young when they first met, it was on his insistence that she moved into his Gracelands mansion and completed her education. As a Capricornian, he was driven to protect and ensure that Pricilla was well looked after. He may have made assumptions about what was good for her, since he was not always in tune with what his partner really needed. While he showed external strength, his chart has some fire elements, making him need emotional support and attention.

Elvis's complexities would have made him difficult to live with. Outwardly he would appear confident and in control yet underlying this was an emotional insecurity that would have required an understanding and patient partner.

Both Pricilla and Elvis's Moon signs were in water elements, which meant they had an empathic bond and could tune into each other's feelings and moods. There would have been an irresistible attraction between them. Priscilla's Moon in Scorpio would have given her a more discerning personality and made her less forgiving and somewhat controlling compared with Elvis, whose Moon in the sensitive and romantic sign of Pisces would have made him emotional and shy, with a strong need for escapism which resulted in his many addictions. Like many gifted and talented people, Elvis's chart shows a strong link between his Sun sign and the planet of creativity and intuition, Neptune. He walked the high and low road of life and, sadly, eventually succumbed to the darker side of his nature.

AQUARIUS (21 January–20 February)

Ruled by the planet Uranus
Air sign
Fixed
Masculine energy

In general ...

Aquarians are the humanitarians of the zodiac. They are independent, free thinkers who are original and rebellious, and are seen in many walks of life marching to the beat of a different drum. Always on the lookout for ways to improve the world, they are attracted to an environment where they can grow through knowledge and where they can move about freely, unhampered by rules and regulations.

Aquarians are known for their sharp wit and intelligence and are often the pioneers of their chosen field. Both male and female water bearers are unselfish lovers, yet they seem to fare better in friendships than in intimate relationships. Aquarians are no stranger to love affairs. They like to play the field rather than commit to a steady union, which might restrict them in their quest to experience as many things in life as they can fit in. They can be committed one moment but gone the next. Then they will be off in pursuit of the next cause, never ones to let the grass grow under their feet.

Aquarians seem to have recurring relationship problems, largely because they are too impersonal and don't know how to relate on intimate terms. Sexually, they are one of the more progressive and sexually experimental signs of the zodiac, yet as an air sign they are removed emotionally, processing their emotions through rationale and intellect. This can lead their partners to feel unwanted and unloved, yet this is not the case. Aquarians do have a desire to be in meaningful relationships, but spend more time thinking about how they can put their energy into universal love rather than into one partnership.

As a fixed sign, Aquarians are never flexible and they will remain stubborn and opinionated, which gives them an air of superiority. Yet they are never social snobs and will engage in friendships with people from all walks of life – the most appealing being those who 'walk their talk'. They are drawn to someone who is individualistic and off-beat and has the same visionary energy. The more bent they are, the more attractive they will seem to a water bearer, who will take them on a guided tour of the zodiac.

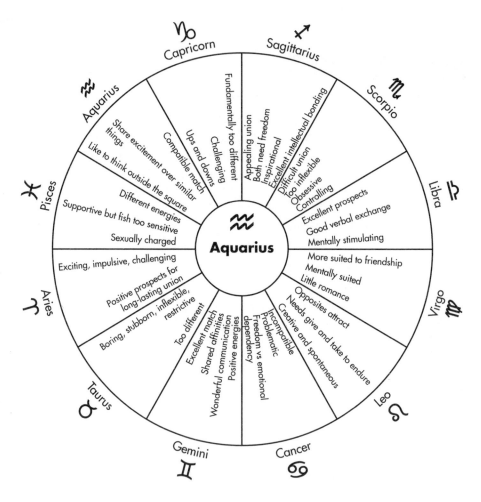

How an Aquarian personality might match up with other star signs

Ms Aquarius – an overview

The Aquarian woman is a blend of tradition and conservatism, and a passionate desire for the unconventional and bohemian. Her ruling planets are Saturn – which gives her the desire for stability – and Uranus – which whets her appetite for the unusual. Most Aquarian women, however, seem to swing to the Uranian camp, where they enjoy the off-beat and unpredictable in their lives.

Ms Aquarius has a friendly disposition yet one could never call her a warm and affectionate woman. Her qualities are directed at mankind rather than a specific man. She is an independent and single-minded girl, who loves relationships but does not depend on just one man. She shares her passion with friends rather than with a man. She is complex and difficult to read and has difficulty showing her emotions and expressing her feelings. Ms Aquarius would prefer to have an intellectual exchange rather than confront her emotions, and often presents as a 'cold fish' and is accused of being too impersonal. She has great difficulty in giving herself intimately and yet is very open-minded when it comes to sexual trysts. She is a woman who loves to experiment and is very open sexually.

Ms Aquarius's intellectual capacity is vast and she will never be content to stay in the background. She would prefer to be actively engaged in a purposeful career rather than playing house. She is attracted to the unusual, which rubs off on her choice of mates. Because she likes to be different, she will be drawn to people from all walks of life and cultures. She doesn't discriminate when it comes to partners, yet her most demanding requirement is that she has the space and freedom to be herself in the union. Like her other air-sign girlfriends, Ms Libra and Ms Gemini, she will not be drawn to hysterical and emotional outbursts, but would rather analyse her feelings logically. She has a detached perspective on things and will never let emotions get in the way.

This woman is an exciting and diverse companion who needs a mate who will share in her love of humanity and also understand her sensitivities. He will need to respect her independent streak and yet will need to be as sharp and as smart as she is, otherwise she will always be one step ahead.

Famous Aquarian women

* Eartha Kitt (singer)
* Germaine Greer (feminist/writer)
* Anna Pavlova (ballerina)
* Virginia Woolf (author)
* Mia Farrow (actor)
* Oprah Winfrey (talk show host)

Combinations

♒ Ms Aquarius + Mr Aries ♈

Sign	Aquarius	Aries
Symbol	Water bearer	Ram
Ruler	Uranus	Mars
Type	Fixed	Cardinal
Element	Air	Fire

This dynamic duo will find much common ground in a relationship. Both idealistic and adventure loving, Ms Aquarius and Mr Aries will entertain and amuse each other to no end. She will find his child-like qualities endearing and, for him, her quirky sense of humour and *joie de vivre* will be a breath of fresh air.

This Aquarian girl will teach her Arian mate to broaden his outlook and perspective on life, which will lead to his own journey of self-discovery. He will admire and respect the intellect of the water bearer and will learn a great deal from her. On the downside, however, he might find her detached, aloof nature a little confusing because he can't really work out what she feels; she has a tendency to hide her emotions under a cool exterior for fear of revealing a vulnerability that her mate might not fully understand.

Despite the obvious compatibility between this pair, Aquarius is a fixed sign, making this woman stubborn and rigid in her outlook on life. This can be frustrating for her Arian partner, who might find her a bit too opinionated and set in her ways. While he enjoys freedom and space in his relationships, it's usually on his terms and he might find his Aquarian mate's equal need for solitude a bit unsettling.

However, Aquarians are altruistic people and if Mr Aries can share his partner's interest in humanitarian causes and intellectual exchange, this could end up a decidedly rewarding union.

In the bedroom: The Aquarian woman is not as sexually needy as her Arian mate and can sometimes be a bit detached when it comes to their lovemaking. She'll need to summon up some enthusiasm and interest in his sexual advances, otherwise this air girl might find she has extinguished his fire.

♒ Ms Aquarius + Mr Taurus ♉

Sign	Aquarius	Taurus
Symbol	Water bearer	Bull
Ruler	Uranus	Venus
Type	Fixed	Fixed
Element	Air	Earth

Ms Aquarius will be too independent, wilful and flamboyant for the Taurean man's more conservative and structured personality. She values her freedom above all else and Mr Taurus will always be trying to tame his free-spirited mate. Unfortunately, because Ms Aquarius has the same fixed mode of expression as him, she will be unwilling to temper her desire for universal love.

At times the Aquarian might show a conservative streak because she is, on the one-hand, traditionally oriented yet, on the other, attracted to a bohemian lifestyle. This can confuse Mr Taurus, who thinks he has her figured out until she is off saving the world on one of her humanitarian pursuits, leaving him out in the cold. When she returns, hoping to pick up where they left off, she'll be most surprised to find that he has finally lost patience, which usually takes some time for the loyal and patient bull, and is fussing over the next woman in his life.

Both these signs are generous spirits and are always willing to lend a helping hand, but while Ms Aquarius expects nothing in return, Mr Taurus is more calculating in his approach. He will find the water bearer too cold and detached for his sensual nature and will feel his efforts to ensure she feels secure and comfortable are not always appreciated.

One of the fundamental differences in this love relationship is that Aquarians are attracted to people from all walks of life, and friendship is sometimes more important than love and intimacy. This can frustrate the single-minded, loyal Taurean, who likes to know the status quo, and lead to feelings of insecurity. This couple's requirements in love will rarely be met by each other, and the sooner each recognises these incompatibilities, the better for all.

In the bedroom: The detached air woman will be a little confusing to read for the down-to-earth Taurean. She's more into a meeting of the minds than a melding of the bodies.

♒ Ms Aquarius + Mr Gemini ♊

Sign	Aquarius	Gemini
Symbol	Water bearer	Twins
Ruler	Uranus	Mercury
Type	Fixed	Mutable
Element	Air	Air

When two in-sync signs collide, it can be the start of a beautiful friendship that blossoms into an even more beautiful relationship. Mr Gemini will notice this zany and effervescent Aquarian enigma across a crowded room and she'll be equally enchanted to finally have met someone who truly understands her.

Although no relationship is perfect, the Aquarian and Gemini union will be close to harmonious compared with the other rocky relationships they have each weathered along the way. She is a true humanitarian who will have no qualms about being the more giving and tolerant partner in this union. She prides herself on her quest for the truth and is likely to become deeply annoyed at Mr Gemini's continuous ability to bend it. But the sharp-witted twin is quick to point out to his fellow air sign that while she speaks the truth, it's often not always at once.

Both love people and neither will have the slightest concern with the menagerie of various souls each gathers into their fold. In this relationship, both Mr Gemini and Ms Aquarius give as much as is needed and expected from their mate which results in satisfaction all round. Since these two value friendship above all else, they often sacrifice love in favour of it because it is less demanding and intense. But if they can weather the trials and tribulations of a love match – she understanding his need for freedom and he recognising and understanding her complexities – then this will be a pairing of soulmates.

In the bedroom: The Gemini and Aquarian understand each other's physical needs and can make beautiful music together. Both tend to favour expressing their love through mental exchanges rather than physical abandonment.

♒ Ms Aquarius + Mr Cancer ♋

Sign	Aquarius	Cancer
Symbol	Water bearer	Crab
Ruler	Uranus	Moon
Type	Fixed	Cardinal
Element	Air	Water

The Aquarian woman and the Cancerian man will share some great intellectual times together and are really better suited to a friendship or business relationship than a love match. Ms Aquarius's strong independent streak, her elusive manner and cool disposition do not give Mr Cancer the validity he needs to embark on the emotional relationship he desires.

The Aquarian woman's strong drive for independence will always leave her mate struggling to possess this girl, especially a Cancerian male who is after a woman who will stand by his side and be there for him in every situation. Ms Aquarius finds it hard to commit to a relationship because she is a lover of humanity and shares her life with many. Her life's journey is to spread her altruistic message to all who wish to listen and, although she has a kind heart, Mr Cancer rarely gets to see it because she does not know how to show emotional depth the same way he does. All air signs seem to have this inability to give themselves completely to a relationship; often their detached and impersonal attitude is misinterpreted as a lack of desire and love.

Mr Cancer needs someone who will openly display affection and be committed to the union. He is the clingy type and his jealous streak will drive Ms Aquarius away because she doesn't have his same possessive or needy disposition. Variety for her is the spice of life, but for Mr Cancer it is finding true love.

In the bedroom: Mr Crab can pull out all his sexual trickery and, as long as he keeps it bright and bubbly and loaded with fun, his Aquarian lover will be only to happy to join the party, However, if Mr Cancer is longing for a long and languid romp with lots of foreplay he'll be walking sideways in the wrong direction.

♒ Ms Aquarius + Mr Leo ♌

Sign	Aquarius	Leo
Symbol	Water bearer	Lion
Ruler	Uranus	Sun
Type	Fixed	Fixed
Element	Air	Fire

The fire and air elements of this combination create a good rapport between Mr Leo and the zany Ms Aquarius, but only if he can play down his domineering persona. Leo men like a partner who can support them and help them shine so he may be a little disappointed that his Aquarian women is off saving the world instead of doting on him and pandering to his needs.

Both might find themselves in the public arena; however, she's more likely to be involved in a humanitarian cause and he'll be in the latest Broadway production. They will admire and respect each other's capabilities and share a great passion for collecting and surrounding themselves with a menagerie of people from all walks of life.

Ms Aquarius will not be the least bit flustered or jealous of her lion's string of adoring female fans. She's more likely to join in the praise for her wonderful, creative and talented man instead of wondering about the motives behind the female flattery. Mr Leo, in turn, will be in awe of Ms Aquarius's amazing mind and intellect and the two will be kept entertained for hours chatting about world peace, politics or what the Martians really look like.

In the bedroom: Ms Aquarius may be a little detached and aloof for the voracious Mr Leo, who is much more tactile and demonstrative. But if she truly admires and respects him, she can soon turn into a passionate playmate for her lion.

♒ Ms Aquarius + Mr Virgo ♍

Sign	Aquarius	Virgo
Symbol	Water bearer	Virgin
Ruler	Uranus	Mercury
Type	Fixed	Mutable
Element	Air	Earth

Mr Virgo is too practical and lacks the vision his Uranian girl needs. While she is often off seeking out her various humanitarian pursuits, Mr Virgo is too focused on his requirements in his immediate environment. He can harbour a secret admiration for this independent and highly intelligent woman and, when it comes to communication, these signs click. However, Mr Virgo lacks the tolerance to handle her detached and impersonal manner and Ms Aquarius doesn't appreciate any form of restraint and will not be curtailed by his constant nagging.

This woman cannot display any tactile forms of affection that her man needs and, although she might not even be aware there are any problems brewing, Mr Virgo will feel rather disillusioned that this airy girl cannot comprehend something is not right.

This pair is more suited to a friendship than a romantic union. Ms Aquarius collects friends from all walks of life and will always want to retain a friendship – even with past lovers. Earth and air signs don't blend well. The solid and grounded male needs a partner he can stay fused with and remain close to, but the airy Aquarian walks around with her head in the clouds and can't be hemmed into any situation.

In the bedroom: It's difficult for their bodies to connect as Mr Virgo needs to analyse everything, and this spills into the bedroom. On the other hand Ms Aquarius is a 'wham bam, thank you m'am' kind of girl who won't stick around for a post mortem.

♒ Ms Aquarius + Mr Libra ♎

Sign	Aquarius	Libra
Symbol	Water bearer	Scales
Ruler	Uranus	Venus
Type	Fixed	Cardinal
Element	Air	Air

These two signs are an excellent combination. Both are interested in social justice and equality, and will always be supportive of each other's needs and projects. Both are skilful communicators and will spend many hours engaged in verbal discussions. These two are not comfortable with emotional intensity, but would rather enjoy an intellectual approach to their relationship, preferring logic and evaluation over emotions.

The main theme that seems to run through this combination is this pair's ability to be open minded and fair. Mr Libra is perhaps more needy because he is a romantic and wants everything to be perfect when he sails into the sunset with his beloved by his side. Ms Aquarius, however, will want to seek adventure independently rather than needing to have her mate constantly under her feet.

She is the more impersonal of the two and is interested in freedom and not becoming trapped, so Mr Libra will need to make some adjustments if he wants a relationship with the water bearer, who is a strange paradox of conservatism and unconventionality. Because Mr Libra has a strong desire to conform to please his mate, he just might find he is the one making more compromises in this relationship.

In the bedroom: Mr Libra will display his usual talent to bring Ms Aquarius to nirvana, yet he'd better not dilly-dally too long as her interest will wane and she will be planning her next move outside the confines of the bedroom.

NIRVANA - GIVING THE ULTIMATE EXPERIENCE OF SOMETHING PLEASURABLE.

♒ Ms Aquarius + Mr Scorpio ♏

Sign	Aquarius	Scorpio
Symbol	Water bearer	Scorpion
Ruler	Uranus	Pluto
Type	Fixed	Fixed
Element	Air	Water

This man and woman are too different in their emotional makeup to become permanent lovers. Mr Scorpio is a man who craves emotional intensity and thrives on the highs and lows of a relationship where he is in control. The more complex it is, the more responsive he is. By comparison, Ms Aquarius is an idealistic, freedom-loving girl, who is more inclined to love her mates than become entangled in a complex tirade of emotions with this intense man.

Her detached and indifferent demeanour will create some discord between them and, because they are both fixed signs, neither will give in and nor will they be receptive to some compromise. Both Mr Scorpio and Ms Aquarius are stubborn and headstrong and will lock horns often. She will not stay in this relationship too long; her scream 'don't fence me in' will be heard far and wide. In turn, he will find that this woman doesn't understand his need for intimacy, commitment and stability. She wants to explore life free from restrictions, in her own time and in her own way. This will not suit Mr Scorpio, who needs a woman by his side – or at least on a short leash that he can reel in when he so desires.

These two are on different wavelengths. He is possessive and controlling and is inclined to jealous outbursts, whereas she has a tendency to provoke him with her insensitive, detached demeanour. He is a private man and wants to be with her; she is a social creature, who wants to the save the world and will only fit him in when she wants to.

Air is detached and non-feeling; water is intense and emotional. She will find it hard to swim in this sea of emotion and will have to keep her head above water to survive this union.

In the bedroom: Ms Aquarius is more interested in discovering life on Mars than flying to the moon and back with her Scorpio lover. He might take some time to float back down to reality after a romantic interlude, while she'll already be thinking about her next adventure.

♒ Ms Aquarius + Mr Sagittarius ♐

Sign	Aquarius	Sagittarius
Symbol	Water bearer	Archer
Ruler	Uranus	Jupiter
Type	Fixed	Mutable
Element	Air	Fire

This highly intelligent and off-beat girl will drive Mr Sagittarius wild with her indifference. She will prove a real challenge: he will chase her up hill and down dale until she finally succumbs and his arrow finds her heart. 'Once you have found her, let her go' should be the advice offered to an archer faced with this scenario, because the water bearer will prove too headstrong for this easygoing man. She is a woman who values independence even more than he does and she will be more involved with humanitarian causes.

Mr Sagittarius will feel somewhat neglected because he is used to being the centre of attention and is, himself, often pursued by a string of admirers. He will view her indifference as somewhat of a slight. But rather than making his needs known, Ms Aquarius will be left guessing as to why her man is brooding in the corner, so unlike his usual sunny disposition.

Ms Aquarius has difficulty in expressing her emotions, which results in her being considered too cold or too impersonal for the hot-blooded archer, whose passionate streak will turn to ice if kept out in the cold too long.

This couple's love of adventure and desire to seek new frontiers will kick-start the relationship, but Ms Aquarius will never get out of the driver's seat and help push this union along. She is a fixed sign and is much too stubborn to be the one to concede when something needs fixing. It will be up to the optimistic Mr Sagittarius to wake up and smell the roses and recognise that this was a wonderful journey, albeit at times frustrating, while it lasted.

In the bedroom: These two will enjoy a good romp under the covers. Rarely will there be strings attached and pressure to perform. Both are freedom-loving but they can be possessive about their property, so it wouldn't be wise for Mr Sag to think his Aquarian lover's unconventional attitude means he can slip between the sheets with another woman.

♒ Ms Aquarius + Mr Capricorn ♑

Sign	Aquarius	Capricorn
Symbol	Water bearer	Goat
Ruler	Uranus	Saturn
Type	Fixed	Cardinal
Element	Air	Earth

Earth and air seem to be at odds with one another. Mr Capricorn likes to have his feet firmly planted on terra firma and needs to know where he is going. So resolved is the mountain goat in his ambition that he plans his path down to the finest detail; Ms Aquarius, however, is a woman who enjoys wandering wherever her mood takes her. She is freedom-loving, rebellious and impulsive – all traits the goat won't allow himself to indulge in. She is a lover of humankind and is on a mission to save the world.

Both share the same energy and passion to achieve, yet Mr Capricorn needs appreciation and validation along the way. He is not as strong and secure as he leads people to believe and will feel left out in the cold by his Aquarian ice-maiden. Even with all his managerial talents, this woman is one he won't be able to control. She is a girl who can create relationship problems because she doesn't know how to give herself emotionally. She can seem impersonal and is often misunderstood as being disinterested and detached.

Air signs are regarded more as thinkers than feeling types. Her emotions run deep, but they will not be easily understood by her Capricornian man. He will see her as single-minded and fixed in her ideas – never the one to compromise. They do, however, share a common bond because Ms Aquarius is co-ruled by the planet Saturn and Uranus, and the Saturnine energy shared by Mr Capricorn will attract her to the trappings of success. She will delight in the finery this man has to offer.

In the bedroom: Mr Capricorn is likely to be too practical and down-to-earth for this ethereal and imaginative Ms – especially when it comes to his bedroom antics. Her changeability will be unsettling, making it hard to know exactly where she's at and what she wants from him.

♒ Ms Aquarius + Mr Aquarius ♒

Sign	Aquarius	Aquarius
Symbol	Water bearer	Water bearer
Ruler	Uranus	Uranus
Type	Fixed	Fixed
Element	Air	Air

These two share a similar vision and value system. Ms Aquarius and her water bearer are both intelligent, freedom-loving and enterprising individuals who have the same drive to venture into new territory and explore what turns them on. However, being together is like looking in a mirror for each of them – reflecting some of their most difficult attributes – which can bring the relationship undone. The weak link is that they both tend to intellectualise rather than feel. This can lead to a detached and undemonstrative relationship: if either needs a dose of tender loving care, it might not be so forthcoming.

Because the water bearers value their space, there may come a time when they are both too independent and will find intimacy elsewhere. On a brighter note, they do have fun in their lives and their love of adventure will not allow boredom to creep in. If they do fall into a rut, this pair will always be seeking ways to radically change their lifestyles.

Intellectually they are on a par and will find each other stimulating and progressive. Mr Aquarius will be drawn to her creative streak and will value her sense of fun, as well as her ability to bring new and innovative ideas into the partnership. As fixed signs, however, they will need to learn the art of compromise as neither will want to admit defeat in times of battle. But if they both learn to expose their vulnerabilities at times and allow each other to see the ray of sunshine in their hearts, this paring will melt away the difficulties, and enjoy a long and lasting union.

In the bedroom: Once these two hit the sack they are likely to spend more time analysing the meaning of life than engaging in sex. That's not to say they won't, but there's a time and place for love, and given that these two are extremely unconventional, it is not surprising when their passion surfaces in off-beat settings.

♒ Ms Aquarius + Mr Pisces ♓

Sign	Aquarius	Pisces
Symbol	Water bearer	Fish
Ruler	Uranus	Neptune
Type	Fixed	Mutable
Element	Air	Water

This can be a wonderful pairing because Ms Aquarius feels this man really understands her. In his own way, he is obtuse and indifferent, but at least she will be comfortable with how he allows her to be herself. She is a fixed sign and is reluctant to change, so Mr Pisces will always be the one to make the adjustments. He is known for his gentle and compassionate nature. Hopefully, he won't make a martyr of himself as this girl can exploit her relationships and will take what she can. She does, however, have a compassionate side, especially when it comes to the underdog. Her passion lies in helping those less fortunate, which is in sync with her Piscean mate, who is also not adverse to humanitarian pursuits when he is not acting like a victim.

These two will share a love of culture and the arts, and Ms Aquarius will be the first to encourage the fish to explore his talents and put them to good use. She craves connection with others, be it socially or in her life's work, whereas Mr Pisces wants to lose himself, retreat from the world and contemplate life. This relationship just might work because she needs her independence and freedom and will allow her fish to swim below the surface, as long as he comes up for air every so often and gives her a dose of compassion and warmth.

On the downside, Ms Aquarius is not so at home with her emotions and will leave her fish undernourished and feeling unloved at times. She doesn't recognise that she can be cold and impersonal. Her Piscean man will be need to tap into his intuition and realise that her detachment is part of her demeanour and not an indicator of her lack of love for him.

In the bedroom: These two will have no trouble about being able to submit to physical pleasures. Both are fairly imaginative and experimental lovers; however, neither is likely to completely give their all until they feel totally secure and committed.

Celebrity Ms Aquarius: Yoko Ono

Artist/John Lennon's wife, born 18 February 1933, in Tokyo, Japan

```
Personal planets:  Sun in Aquarius
                   Moon in Sagittarius
                   Mercury in Pisces
                   Venus in Aquarius
                   Mars in Virgo
```

I saw that nothing was permanent. You don't want to possess anything that is dear to you, because you might lose it.

– Yoko Ono

Yoko Ono, the avant garde artist, was the second wife of the late John Lennon of Beatles fame. Theirs was the classic air sign union: their lives revolved around their shared intellectual and communicative bond. To some onlookers, it appeared that Ono and Lennon's focus was to create a magical perception of sensuality by way of their public displays of naked bodies and 'love-ins'. But their strongest connection was a shared philosophical world view.

As an Aquarian, Ono would have helped to arouse Lennon's interest in the brotherhood of man and develop his awareness for humanitarian and social reforms. They had similar values and were supportive of each other's creative self-expression. As two air signs, they had a natural affinity with expressing themselves and shared a desire to influence others. Their vision for world peace fitted well with Ono's Aquarian disposition to help humankind and Lennon's Libra Sun, which sought peace and harmony, personally and universally. They both sought some emancipation from the trials and tribulation of the world, and wanted to make a difference with the talents they shared.

Lennon's song 'Imagine' demonstrated his own spiritual aspirations. His Neptune–Mars connection gave him the impetus to make a difference, although it also gave him a delusional perception of what could be achieved. Ono's chart also has the same level of magnetism and spiritual liberation. She, too, has Mars connected to Neptune, which gives her a mystical, artistic and visionary bent.

Together, Ono and Lennon shared the same dream. Both their charts contain an earth quality, giving them dutiful and even traditional qualities. As unconventional as they both appeared, they were totally committed to one another. Ono's strong Aquarian theme makes her a more detached persona; her unconventional attitude to Lennon's indiscretions show her to be a strong and independent woman who stood by her man, but didn't live through him. Their charts also show a desire to achieve some meaningful results in their lifetimes. Both had the same endurance and drive to take their ambitions to a higher plane and connect as one.

Mr Aquarius – an overview

Mr Aquarius is a great mate – fun, interesting and diverse – and is someone with whom you can communicate on all levels, bar the emotional. He will be understanding, thoughtful and helpful, but never expect this man to understand you emotionally because he feels uncomfortable talking about feelings – his own or those of others. This is a man who values his freedom and will be very understanding of a mate who needs the same space and independence. Mr Aquarius is genuine and honest when he says he loves you. This man doesn't play games and is an open book when it comes to his relationships. He will be fair in his attitudes and upfront about what he wants from a partner.

So now, you ask, does he have a negative side? Well, this man is not good at attending to emotional responses, and he considers displays of sentimentality and vulnerability to be a weakness. He bases life on what is rational and he tends to process his problems intellectually rather than emotionally. He abhors the idea of exposing the gentler and more poignant side of his nature because he sees this as a sign of weakness and yet, ironically, he is particularly compassionate when it comes to worldwide humanitarian affairs. As a fixed sign, he has an inflexible quality and seems to fear change, so he will be resolute in his ideas and opinions when it comes to his relationships. Yet here again we see the paradox: he seems to fear change, but feels it necessary to change the world through his humanitarian concerns.

Like Ms Aquarius, he has a fear of intimacy and, by seeming indifferent, will often send out the wrong signals to his mate, causing her to feel rejected and unloved. Mr Aquarius is highly individual and, through his bohemian attire, will often stand out in a crowd. True to form he is a man who appreciates something different. His choice of mate will see him attracted to women who are also unconventional and who share the same sense of humour and intellect. Above all, this man is interested in ideas and concepts, so he will seek a woman with whom he can exchange his ideas and who shares his passion for contributing to world reform.

Famous Aquarian men

* James Dean (actor)
* Charles Dickens (author)
* Jack Nicklaus (golfer)
* Paul Newman (actor)
* Wolfgang Amadeus Mozart (composer)
* John Travolta (actor)

Combinations

♒ Mr Aquarius + Ms Aries ♈

Sign	Aquarius	Aries
Symbol	Water bearer	Ram
Ruler	Uranus	Mars
Type	Fixed	Cardinal
Element	Air	Fire

This dynamic duo will find much common ground in a relationship. Both idealistic and adventure loving, Mr Aquarius and Ms Aries will entertain and amuse each other to no end. Mr Aquarius will find her child-like qualities endearing and, for her, his quirky sense of humour and *joie de vivre* will be a breath of fresh air.

There's no stopping this pair, who'll share an insatiable thirst for new adventures. They embrace life with open arms and are interested, particularly Mr Aquarius, in the greater good of mankind. Mr Aquarius will teach Ms Aries to broaden her outlook and perspective on life, which will lead to her own journey of self-discovery. Ms Aries will admire and respect the intellect of the water bearer and will learn a great deal from him. But she may find his detached, aloof nature a little confusing because she can't really tell what he feels. The Aquarian guy might hide a sea of emotions under his cool exterior for fear of revealing a vulnerability that may not be fully understood by the Arian woman.

Despite their obvious compatibility, Aquarius is a fixed sign, making this guy stubborn and rigid in his outlook on life. This can be frustrating for Ms Aries, who may find him a bit too opinionated and set in his ways.

In the bedroom: She likes to lead but, being a fixed sign, he doesn't like to follow. However, her frankness – especially about what she needs physically – will appeal to her Aquarian lover, who can be as adventurous in bed as she can be hungry for sexual gratification.

♒ Mr Aquarius + Ms Taurus ♉

Sign	Aquarius	Taurus
Symbol	Water bearer	Bull
Ruler	Uranus	Venus
Type	Fixed	Fixed
Element	Air	Earth

Too many fundamental differences exist between the rebellious and independent water bearer and the straight and inflexible Taurean. Mr Aquarius loves nothing better than adventure, excitement and surprises, while Ms Taurus is attracted to predictability and safety, and will not dip her toe into unchartered waters. Both are fixed signs and as such are inflexible in their ability to compromise – neither will be pushed into doing anything they don't want to, making it difficult for them to find common ground.

Ms Taurus will not find Mr Aquarius reassuring enough because he will always display an impersonal and aloof detachment that will frustrate the security-conscious bull. He seeks adventure, attracting him to the unconventional – he would prefer to live in a commune where he can spread love everywhere, unlike the domestic goddess Ms Taurus, who could think of nothing worse than not having a cosy, comfortable home.

One of the fundamental differences in this love relationship is that Aquarians are attracted to people from all walks of life, and friendship is sometimes more important than love and intimacy. This can be frustrating for the single-minded, loyal Taurean woman who might not know where she stands in the relationship. Such uncertainty can lead to feelings of insecurity in Ms Taurus, who likes to know the status quo.

Such differences can be insurmountable, with each's requirements in love rarely being met by the other. The sooner they recognise the incompatibilities, the easier it will be to move on and find a more suitable partner.

In the bedroom: The element of surprise will feature strongly in the bedroom of Ms Taurus and her Aquarian lover. He will shock her with his wacky and outlandish sexual antics; she should try to lighten up and enjoy the ride!

♒ Mr Aquarius + Ms Gemini ♊

Sign	Aquarius	Gemini
Symbol	Water bearer	Twins
Ruler	Uranus	Mercury
Type	Fixed	Mutable
Element	Air	Air

Ms Gemini and Mr Aquarius will have a great time together because both are communicative and love to be surrounded by people. They share a passion for the unpredictable, especially the Aquarian, so these two will have no trouble striking up a friendship.

Since neither likes to be fenced in, they will respond well to the other's need for independence. Both are a little zany and have a sense of adventure and will be willing to try something new at the drop of a hat. Ms Gemini is more adaptable than her fixed-sign Aquarian mate and is likely to be more flexible in the relationship. Although he has an appetite for the new and exciting, he can be strong-willed when he wants his own way – a stubborn streak that might frustrate his Gemini mate. Both seem to have an erratic disposition but, as long as they can temper this side of their personalities, they will have a great meeting of the minds.

Both air signs, this pair can be a little cool in their expression of affection and might be accused of not knowing how to give themselves properly in love. However, since they share this trait, they seem to understand each other very well. Neither is romantic by nature and both like to experiment in love, often leaving them open to being labelled promiscuous. It is not that they are fuelled by sexual desire; instead they love people from all walks of life and are naturally drawn to different experiences and situations.

In the bedroom: 'It will happen but it won't happen overnight' is the best way to sum up the consummation of the relationship between these two air signs. Sex is not a priority for either and they might end up spending more time on mental stimulation than the physical. But when they eventually remember that lovers actually do have sex, it is sure to be uncomplicated and exciting.

♒ Mr Aquarius + Ms Cancer ♋

Sign	Aquarius	Cancer
Symbol	Water bearer	Crab
Ruler	Uranus	Moon
Type	Fixed	Cardinal
Element	Air	Water

This is not the ideal relationship pairing. Mr Aquarius is independent, freedom-loving and open to new ideas, which make him extremely unpredictable, while Ms Cancer, on the other hand, is all about family and home life. Her need for conventionality is marred by his desire to explore different and untried territory. He thrives on change; she abhors it. She values tradition; he's unconventional.

The Aquarian male is detached and aloof in relationships, something Ms Cancer will interpret as a form of rejection, leaving her feeling unloved and unsupported. However, this will not worry the water bearer. He loves a challenge and the more the crab tries to hold him down, the more distant he will become. The Aquarian man will not want to be told what time he's expected home – possessiveness will stifle his need for freedom and self-expression. Another hurdle in this pairing is that Aquarians tend to intellectualise their feelings in comparison with Cancerians, who are more swayed by emotions. At times his behaviour might appear odd and reduce his crab to tears, but he probably won't even be aware of it.

These two seem to make a greater success of a friendship rather than an intimate union. Both are humanitarians, always fighting for the greater good and often using their creative talents for a good cause. In a work scenario they will encourage each other's ideas and thoughts, pushing them to achieve greater heights.

In the bedroom: Sexually these two will share great passion. And Mr Aquarius, who never likes to be pinned down, will feel that he really has caught his own moonbeam and love it.

♒ Mr Aquarius + Ms Leo ♌

Sign	Aquarius	Leo
Symbol	Water bearer	Lion
Ruler	Uranus	Sun
Type	Fixed	Fixed
Element	Air	Fire

Both Mr Aquarius and Ms Leo have an air of flamboyancy and attract excitement into their lives. She is drawn to the spontaneity and unexpected treats that her Aquarian mate seems to hand out regularly. The lioness is a fun-loving individual and will relish her partner's last-minute surprises, which might require her to pack her bags on a minute's notice – destination unknown.

Both are fixed signs and know their own minds well, and both are involved in world pursuits: Ms Leo wants to be on stage – she loves the entertainment industry and wants her name up in lights, whereas Mr Aquarius is passionate about humanitarian affairs. Both are likely to have careers that involve public recognition. They are well-respected and well-liked individuals who make friends easily.

On the relationship front, these two don't muck around; they like to get to the core of what they want and can be quite forthright when asking for it. Ms Leo will give her Aquarian mate the space he needs but will still be able to tighten the reins when she needs to tame him. If he is willing to be a little more demonstrative in his affections, these two can sustain a fun-packed life filled with great variety, fun and spontaneity.

In the bedroom: Mr Aquarius can teach his lioness a few tricks in the bedroom; he is an experimental and experienced lover and anything goes in this relationship. However, it's more a physical exchange than a sensual experience for these two.

♒ Mr Aquarius + Ms Virgo ♍

Sign	Aquarius	Virgo
Symbol	Water bearer	Virgin
Ruler	Uranus	Mercury
Type	Fixed	Mutable
Element	Air	Earth

The initial attraction in this relationship is a meeting of the minds. Ms Virgo will find Mr Aquarius exciting, independent and informative. He will find not only a stimulating muse but someone who shares his vision to create a better world. The relationship between these two will be more in the mind than on a physical level, and they will spend many hours conversing. She will discuss her need to be of service in a personal sense while Mr Aquarius will be more visionary, looking at how he can improve the universe.

But Ms Virgo is too reserved and insular for the Aquarian male, who is known for his unusual and off-beat ideas and interests and his collections of friends from all walks of life. She will be much more discerning in her choice of friends and won't understand his need to be in the company of many, especially since she is such a warm, committed and devoted lover.

Ms Virgo is an extremely loyal partner and Mr Aquarius can often take advantage of this self-sacrificing woman. He is likely to neglect her while he is out searching for rainbows and she will be annoyed if he doesn't include her in some of his outlandish pursuits.

Ms Virgo has the physical drive and the mental dexterity to face any challenge that the water bearer throws at her and she will be only too willing to show him that he needs a woman like her, who can keep him on the straight and narrow and organise him when his life – with its many commitments – becomes too challenging. Her success only adds to her confidence and self-esteem and this can only have productive consequences. Mr Aquarius just needs to show this virgin some patience and he will be in for a surprise or two when he least expects it.

In the bedroom: Sexually, there may be a few surprises in store for Ms Virgo as far as Mr Aquarius's tendency to throw an element of shock into the mix. She'll be intrigued by her mysterious Uranian man, and passion will not be lacking between the practical earth girl and her wacky lover.

♒ Mr Aquarius + Ms Libra ♎

Sign	Aquarius	Libra
Symbol	Water bearer	Scales
Ruler	Uranus	Venus
Type	Fixed	Cardinal
Element	Air	Air

These two make great friends as well as lovers because both gravitate towards people and will always maintain a connection, even if their romantic relationship ends. Because both are air signs, they share a mutual passion for mental and physical exploration, and will encourage each other to experience as much texture and diversity as they can fit into their lives. And they will give each other room to move in the relationship. Although Ms Libra will want to keep her Aquarian man in tow – her need for commitment is more strongly developed than his – her sense of fair play will allow him the periods of freedom he needs to stay happy.

Ms Libra and Ms Aquarius will always keep their channels of communication open. They come from an intellectual perspective and need to share knowledge and be intellectually stimulated. The only difficulty these two might have is on the occasions that Aquarian instincts lead this guy to indulge in off-beat and unconventional behaviour, which is when Ms Libra might need to keep the peace by dropping her airs and graces and letting it all hang out.

Air signs seem to lack in the feeling department and this relationship will be based more on a mental connection than instinctive feelings, which means the old 'you don't understand me' phrase is less likely to pop up. Both have a tendency to repress or disguise their emotions on an intimate level. However, when it comes to social justice, human rights and equality, they are both on the same wavelength – deeply committed to such causes. They both have a strong social conscience and a sense of fair play, which further strengthens their bonds.

In the bedroom: These two make great bedfellows because they both enjoy and take pride in the art of lovemaking. The open Mr Aquarius will pull a few tricks out of his bag to tantalise his Libran love and she will always express her appreciation in ways he has only dreamed of.

♒ Mr Aquarius + Ms Scorpio ♏

Sign	Aquarius	Scorpio
Symbol	Water bearer	Scorpion
Ruler	Uranus	Pluto
Type	Fixed	Fixed
Element	Air	Water

Mr Aquarius will be too detached and indifferent for Ms Scorpio. Air signs appear cold and impersonal in their intimate relationships and Ms Scorpio is a woman who thrives on emotional and physical intimacy. She needs to feel appreciated and very much acknowledged, and her Aquarian man will not have the awareness and intensity she requires to feel secure in the relationship.

The water bearer is often unpredictable and unconventional; he needs a partner who lets him do his own thing rather than confining him, and it is unlikely to be Ms Scorpio. She is a control freak and won't be at all comfortable to see her man pursuing universal love instead of concentrating all his love and attention on her. Her need for a relationship is far greater than his and she may feel his detachment hurtful and unsympathetic.

Both these signs are fixed elements, so a certain degree of stubbornness and wilfulness will creep into this relationship. Who will be the one to compromise? Ms Scorpio and Mr Aquarius are strongly opinionated people and will rarely concede they are in the wrong. Because they have firmly entrenched personalities, they rarely make allowances for the differences of others.

Ms Scorpio is too sensual and passionate for Mr Aquarius, who is intimidated by her sexual prowess and would rather have a playful companion with whom he can carry on a conversation than a partner who stretches him emotionally. He comes from an intellectual perspective and she comes from an emotional standpoint.

In the bedroom: Although their libidos are quite different, Ms Scorpio's innate ability to turn him on will excite Mr Aquarius, who is open to all things new, especially when it comes to sex! He loves to experiment and learn new tricks and couldn't ask for a better teacher than Ms Scorpio. The bedroom is where this pair will leave their differences at the door and get to have the most fun together.

♒ Mr Aquarius + Ms Sagittarius ♐

Sign	Aquarius	Sagittarius
Symbol	Water bearer	Archer
Ruler	Uranus	Jupiter
Type	Fixed	Mutable
Element	Air	Fire

These are two cool customers, although Mr Aquarius is the cooler and more detached of the two. Despite their need for independence, fire signs also need lots of admiration and attention. These are not qualities Mr Aquarian easily bestows on his woman, who will feel neglected as a result. He is not as responsive and as personal as she would like, yet she cannot be too critical of this man, as she doesn't like to be possessed herself.

However, they have much in common. Each values their freedom and independence and has a desire to grow intellectually. They share a passion for communication and will stimulate each other with their insights and wisdom. Ms Sagittarius will value this man's loyal and honest approach. Both are interested in serving mankind and will be able to support each other's vision for global peace and harmony. But this is where the similarities end. The Aquarian man is unconventional and open to all things and, although his archer maiden is far from straight-laced, she has a strong moral code and will not indulge in this man's off-beat ways.

He can always justify his behaviour intellectually, which won't suit the romantic and idealistic Ms Sagittarius, who needs her man to show some emotion rather than repress his feelings. And because of his fixed nature, she will be the one making the compromises. Her mutable mode of expression makes her more adaptable and tolerant.

This duo will make far better friends than lovers because they will enjoy each other's attributes without the strings attached, which is ideal – especially because neither is very good at tying the other's laces.

In the bedroom: Mr Aquarius's love of experimentation is at its best in this room, where he can try out his new tricks. Ms Sagittarius – the perpetual and eager student – will be only too willing to learn something new.

♒ Mr Aquarius + Ms Capricorn ♑

Sign	Aquarius	Capricorn
Symbol	Water bearer	Goat
Ruler	Uranus	Saturn
Type	Fixed	Cardinal
Element	Air	Earth

The goat and the water bearer have much in common: each has a certain mission in life. Both have excellent minds and will respect each other's skills and talents, but they do have their differences. Ms Capricorn is focused on personal success and achievement, whereas Mr Aquarius has humanitarian aspirations and is focused on helping the world.

Even though they are individuals who don't need to bask in each other's glory, Ms Capricorn might feel her man is too detached and indifferent at times and is not as attentive as she would like him to be. But both lack the ability to be responsive on an emotional level and, when things get tough, will find it hard to get through to each other. Her good deeds will never go unnoticed or be taken for granted but the Aquarian man is not good at knowing how to be responsive. His manner is unpredictable: he will be all lovey-dovey one minute and impersonal the next. Yet he is completely in the dark about this pattern of behaviour. His ruling planet Uranus, which is rebellious and unpredictable, can be blamed when he is off doing his own thing. But Saturn, who co-rules Aquarius, is responsible when he is attentive and supporting his mate.

Ms Capricorn has a traditional side to her personality and, with her, everything has an order and fits into a plan. Her off-beat man will never be that conventional and, in fact, will be much more unorthodox in his approach to life. She may see glimmers of hope at times; however, Ms Capricorn loves consistency and Mr Aquarius will be consistent only in his inconsistency! Both are visionaries yet how they accomplish their dreams will differ. If she is willing to sit back and take a magic carpet ride with Mr Aquarius, she might find she enjoys being swept off her feet.

In the bedroom: Sex is not an obsession for either Capricornians or Aquarians. But she will relish the unpredictable bedroom antics of her zany lover and together, they will dedicate themselves to the task at hand.

≈ Mr Aquarius + Ms Aquarius ≈

Sign	Aquarius	Aquarius
Symbol	Water bearer	Water bearer
Ruler	Uranus	Uranus
Type	Fixed	Fixed
Element	Air	Air

These two share a similar vision and value system. Ms Aquarius and her water bearer mate are both intelligent, freedom-loving and enterprising individuals who have the same drive to venture into new territory and explore what turns them on. However, being together is like looking in a mirror for each of them – reflecting some of their most difficult attributes – which can bring the relationship undone. The weak link is that they both tend to intellectualise rather than feel. This can lead to a detached and undemonstrative relationship: if either needs a dose of tender loving care, it might not be so forthcoming.

Because the water bearers value their space, there may come a time when they are both too independent and will find one might find intimacy elsewhere. On a brighter note, they do have fun in their lives and their love of adventure will not allow boredom to creep in. If they do fall into a rut, this pair will always be seeking ways to radically change their lifestyles.

Intellectually they are on a par and will find each other stimulating and progressive. Mr Aquarius will be drawn to her creative streak and will value her sense of fun, as well as her ability to bring new and innovative ideas into the partnership. As fixed signs, however, they will need to learn the art of compromise as neither will want to admit defeat in times of battle. But if they both learn to expose their vulnerabilities at times and allow each other to see the ray of sunshine in their hearts, this paring will melt away the difficulties, and enjoy a long and lasting union.

In the bedroom: Once these two hit the sack they are likely to spend more time analysing the meaning of life than engaging in sex. That's not to say they won't, but there's a time and place for love, and given that these two are extremely unconventional, it is not surprising when their passion surfaces in off-beat settings.

♒ Mr Aquarius + Ms Pisces ♓

Sign	Aquarius	Pisces
Symbol	Water bearer	Fish
Ruler	Uranus	Neptune
Type	Fixed	Mutable
Element	Air	Water

Mr Aquarius is often drawn to this woman. Ms Pisces is different and has a mystical quality that the water bearer finds alluring and seductive, although she is far more emotional and vulnerable than he. Mr Aquarius will make some allowances for this lady because he feels she is coming from the same philosophical space – universal love and helping mankind. She will be the passive and compromising one in this union, and yet she will rarely feel like a martyr because she will constantly be stimulated by his diversity and active mind. His visionary quality and her compassion will see them bond closely. Ms Pisces might be just the one to expose the water bearer's inability to give of himself emotionally, and her kindness and humility will draw him out.

The relationship between these two is often founded on empathy. Each will want to contribute tools to assist their union. The differences that set these two apart are that Mr Aquarius is a much more gregarious and social being than Ms Pisces, and she might not always feel comfortable being dragged here and there. Her need for solitude and quiet time is foreign to Mr Aquarius who loves being engaged on a social level and is uncomfortable with silence. Escapism is something they both have an affinity with, but for Ms Pisces, her solitary world is one of addiction to love or other aphrodisiacs that may not be good for her health or mind. That's not to say Mr Aquarius won't mind indulging in a puff or two – after all, he is the flower child from the Age of Aquarius and, when Jupiter aligns with Mars, peace will shine on this union.

In the bedroom: This Neptunian woman will captivate Mr Aquarius and there will be definite fireworks when these two go behind closed doors. She's all woman and he's all man, making this a match high up in the solar system.

Celebrity Mr Aquarius: John Travolta

Actor, born 2.53 pm 18 February 1954 in Englewood, New Jersey, USA

```
Personal planets: Sun in Aquarius
                  Moon in Virgo
                  Mercury in Pisces
                  Venus in Pisces
                  Mars in Sagittarius
```

I wanted my own little airliner in the backyard. I'd have my girlfriends use their Brownie uniforms to be the flight attendants, and I was the captain and they would have to pretend they were serving people.

– John Travolta

John Travolta is famous for his multi-talented skills and can act, dance and fly. He is a man who is true to the Aquarian spirit – in love with life and what it has to offer. Travolta's passion for his craft, be it acting or his love of flying, demonstrates his desire to be emotionally absorbed – not only in his relationships, but in the world beyond. His interest in aviation is perhaps reflective of his desire to be independent and free from restraint, which is a typical Aquarian trait. Travolta also has a strong water composition in his chart that gives him a caring, sensitive and intuitive nature.

Travolta's relationships also reflect his ability to intuit what can work for him. He has had a particularly harmonious and compatible link with the women who have shared his life.

His first major love affair was with actor Diana Hyland, an Aquarian he met in 1976 and who was 17 years his senior. It was a compatible union because they shared similar visions, a love of adventure and an attraction to being different; hence the age gap was of little consequence to them. Her Venus in the freedom-loving sign of Sagittarius complemented his Mars in Sagittarius, so they both valued an honest, direct approach to relationships. Each would have had a desire to learn from the other, but incorporated plenty of play and fun time into their partnership. His Venus and her Mars, both in the sign of Pisces, gave them a spiritual connection and a close emotional identification.

Travolta's Libran wife Kelly Preston has a similar astrological configuration and identification to him. As an air sign, communication is of primary importance. Travolta values a partnership that shares a communicative yet non-restrictive bond, which allows him to pursue his interests. Both Travolta and Preston have their Mars in fire signs, giving them a dynamic and powerful union, with an element of competitiveness. They both have a high energy level and need to express this through their personal interactions. Both are highly idealistic yet have the ability to express their ideas and be firm friends as well as lovers.

PISCES (21 February–20 March)

Ruled by the planet Neptune
Water sign
Mutable
Feminine energy

In general ...

So here we come to the end of the journey and find the last catch of the day: the spiritual, paradoxical hard-to-define Pisces. The Piscean symbol represents two fish swimming in opposite directions, each looking into the mystical depths of humankind. Yet their search is an elusive one and they spend their lives searching for the perfect mate. Although some Pisceans find true happiness, many more who think they have found 'the one' become disenchanted when their rose-coloured glasses start to mist up.

Pisceans are idealistic, mystical and intuitive when they are channelling their creativity in a positive way, yet they have the tendency to lose themselves in their own fantasies and fall into addictive habits when they are walking the low road of life. Neptune, the mythological god of the sea, rules this sign, which gives some understanding as to why the Piscean energy is hard to contain. This sign has ill-defined boundaries and will move like the ebbs and flows of the ocean's tide. When the fish surfaces from his reveries to partake in life, he often feels ill at ease, and likes to escape to find the treasures of the world beyond the confines of the daily grind of life.

Pisceans are talented and gifted individuals and have a natural attraction to the theatrical and artistic world, where their strong romantic energy can come to the fore. They are often rescuers in their relationships because they sacrifice their own needs, and can sometimes be taken advantage of. Even though Pisceans are intuitive, they are also very impressionable, and their need for love overrules their rationale. This causes many Pisceans to fall in love quickly, rarely allowing enough time to ascertain if it is a suitable partnership for them.

The fish is most satisfied when a bond with another is established which transcends the physical and becomes spiritual. This can be hard to achieve, however. As much as Pisceans needs that bond, they can appear too elusive – wavering between total selflessness and a total preoccupation with their own world. This is a reflection of their need to have some solitude to process their fantasies and return to their blissful state of subconsciousness.

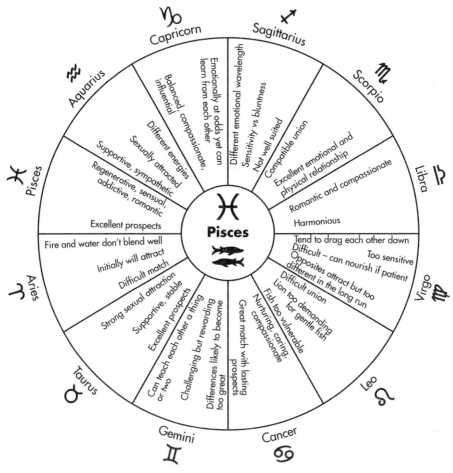

How a Piscean personality might match up with other star signs

Ms Pisces – an overview

Ms Pisces is a quixotic woman who will never give up her dream of finding the perfect spiritual union. In her quest to find true happiness, she sometimes takes the wrong turn and ends up in the depths of despair. She is a giver in every sense of the word and her need to be in a relationship causes her to lose her own identity. She projects her fantasies onto her partner and reveres him quite unrealistically.

She is a woman of extremes and oscillates between her need to escape the perplexities of life and her desire to contribute her talents in a tangible way. This woman needs a partner who can see beyond her grace and compassion and into the depths of her soul. Under her veil of mystique and spirituality, she is a deeply sensitive and complex woman, but one who has an air of secrecy about her. A prospective partner will find her perplexing because she never gives too much away. Just when he thinks he has his fish on a silver platter, she will squirm away, only to be hooked by the next eager fisherman.

Ms Pisces's instincts are her ally, yet she doesn't always make the best use of this gift and often ends up the martyr in a relationship. This is a woman who often shuns her talents and jettisons her own needs in response to her man's demands. Because she is often reluctant to voice her own desires, she needs a partner who will encourage her creative and artistic side. When operating in the positive, she can achieve beyond her wildest dreams, but dreams need to be put into reality. That is her challenge.

Romance means the world to Ms Pisces and if her mate can indulge her fantasies, he will be more than halfway to netting his fish and taking her home. He will be rewarded because this woman is receptive to her man's needs and will indulge him with a passion; and in times of need, he will find solace in her compassionate heart.

Ms Pisces craves love and plays the damsel in distress very convincingly, always on the lookout for her knight in shining armour. It may take a lifetime for this woman to find the 'one', yet she will be well practised in the art of love, as she personifies love and romance. The man who is lucky enough to win her can look forward to a lifetime of bliss.

Famous Piscean women

* Elizabeth Taylor (actor)
* Elizabeth Barrett
  Browning (poet)
* Anais Nin (writer)
* Jean Harlow (actor)
* Joanne Woodward (actor)
* Liza Minelli (singer)

Combinations

♓ Ms Pisces + Mr Aries ♈

Sign	Pisces	Aries
Symbol	Fish	Ram
Ruler	Neptune	Mars
Type	Mutable	Cardinal
Element	Water	Fire

The sensitive, intuitive, gentle Piscean woman will be highly attractive to Mr Aries. Pisceans yearn for an ideal love and are romantic by nature, so these two signs will be able to give each other the passion they need. A Piscean woman tends to give her all in a relationship and will make her mate her number one priority, which her Arian mate will find very appealing. He will be attracted to the Piscean's sense of adventure and his need for a soulmate, and loves the fantasy world she lives in and her desire to nurture his every need.

His ability to be open, honest and direct in the relationship will comfort Ms Pisces because she is often unsure of her direction in life and likes her mate to take control. She has a vivid imagination and is highly creative, both qualities that can stimulate the ram in and out of the bedroom. Her sixth sense will be tuned into just the right frequency to know what her Arian mate wants.

Ms Pisces will have a tendency to tire easily from the mundane rituals of life, providing Mr Aries with a legitimate reason not to let the grass grow under his feet. However, as long as Ms Pisces sticks to the higher road of her persona and does not fall prey to her addictive, destructive side, then this union will have no boundaries. Mr Aries will never allow himself to become the rescuer or the martyr in this relationship.

In the bedroom: Think Romeo and Juliet or Adam and Eve and you've got a sexual union like no other. The sensitive and intuitive Piscean will know exactly how to satisfy and fulfil her ram lover's every desire.

♓ Ms Pisces + Mr Taurus ♉

Sign	Pisces	Taurus
Symbol	Fish	Bull
Ruler	Neptune	Venus
Type	Mutable	Fixed
Element	Water	Earth

These two romantics of the zodiac will find a loving partner in each other. The attraction between them lies in Mr Taurus's ability to ground the dreamy Piscean and create stability and structure in her life. Ms Pisces, in turn, will introduce her mate to a more spiritual and creative way of life.

Pisceans are particularly intuitive and have an innate knowledge of what their partner needs, and Taureans love the closeness and intimacy that their Pisces mate injects into the partnership. The Taurean man loves to be wanted and needed, and will value his partner if he feels appreciated, while Ms Pisces will always feel grateful for the loving and stable environment her mate can provide. His pragmatic and practical approach to life enables the bull to keep his dreamy, and sometimes wayward, escapist Ms Pisces on the straight and narrow. If she receives the right encouragement and nurturing, Mr Taurus will be privy to a Pandora's box of amazing spiritual, artistic and aesthetic delights.

Although the Taurean man is not always seen as the most exciting partner of the zodiac, his Piscean companion has the ability to transform his earthly approach to life and create a more ethereal and spiritual affair. This really is a wonderful union with both having the ability to nurture and encourage each other's more positive aspects. She likes to lead but, being a fixed sign, he doesn't like to follow. However, her frankness – especially about her physical needs – will appeal to her Aquarian lover, who can be as adventurous in bed as she can be hungry for sexual gratification.

In the bedroom: It might not be the thunderbolt sex experienced by some other combinations but there'll be a fair share of tenderness and affection between Mr Taurus and his gentle Piscean lover. They are both extremely sensual; he's into romance and she's into fantasy, which creates a utopian union.

♓ Ms Pisces + Mr Gemini ♊

Sign	Pisces	Gemini
Symbol	Fish	Twins
Ruler	Neptune	Mercury
Type	Mutable	Mutable
Element	Water	Air

Mr Gemini's changeable attitudes and actions will be both attractive and abhorrent to the sensitive and intuitive Ms Pisces, who will be continually striving to understand what makes her man tick. Neither the air or water signs are particularly warm and demonstrative types, but their combined essence makes them value the need for freedom.

Mr Gemini and Ms Pisces are both elusive, imaginative types but she lives more in a fantasy world and will frustrate the twin, who wants to know what's going on in her mind. She needs a deep and meaningful union to feel spiritually connected and at times will be frustrated by his flighty and fanciful ways. Ms Pisces often plays the role of the rescuer, sacrificing her own needs in order to sustain a relationship. She will tolerate the excesses of her Gemini guy because she will always want to see her partner as the perfect, ultimate mate. Even if he is not her King Neptune, she will continually make allowances in the union.

Pisces represents the 'I believe' motto of the zodiac, so when this fish puts her trust in a relationship she believes it will lasts forever. Mr Gemini is more interested in instant gratification than his Piscean companion, who is more emotional and needs to create the perfect mood before she can give herself completely. If this Gemini guy is willing to spend time on the relationship, looking into the depths of his love's deep Piscean soul, he will find many hidden delights in Neptune's treasure chest.

In the bedroom: These two can have a very fulfilling and sensual physical connection when they join as one. Their imaginations will take them to great heights of pleasure.

ℋ Ms Pisces + Mr Cancer ♋

Sign	Pisces	Cancer
Symbol	Fish	Crab
Ruler	Neptune	Moon
Type	Mutable	Cardinal
Element	Water	Water

The sensuous, passionate and mysterious Ms Pisces will hold great allure for Mr Cancer. He immediately senses that this woman shares his compassionate, intuitive and nurturing instincts. Cancerians and Pisceans are in touch with their feelings and will share a give-and-take approach in their relationships.

Mr Cancer will delight in Ms Pisces' rescuing qualities and she will thrive on his support. At the same time, she is a dreamer who has high expectations of a relationship, and will adore her crab mate who can fulfil her fantasies. There are plenty of romantic and passionate exchanges between these two. The combined energy of Cancer's ruling planet, the Moon, and Pisces' rulers – Jupiter and Neptune – creates an easy and dynamic flow. Mr Cancer's Moon shines brightly on Neptune's great oceans and like a mirror at night will reflect the alluring qualities of his Piscean lover.

This pair will be perceptive enough to see each other's positive qualities and she in particular will recognise the long-term potential of this caring and gallant man, who shares a mutual interest in the arts and has the same value system.

In the bedroom: There will be no denying the deep and passionate attraction between these two signs and it will be in the bedroom where the crab and fish give themselves completely. This will not be a hurried affair, more a languid process that will see them float on a wave of pleasure.

♓ Ms Pisces + Mr Leo ♌

Sign	Pisces	Leo
Symbol	Fish	Lion
Ruler	Neptune	Sun
Type	Mutable	Fixed
Element	Water	Fire

The watery Piscean is too evasive, dreamy and slippery when it comes to a relationship with Mr Leo. The lion needs to know he's being acknowledged and respected; however, Ms Pisces seems to be too distant and wrapped up in her own dreamy world.

She is a woman who needs to retreat and regroup to become revitalised, which will leave her Leo mate feeling left out in the cold, not really understanding what makes this deep and soulful creature tick. Mr Leo often lacks the depth and spirituality to make a fulfilling partner for Ms Pisces. She will unnerve the Leo man with her intuitive abilities and he will be unsettled when she can read his mind and know his motives.

Although these two are both romantics, they have unrealistic expectations of one another. Mr Leo may see this giving, vulnerable woman as a victim rather than his equal and won't have the patience or inclination to nurture and be compassionate enough to understand her vulnerabilities. His roar is much too loud for the demure and gentle fish, who would rather swim upstream in search of someone who understands her. Dreamy Ms Pisces prefers to be in a relationship where she can nurture her man and envelop him with her compassionate nature, but Mr Leo is too arrogant and self-centred to appreciate her martyr-like qualities.

In the bedroom: The watery nature of the fish tends to cause the Leo's fire to fizzle. The lion will need to be a mind-reader to know what will turn on his sensitive and secretive lover. The fish has a tendency to slip far too easily in and out of the sheets, keeping her lion on his paws!

♓ Ms Pisces + Mr Virgo ♍

Sign	Pisces	Virgo
Symbol	Fish	Virgin
Ruler	Neptune	Mercury
Type	Mutable	Mutable
Element	Water	Earth

Water and earth are an ideal combination. Both Ms Pisces and Mr Virgo are feeling people with deep emotions and share a reputation for being compassionate and caring individuals. As polar opposites in astrological terms, they can bring about the best and worst in each other. Mr Virgo is attracted to Ms Pisces' responsiveness and she is turned on by his encouragement and support. He will be intrigued by her intuitive nature and secretly wish he could understand the deeper meaning of life and be more spiritual like her. However, his non-nonsense, pragmatic approach will never allow him to explore his mystical side.

Ms Pisces has strong escapist tendencies, which Mr Virgo can curtail. He will be able to ground her by keeping her on the straight and narrow and tempering her addictions. Mr Virgo has an appreciation for life's aesthetic pleasures, an interest that his Pisces partner will nourish because she too loves the arts and creative pursuits.

Although both have high expectations from their relationships, Mr Virgo has a better grasp of reality than his dreamy Piscean mate, who can be delusional and idealistic in love. They both have plenty of similarities on which to build a strong relationship.

In the bedroom: Sexually, there will be fireworks between Mr Virgo and Ms Pisces, mainly because they share a deep trust and understanding that allows them to be open and honest with their emotions. Since these two are at times unsure of themselves and self-critical, this union will provide a comforting blend of the elements, as the watery woman nourishes her earthly man.

♓ Ms Pisces + Mr Libra ♎

Sign	Pisces	Libra
Symbol	Fish	Scales
Ruler	Neptune	Venus
Type	Mutable	Cardinal
Element	Water	Air

These two are romantics at heart. They will have an interesting exchange because both are interested in love and relationships and will be totally committed to each other. Ms Pisces takes the award for being the most sensitive and intuitive of the water signs. She comes from a feeling perspective and her passion can be a little overwhelming for the Libran guy, who is very much in his head and will rarely understand the depth of this woman. They each seek perfection from their relationships and will project their ideals onto each other, only to feel disappointed in the light of day.

This pair shares a flair for the artistic and the creative and will stimulate each other by expressing their mutual talents. The fish has escapist tendencies and will be somewhat self-deluded, always making adjustments and compromises for her mate. Mr Libra will also make compromises for his lady because he will see her as a gifted, sensitive and gentle person.

Water and air don't usually mix well, but these two are an exception as both will be interested in plain sailing on calm waters rather than bobbing about in turbulent seas. This combination has a magical quality based on the ruling planets. He is ruled by the planet Venus, so love and harmony are his focus, while the little mermaid has Neptune ruling over her, which gives her a sensitive and highly-idealistic flavour, making their relationship harmonious.

In the bedroom: She needs little encouragement – one touch and she is away in her own space, taking her Prince Charming to a place he has never been, let alone even dreamt of.

♓ Ms Pisces + Mr Scorpio ♏

Sign	Pisces	Scorpio
Symbol	Fish	Scorpion
Ruler	Neptune	Pluto
Type	Mutable	Fixed
Element	Water	Water

These two will share a strong bond based on intuition and compassion. The water elements that bind them are a powerful force that gives a deep and intense quality to this relationship. Mr Scorpio and Ms Pisces are aware of each other's shortcomings, yet will be tolerant and supportive of them.

The fish will often make the sacrifices in this relationship because she is the softer and more submissive of the two. She can be seduced by this man because she has she has a tendency to view her relationships through rose-coloured glasses. She needs a strong man that can anchor her emotionally, and no man could do it as efficiently as Mr Scorpio, who is the master of control.

Ms Pisces will value this man's attention and interest in her. She needs validation and Mr Scorpio will cherish her devotion and selfless love. Both are inclined, at times, to repress their emotions and will need to keep their channels of communication open if they want to feel secure with each other.

Water signs are complex creatures who doubt their self- worth yet, in time, they can learn to trust each other with their love. This can be a mystical union because both can conjure the intrigue that is characteristic of their signs. They share a desire to turn their union into a purposeful relationship that transcends all boundaries. If Mr Scorpio can hang on to his fish and not let her swim downstream to escape to the underworld – where they indulge in sex, drugs and rock'n'roll – these two are looking at a long and successful union.

In the bedroom: Sex will be an all-consuming experience when the fish and scorpion unite. It will be a melding of the mind, body and spirit in a sea of emotions.

♓ Ms Pisces + Mr Sagittarius ♐

Sign	Pisces	Sagittarius
Symbol	Fish	Archer
Ruler	Neptune	Jupiter
Type	Mutable	Mutable
Element	Water	Fire

This risque man will attract Ms Pisces, who will see him as a dashing knight who will pluck her from the depths of the ocean and transport her to nirvana. Ms Pisces will, of course, have her rose-coloured glasses on and will see only what she wants. She is a true romantic and will ignore the more negative sides of her mate, namely his lack of subtlety and his hedonistic demeanour. Instead she will focus on his optimistic, outgoing and honest attributes. In turn, he will be attracted to her creativity and her subtle disposition. Ms Pisces will bring out the gentle side of the archer's nature and he will feel a sense of protectiveness towards this seemingly demure and compassionate woman.

Both need to be spiritually bonded and enjoy the romantic aspects of the partnership, rather than the daily grind. Mr Sagittarius and Ms Pisces could be together forever if they could indulge in the excesses of life without having to come down to earth. But they both have an aversion to commitment and don't like to be pinned down. All will run smoothly until Mr Sagittarius wants to stretch his legs and wanderlust sets in.

Essentially, the archer will be too energetic and restless for the fish, who is much more laid back and contented to just sail along. And although Ms Pisces will be happy for her mate do his own thing, she will start to feel disillusioned when she realises she is the one always making the sacrifices, and she is likely to end up the martyr in the relationship. In restless times, she will keep the peace by retreating to her cave and burying herself into her own private world, not letting the wayward Mr Sagittarius in until he has redeemed himself and carried her off to conquer new horizons.

In the bedroom: The archer will find the fish extremely alluring, but she needs deep, sensitive loving rather than just the physical closeness he seeks. But, if they can tune into each other's psyches, their bodies will follow suit in spectacular fashion.

♓ Ms Pisces + Mr Capricorn ♑

Sign	Pisces	Capricorn
Symbol	Fish	Goat
Ruler	Neptune	Saturn
Type	Mutable	Cardinal
Element	Water	Earth

She is a romantic and he is pragmatic. She lacks discernment and he is discriminating. She is an escapist and he is ambitious. She is a victim and he is a saviour. Will these two really make it as a couple? Yes, but only if they are willing to learn and develop, and incorporate a little portion of each other's virtues into their psyches.

The fish and the goat seem worlds apart. He stands firmly on the mountain top for all to see and revels in his accomplishments, while the fish hides deep in the ocean with King Neptune by her side, swimming free of restraints.

This is a relationship in which each can see what they are lacking and will appreciate the other's efforts to make things work. Mr Capricorn will love the artistic and gentle qualities this soft lady can provide, while she will be grateful for his physical support and his encouragement of her talents. As different as these two seem, it is a partnership that has much potential. Earth needs water to sustain it, so Mr Capricorn will be grateful to his Piscean mate for keeping him from perishing and allowing him the opportunity to grow spiritually.

Their challenges provide a landscape of opportunity for learning and developing. Ms Pisces will make the adjustments and sacrifices for this man because she can see he is honourable and, above all, virtuous in his pursuits. This thoughtful woman will suit Mr Capricorn, because beneath his veneer of strength and composure lies a vulnerable man who needs a gentle soul to coax out his well-hidden soft side. She can guide him on his quest for power for the good of all rather than for his own selfish desires.

In the bedroom: There's no stopping the unbridled passion between a sensitive and seductive fish and her eager goat. He will feel relaxed and comfortable in the arms of a woman who is happiest when giving pleasure to others.

♓ Ms Pisces + Mr Aquarius ♒

Sign	Pisces	Aquarius
Symbol	Fish	Water bearer
Ruler	Neptune	Uranus
Type	Mutable	Fixed
Element	Water	Air

Ms Pisces holds a special allure for Mr Aquarius. Ms Pisces is different and has a mystical quality that the water bearer finds alluring and seductive, although she is far more emotional and vulnerable than he. Mr Aquarius will make some allowances for this lady because he feels she is coming from the same philosophical space – universal love and helping mankind. She will be the passive and compromising one in this union, and yet she will rarely feel like a martyr because she will constantly be stimulated by his diversity and active mind. His visionary quality and her compassion will see them bond closely. Ms Pisces might be just the one to expose the water bearer's inability to give of himself emotionally, and her kindness and humility will draw him out.

The relationship between these two is often founded on empathy. Each will want to contribute tools to assist their union. The differences that set these two apart are that Mr Aquarius is a much more gregarious and social being than Ms Pisces, and she might not always feel comfortable being dragged here and there. Her need for solitude and quiet time is foreign to Mr Aquarius who loves being engaged on a social level and is uncomfortable with silence. Escapism is something they both have an affinity with, but for Ms Pisces, her solitary world is one of addiction to love or other aphrodisiacs that may not be good for her health or mind. That's not to say Mr Aquarius won't mind indulging in a puff or two – after all, he is the flower child from the Age of Aquarius and, when Jupiter aligns with Mars, peace will shine on this union.

In the bedroom: This Neptunian woman will captivate Mr Aquarius and there will be definite fireworks when these two go behind closed doors. She's all woman and he's all man, making this a match to light up the solar system.

♓ Ms Pisces + Mr Pisces ♓

Sign	Pisces	Pisces
Symbol	Fish	Fish
Ruler	Neptune	Neptune
Type	Mutable	Mutable
Element	Water	Water

Ms and Mr Pisces are on the same spiritual platform and their love has no boundaries. They share the same vision of life and reinforce each other's positive and negative sides, whether they're 'the good, the bad or the ugly'. This union experiences the agony and the ecstasy of love and works best when each confronts the other's shortcomings, rather than pursuing a dream that is idealistic and intangible. These two fish swim in synchronicity with each other, dipping into a sea of turbulence and calm. When they are on their life's true mission, they can support and encourage each other's virtues and lead a serene and peaceful existence; however, if they succumb to their vulnerabilities, they can share a world of chaos and suffering.

The waters run deep in this connection. Both share a yearning to transcend the physical and make their relationship a spiritually unifying bond. There is a magical quality that ties Ms Pisces to her fish; however, they will need to keep their channels of communication open because they both can be evasive in their emotions. This deceptive quality will manifest itself in periods of escapism where they will succumb to their addictive tendencies to numb their pain and suffering. Their devotion to each other, however, is very strong and they are responsive to the other's needs.

The Piscean pair will strive to fulfil each other's dreams of forming an invincible union that can surmount any of life's challenges. Their journey together will be a kaleidoscope of colour and texture, and their passion will rarely fade.

In the bedroom: These two are natural aphrodisiacs for each other, and their physical needs come from the same place. There is both a spiritual and physical connection between the two fish. Each knows how to turn the other on and all it takes is the slightest touch to transport them to a universe that only they can inhabit.

Celebrity Ms Pisces: Elizabeth Taylor

Actor, born 2 am 27 February 1932 in London, England

```
Personal planets: Sun in Pisces
                  Moon in Scorpio
                  Mercury in Pisces
                  Venus in Aries
                  Mars in Pisces
```

I've only slept with men I've been married to. How many women can claim that?

– Elizabeth Taylor

Liz Taylor, as she is affectionately known, has been an inspiration to many women and has been adored by many men. Her life has been coloured by numerous highs and lows, so characteristic of the Piscean chameleon. Taylor has been married eight times and would probably try it again if another Prince Charming came along.

Throughout her life, she has indulged in romance and flirted with the magic of love, yet has not always found the bliss she was searching for. Her chart shows a powerful Piscean theme, which drenches her in sensitivity, romanticism and intuition. Yet her idealistic nature gives her unrealistic expectations for life and her relationships.

In some way Taylor transports her fantasies into her love life, only to become disillusioned when, in typical Piscean fashion, her 'lenses' become blurred and her dreams are shattered.

Taylor's Venus connected to Uranus compels her to make sudden changes, a characteristic that has been reflected in some of her marriages which have ended abruptly. Her Mars in the sensual sign of Pisces makes her attractive to men who share her sensitive side and her need for emotional and spiritual intimacy.

Of the seven men Taylor has been married to, four have been water signs. Her greatest love affairs were with Mike Todd, a Cancerian, who died tragically after they had been married for one year, and with

Richard Burton, whom she married twice, for 10 years and then for one. Burton, a Scorpio, had a strong and powerful connection with Taylor. Both water signs, they devoured each other both physically and emotionally. Their charts are threaded by some powerful connections. Her Scorpio Moon and his Scorpio Sun gave them both an awareness that their relationship would hold some transformational qualities and cross the normal boundaries of love and develop into a truly mystical bond. This magnetic duo had some challenges because both wanted to be in control, even though they handled their emotional issues differently.

Although Taylor sought to find herself through her relationships, she has a strong independent streak with her Venus in the sign of Aries. Hence, she would want to have things her way. Burton, on the other hand, with his Mars in Libra, would be able to handle things with more balance and a clearer perspective. Regardless of their affinities and differences, Taylor will always be remembered as the Cleopatra who won the heart of her Prince Charming, and together they shared the agonies and ecstasies of love.

Mr Pisces - an overview

A quote from Indian spiritual leader Meher Baba, who is a Piscean, best describes the male fish's take on love: 'Love is a gift from God to man'. Mr Pisces, a water sign, is a blend of mystery and receptive and sensual energy. This man has a sympathetic and romantic demeanour which many women find appealing. He is a spiritually conscious man who flirts with the realities and the fantasies of life. The more involved he is, the more he achieves his true purpose in life. The dilemma is to find his true mission: Mr Pisces has a difficult time determining which direction to take. When he is on track, he is an exceptionally gifted and artistic individual and yet, when he drifts to the bottom of the ocean, he becomes lost in a sea of confusion and addictions.

Mr Pisces's innate desire to connect with a mate will see him sacrifice his own needs in order to make the union work, which could end in rejection despite having given his all. His idealistic and impressionable qualities often see him a victim of his own circumstances. Because he doesn't have a clear view of the situation or the person, he will often ignore the truth, preferring to see things optimistically.

Mr Pisces is a true romantic who will rarely get into a relationship purely to satisfy his lust. He needs to be connected on a intense level and, to be completely satisfied, his passion needs to transcend the boundaries of human endeavour and become spiritually fulfilling. This man tends to fall into emotional chaos, which can cause him to resort to addictive comforts at times, which has a detrimental effect on his relationships. On the flip side, he has a clarity of mind that gives him the desire to achieve his dreams and be wildly successful. Mr Pisces has an elusive air about him, which can cause him to be seen as detached and distant. If he has been wounded by his partner, he rarely shows his emotions, instead retreating to the confines of his private world.

Mr Pisces needs a mate who will encourage his talents and help him to direct his gifts into a purposeful existence. His requirements are simple: he needs to be loved. And once he feels his partner is tuned into him, he will plunge her into hidden depths of passion.

Famous Piscean men

* Rudolf Nureyev (dancer)
* Harry Belafonte (singer)
* Rupert Murdoch (publisher)
* John Steinbeck (writer)
* Michael Caine (actor)
* Pierre Renoir (artist)

Combinations

♓ Mr Pisces + Ms Aries ♈

Sign	Pisces	Aries
Symbol	Fish	Ram
Ruler	Neptune	Mars
Type	Mutable	Cardinal
Element	Water	Fire

The longevity of this relationship will depend on how patient Ms Aries is getting to know this sensitive, romantic, idealistic man. The ram, known for her impulsive and headstrong persona, will appeal to Mr Pisces. He will be attracted to her direct and confident approach, but can he use his sixth sense quickly enough to tune in to what this woman wants, and not let her get away? Mr Pisces needs to act quickly and show her his mystical and creative qualities, and then he may start a fire in her heart.

Both Ms Aries and Mr Pisces can bring some wonderful delights into their union, as they share a love of adventure and excitement. This duo need to live their lives in creative and spirited ways, exploring all the possibilities that lie before them, instead of being bogged down by the mundane aspects of life.

Fire and water are often at odds with one another and, true to form, this Arian girl may be rather blunt and insensitive to the more passive and gentle Mr Pisces. If he can keep his over-sensitive nature under wraps and recognise that her outbursts are over in a flash, this duo could have a lot of fun. Mr Pisces should be aware that his brooding and, at times, detached and private temperament can dampen the spirits of this bubbly girl.

Ms Aries will be the stronger and more controlling of the two, as Mr Pisces will always make the sacrifices in the relationship. However, that is just what this girl desires and needs. As long as Mr Pisces is living the higher side of his persona and not falling prey to the addictive, destructive side, this relationship will teach the Arian girl and her Piscean man a thing or two about love.

In the bedroom: They both want a sexually experience that offers great intensity and passion. Often these two will have the chance to fulfil their fantasies behind closed doors. They are both extremely creative when it comes to sex, which can lead to endless possibilities!

♓ Mr Pisces + Ms Taurus ♉

Sign	Pisces	Taurus
Symbol	Fish	Bull
Ruler	Neptune	Venus
Type	Mutable	Fixed
Element	Water	Earth

Mr Pisces and Ms Taurus seem to have a mutual respect for each other and their qualities. The fish may be seen at times to be swimming in a sea of his own emotions, but his lady bull's sensitivity, understanding and patience will nurture and support his fragile and introspective soul.

He will be drawn to the practical, earthed and stable influence of Ms Taurus, who will not pander to the escapist tendencies he displays at times. She will never take advantage of her vulnerable mate, instead instilling in him a sense of confidence and self-worth because she appreciates and admires his creative flare, kindness and compassion. The bull will ensure her fish swims upstream instead of going in different directions and will not tolerate any wayward behaviour.

Ms Taurus is more pragmatic, predictable and self-assured than her Piscean mate, making her able to keep him on the straight and narrow and steer him away from his negative addictions. In turn, he will thrive and enjoy the supportive and nurturing home environment the bull creates. Both share a passion for music and the arts, creating a strong bond between them. Ms Taurus loves to be wooed and pursued and is a true romantic at heart, like her equally sensual Piscean man. Both will find solace and comfort in a happy and harmonious love relationship.

In the bedroom: He'll be a sensuous and romantic bedmate for the equally loving and caring bull. Her feminine energy will be hugely appealing to her ethereal and intuitive Piscean lover, and these two will unleash pleasures from out of this world!

♓ Mr Pisces + Ms Gemini ♊

Sign	Pisces	Gemini
Symbol	Fish	Twins
Ruler	Neptune	Mercury
Type	Mutable	Mutable
Element	Water	Air

Although these two signs are challenging astrologically, they are often drawn to one another. Ms Gemini is attracted to the Piscean's complex, sensitive nature and is fascinated by what lurks in the depth of his mind. He is intrigued by the verbal agility she displays. Both have very different personalities but share an inability to commit, giving them both their own time and space.

The main challenge in this Gemini–Piscean relationship is that they are both elusive and fail to adequately express their needs, which can result in difficulties when it comes to cementing their union. Ms Gemini will try to accommodate her partner's needs, only to become resentful down the track when she finds out that her needy-in-love Piscean relies on her strength to give him the self-esteem that he needs to keep him on the straight and narrow. Ms Gemini, however, is unlikely to have the commitment and endurance to support the needy Mr Pisces; often he will be the one having to prop up his unpredictable and highly strung Gemini mate.

Geminis and Pisceans carry too much baggage and, in a relationship, will allow each other to indulge in their addictive tendencies. Although Ms Gemini values her freedom, she also needs a strong arm to lean on at times and can take advantage of her compassionate and devoted Piscean, who may be too weak to stand up to his demanding mate. Ms Gemini, despite her reliance on him, will see his martyr-like qualities as a sign of weakness and will walk all over him on her way to the next challenge.

In the bedroom: With both approaching sex from a different perspective, Ms Gemini is likely to be too selfish and immature for the sensitive and ethereal Pisceans. The fish may also become insecure and jealous of her sometimes casual attitude to lovemaking.

♓ Mr Pisces + Ms Cancer ♋

Sign	Pisces	Cancer
Symbol	Fish	Crab
Ruler	Neptune	Moon
Type	Mutable	Cardinal
Element	Water	Water

There is a mutual rapport and empathy between these two water signs. Each can indulge the other and feed off their strengths and weaknesses. Ms Cancer will appreciate the depth, sensitivity and talents of her creative mate who, in turn, will share her interests in the arts and other aesthetic pursuits. She will have the strength and determination needed to help her Piscean mate combat his excessive and needy qualities, and will ground his idealistic nature and delusional state of mind.

Water signs seem to have a flair for providing their mate with sentimentality and romance, and Mr Pisces will appreciate his crab's loyalty and protective nature. She, in turn, will feel needed and loved unconditionally. Because each is intuitive, this couple can pick up on the other's moods and overall disposition, making them ideally suited.

At times the more security-oriented crab will find her Piscean mate's elusive nature and lack of commitment and drive frustrating. In turn, he might find her too intense, stifling and protective, but they can find common ground with their watery natures. He will find always find his crab nurturing and protective, while she will find the layers of his personality both magical and alluring.

In the bedroom: On the plus side, the crab and fish will have a very passionate relationship in the physical sense, which can fuse them together as one. Their shared sixth sense makes these two particularly sensitive to each other's thoughts, needs and desires – a dynamic combination in the bedroom.

♓ Mr Pisces + Ms Leo ♌

Sign	Pisces	Leo
Symbol	Fish	Lion
Ruler	Neptune	Sun
Type	Mutable	Fixed
Element	Water	Fire

Mr Pisces' tendency to appear helpless and in need of direction will appeal to Ms Leo, who likes to take charge and be acknowledged for her strengths and capabilities. She seems to take on responsibility particularly keenly, so she will feel she's well in command of this union.

The Piscean man is self-sacrificing and instinctively knows what turns this lioness on. She, in turn, will be flattered by his constant attention. However, the fish also has a predisposition to retreating periodically and a confused Ms Leo, who will interpret his actions as submissive, will see this introspective quality as a weakness. She will be left out in the cold, wondering what this personality change is all about. Leo is a fixed sign; she thrives on consistency and needs to know where she stands at all times. Mr Pisces is known for his escapist tendencies and will disappoint Ms Leo with his changeability. If he can stay focused and balanced somewhere between his intensity and detachment, this fish might be able to keep Ms Leo's flame burning – or at least flickering.

The lioness and the fish sound like an unusual pair but if they can find their way into each other's hearts, she will discover a gentle, sensitive and inspiring man; he, in turn, will find her confident and bold persona inspiring. Both romantic idealists, they are attracted to artistic or musical pursuits, which can give them much in common.

In the bedroom: Sexually speaking, this duo might miss the mark: the Piscean is a spiritual being whereas the lion is more focused on the physical. The fish will want to swim upstream, away from what he perceives to be an overbearing, dogmatic lover who is more about physical gratification than emotional fulfilment.

♓ Mr Pisces + Ms Virgo ♍

Sign	Pisces	Virgo
Symbol	Fish	Virgin
Ruler	Neptune	Mercury
Type	Mutable	Mutable
Element	Water	Earth

This union typifies the ideal give-and-take relationship because each will try to make adjustments to accommodate the other. Mr Pisces will be delighted to find a mate who listens to him and Ms Virgo will find the lure of the fish extremely seductive. On some levels they have a mutual understanding and both are extremely compassionate beings, but Ms Virgo will find she'll need to be the director of the relationship, as her watery man has a way of occasionally swimming up the wrong stream and she'll often have to throw him a lifeline.

He'll be frivolous with his money and she will be overly cautious and protective of hers. Sensitive Mr Pisces won't be able to handle Ms Virgo's constant nagging, especially since the sensitive fish will feel he must have let her down in some way. He is a dreamy, romantic visionary and is often spaced out after too many wines (maybe just to escape her constant criticisms), while she is a practical, level-headed, commonsense woman who won't tolerate such wayward behaviour.

Ms Virgo will also become extremely worried if she feels her Piscean lover is hiding secrets, especially since she is such an up-front girl. If these two can communicate their concerns and worries to each other – and find resolutions – they just might become a caring and compassionate couple.

In the bedroom: Neither is selfish, especially when it comes to sex, which they will consider an extension of their love for each other. The delicate and sensual touch of the fish will be a big turn on for the earthy virgin.

♓ Mr Pisces + Ms Libra ♎

Sign	Pisces	Libra
Symbol	Fish	Scales
Ruler	Neptune	Venus
Type	Mutable	Cardinal
Element	Water	Air

Mr Pisces and Ms Libra are both romantic and creative individuals who share a strange mix of positive and negative energy. They have the same unrealistic expectations of what they need and desire from a relationship and will always want to seek a perfect mate who fulfils their wildest dreams and fantasies.

Mr Pisces is a man who seeks perfection and Ms Libra – his dream woman – will be high on his agenda. This is the best water and air mix of the signs: both crave harmony and peace, and both will make some compromises if the union turns out less than ideal. However, the fish might be too emotional and needy for the controlled Libran woman who is not comfortable with having to confront her feelings. She would rather analyse how she feels in a more detached way. He is the more emotional of the two and will wear his heart on his sleeve. His water element allows him to be swept up in a sea of emotions, which can make the cool Ms Libra rather uncomfortable. She is more selfish and narcissistic than the self-sacrificing fish, who will swim whichever way his lady wants, yet will never mind that he is the one making all the compromises.

On a romantic level, however, this pair can feel very much at one with each other. Ms Libra likes nothing more than having her man tell her how passionate he is about her – the more often the better – and Mr Pisces is a genius at this.

In the bedroom: Ms Libra and her Piscean lover will take great delight in seducing each other with skill. He will take her to depths of emotion that she has never experienced and to mystical places she will never want to leave.

♓ Mr Pisces + Ms Scorpio ♏

Sign	Pisces	Scorpio
Symbol	Fish	Scorpion
Ruler	Neptune	Pluto
Type	Mutable	Fixed
Element	Water	Water

This man and woman come together harmoniously, especially as both share water elements that contain the same deep, sensitive and intuitive qualities. Water has no boundaries, so this couple will be constantly overflowing with passion and feeling.

Mr Pisces is perhaps the nurturer in this union and will temper his Scorpio woman when she gets up to her stinging and controlling ways; she, in turn, will lend a willing ear to his emotional hang-ups and escapist tendencies. The water signs tend to be emotionally sensitive and vulnerable people and are reluctant to express their intimate feelings. At the outset, the crab and the fish might dance around each other for a while to build up a protective wall. When at last they feel secure, it will be a union of substance.

They are both interested in some form of spiritual development and growth, which is where Mr Pisces can teach his woman a thing or two about the aesthetic side of life. Ms Scorpio, on the other hand, can encourage him to develop his creative and intuitive side. These two have well-developed instincts, allowing them to tap into each other's minds. Although Mr Pisces may lose his way on occasions – he is well known for his escapist's tendencies – Ms Scorpio will always save him from a sea of confusion. She is a master analyst who can bring this man to his senses. The fixed and rigid partner in this relationship, she will always be one step ahead of this vulnerable man. He, in turn, will win her over with his sensitive and compassionate manner. The fish needs to feel a powerful connection with his woman and who better to fit the role than the intense, magnetic Scorpio.

In the bedroom: Sex between the Piscean man and Scorpio woman will be more then just a physical expression of their love for each other. She will be moved to find that she's found a mate who understands her needs on a deeper and more spiritual level.

♓ Mr Pisces + Ms Sagittarius ♐

Sign	Pisces	Sagittarius
Symbol	Fish	Archer
Ruler	Neptune	Jupiter
Type	Mutable	Mutable
Element	Water	Fire

The water and fire in the hearts of these two will attract each other initially but may not be sustaining in the long run. She will be drawn to the mystical and sensitive fish and he will be attracted to her outgoing and adventurous spirit. They both have a love of transcending boundaries: Ms Sagittarius with her quest to search for spiritual truth, and Mr Pisces with his desire to escape the confines of his mundane existence to find his soulmate.

With both being mutable signs, there will be much give and take in their relationship. However, it will be more take than give if Ms Sagittarius has her way. Mr Pisces is into making sacrifices for this optimistic woman and she will not allow him to wallow in his world of escapism. She will encourage her man to follow the high road of life and lead him to a place where he can pursue his talents.

These two share the same romantic ideals and have a harsh time facing the realities of a relationship when it carries too much baggage. It is best that they keep the target of domestic bliss out of their lives and concentrate more on the creative aspect of their romance. The archer may have to temper her critical side because Mr Pisces' sensitive nature will cause him to lose faith in her if she is too blunt.

He is a man who needs encouragement and support, and he might find Ms Sagittarius too dogmatic and impatient for him. The dreamy fish likes to swim to the bottom of the ocean occasionally to indulge in his own private fantasies. Ms Sagittarius will be left up in the air, wondering where her lover has escaped to this time.

In the bedroom: The fish is a creature who loves to escape and where better than into the arms of Ms Sagittarius, whose lusty appetite will devour this man in one swoop. She will be licking her lips for more of that tasty morsel.

♓ Mr Pisces + Ms Capricorn ♑

Sign	Pisces	Capricorn
Symbol	Fish	Goat
Ruler	Neptune	Saturn
Type	Mutable	Cardinal
Element	Water	Earth

Ms Capricorn loves to have something to pursue but fishing is not high on her list. But it might be just what she needs to relax and enjoy herself instead of playing the busy wife and homemaker or the determined, driven entrepreneur. To catch the elusive Piscean is challenging, yet Ms Capricorn will have all the skills she needs to snare this man. But will she be happy with her catch? This is the million-dollar question.

Both can benefit from this association. Ms Capricorn can learn to express the more feeling side of her nature, while she can teach the fish a thing or two about order and management. If they have the patience to learn to adjust to their differences, this can be a wonderful meeting of the minds as well as a strong physical connection. Ms Capricorn is not one to show her sensual and lusty appetite readily, yet beneath her reserved demeanour is a girl who needs to be appreciated and loved. Mr Pisces will be that man. He can sense what this lady needs and will be able to draw out her more charismatic side. She, in turn, will ground her fish and help him consolidate his talents with her practical approach and flair for achievement.

Ms Capricorn will be the one in charge of this relationship, which will suit her fish. He will be only too happy for her to take the lead and show the way, because he recognises that he can't stay submerged forever. Ms Capricorn is well able to take control if she sees her fish dive too deeply into his own private world and indulge in his one or two addictions. She will be the discriminating one and will endeavour to bring this romantic man back to earth where he will soak up the earthly pleasures his Capricornian lover can provide.

In the bedroom: Ms Capricorn will be direct and assertive when it comes to sex, like she is about most things in her life. Water and earth signs share a depth of passion that will set the room on fire. She will want to get down to business, while the imaginative and creative fish will be only too happy to lead her on a sexual journey of self-discovery.

♓ Mr Pisces + Ms Aquarius ♒

Sign	Pisces	Aquarius
Symbol	Fish	Water bearer
Ruler	Neptune	Uranus
Type	Mutable	Fixed
Element	Water	Air

This can be a wonderful pairing because Ms Aquarius feels this man really understands her. In his own way, he is obtuse and indifferent, but at least she will be comfortable with how he allows her to be herself. She is a fixed sign and is reluctant to change, so Mr Pisces will always be the one to make the adjustments. He is known for his gentle and compassionate nature. Hopefully, he won't make a martyr of himself as this girl can exploit her relationships and will take what she can. She does, however, have a compassionate side, especially when it comes to the underdog. Her passion lies in helping those less fortunate, which is in sync with her Piscean mate, who is also not adverse to humanitarian pursuits when he is not acting like a victim.

These two will share a love of culture and the arts, and Ms Aquarius will be the first to encourage the fish to explore his talents and put them to good use. She craves connection with others, be it socially or in her life's work, whereas Mr Pisces wants to lose himself, retreat from the world and contemplate life. This relationship just might work because she needs her independence and freedom and will allow her fish to swim below the surface, as long as he comes up for air every so often and gives her a dose of compassion and warmth.

On the downside, Ms Aquarius is not so at home with her emotions and will leave her fish undernourished and feeling unloved at times. She doesn't recognise that she can be cold and impersonal. Her Piscean man will be need to tap into his intuition and realise that her detachment is part of her demeanour and not an indicator of her lack of love for him.

In the bedroom: These two will have no trouble about being able to submit to physical pleasures. Both are fairly imaginative and experimental lovers; however, neither is likely to completely give their all until they feel totally secure and committed.

♓ Mr Pisces + Ms Pisces ♓

Sign	Pisces	Pisces
Symbol	Fish	Fish
Ruler	Neptune	Neptune
Type	Mutable	Mutable
Element	Water	Water

Mr and Ms Pisces are on the same spiritual platform and their love has no boundaries. They share the same vision of life and reinforce each other's positive and negative sides, whether they're 'the good, the bad or the ugly'. This union experiences the agony and the ecstasy of love and works best when each confronts the other's shortcomings, rather than pursuing a dream that is idealistic and intangible. These two fish swim in synchronicity with each other, dipping into a sea of turbulence and calm. When they are on their life's true mission, they can support and encourage each other's virtues and lead a serene and peaceful existence; however, if they succumb to their vulnerabilities, they can share a world of chaos and suffering.

The waters run deep in this connection. Both share a yearning to transcend the physical and make their relationship a spiritually unifying bond. There is a magical quality that ties Ms Pisces to her fish; however, they will need to keep their channels of communication open because they both can be evasive in their emotions. This deceptive quality will manifest itself in periods of escapism where they will succumb to their addictive tendencies to numb their pain and suffering. Their devotion to each other, however, is very strong and they are responsive to one another's needs.

The Piscean pair will strive to fulfil each other's dreams of forming an invincible union that can surmount any of life's challenges. Their journey together will be a kaleidoscope of colour and texture, and their passion will rarely fade.

In the bedroom: These two are natural aphrodisiacs for each other, and their physical needs come from the same place. There is both a spiritual and physical connection between the two fish. Each knows how to turn the other on and all it takes is the slightest touch to transport them to a universe that only they can inhabit.

Celebrity Mr Pisces: Kurt Cobain

Singer, born 7.20 pm 20 February 1967 in Aberdeen, Washington, USA

```
Personal planets:  Sun in Pisces
                   Moon in Cancer
                   Mercury in Pisces
                   Venus in Pisces
                   Mars in Scorpio
```

Never met a wise man; if so, it's a woman.

– Kurt Cobain

The late Kurt Cobain, lead singer and guitarist in the band Nirvana, was a classic Pisces with an abundance of planets in water. To intensify matters, his Moon in the sign of Cancer made him a sensitive and vulnerable man whose life was marred by a series of melancholy moods and addictive behaviour. Cobain's chart shows an overdose of water, which seemed to have drowned his ability to rise above the surface. His talent was submerged in a pool of emotional intensity and he could not release himself from the past: 'I had a really good childhood up until I was nine, then the classic case of divorce really affected me,' Cobain said.

His chart shows a deficiency of fire and air, the predominance of water giving him an unbalanced perspective on life. His emotions were deep but also contained, yet his need to be loved was overwhelming. He sought to fill this need through his relationships. None of these were sustaining because the void in his heart could not be filled by a mere mortal, but only by banishing his own demons.

Cobain and his wife Courtney Love shared may of the same qualities, both needing validation and reinforcement in their relationship. His attraction to her was particularly significant because she has both her Sun and Moon in the sensitive sign of Cancer, which fitted perfectly with his requirements – a nurturing and protective lover who would cater to his sensitivities and vulnerability. Love would have felt his pain and emotions, and also had the spark to draw him out with her zest for life and her outgoing demeanour. Her Venus and Mars in the fickle sign of Gemini could be seen as engaging, and her need to communicate was very strong, as well as her desire to be in a continuous whirlwind of change.

Cobain was a more evasive and detached person. He was a romantic who didn't discriminate well and, true to the Piscean form, he needed a woman who appreciated his compassion and his need for emotional closeness. Cobain, however, had a strong resolve and was not a man to be changed. The significant astrological bond he and Love shared was their Cancerian Moon, which gave their relationship a natural affinity and mutual understanding. It also made them both very receptive to one another's moods and vulnerabilities, often highlighting their excessive natures and weaknesses. Cobain's life was bittersweet and his longing for peace came true sooner than he might have thought when he passed away through suicide.

Index

D

E

F

G

M

N

O

P

Index

Index

NELLIE MCKINLEY

Nellie has been an astrologer for over 15 years, offering relationship, career and personal development counselling through birth chart analysis. A descendant of the famous Danish astronomer Tycho Brahe, Nellie has earned a reputation as one of Australia's leading astrologers. She is passionate about relationship counselling and couple compatibility and specialises in assisting parents through child chart analysis.

Nellie has appeared in publications such as the Gold Coast Bulletin, Sunday Mail and For Me magazine and provides astrology commentary for newspapers and magazines. She also writes an annual 12-day double-page astrology feature for the Gold Coast Bulletin.

A weekly guest on ABC Radio, Nellie has also presented a 12-month program on the Nitemix Around Australia radio show. She has appeared as a guest on television, discussing how parents can understand their children through astrology, as well as being featured on news programs.

A dynamic and entertaining speaker, Nellie conducts regular astrology workshops and has been a guest at the Somerset Celebration of Literature festival. She has also worked as the astrologer-in-residence at the Hideaway Retreat on Queensland's Gold Coast.

'I have been following astrology since I was 16. It provides a great insight into all aspects of your life and Nellie always manages to pick up on key issues.'
Sophie Marshall, director of the Relaxation Corporation